Journeys in the Canyon Lands of Utah and Arizona

Journeys
in the
Canyon Lands of
Utah and Arizona
1914–1916

George C. Fraser

Edited by
Frederick H. Swanson

With a Foreword by
Hal K. Rothman

The University of Arizona Press
Tucson

The University of Arizona Press
© 2005 The Arizona Board of Regents
All rights reserved
☉ This book is printed on acid-free, archival-quality paper.
Manufactured in the United States of America

Library of Congress Cataloging-in-Publication Data
Fraser, George C. (George Corning), 1872–1935.
Journeys in the canyon lands of Utah and Arizona, 1914–
1916 / George C. Fraser ; edited by Frederick H. Swanson,
with a foreword by Hal K. Rothman.
p. cm.
Includes bibliographical references and index.
ISBN 0-8165-2440-8 (pbk. : alk. paper)
1. Utah—Description and travel. 2. Arizona—Description and
travel. 3. Canyons—Utah. 4. Canyons—Arizona. 5. Fraser,
George C. (George Corning), 1872–1935—Diaries. 6. Fraser,
George C. (George Corning), 1872–1935—Travel—Utah. 7.
Fraser, George C. (George Corning), 1872–1935—Travel—
Arizona. 8. Camping—Utah—History—20th century. 9.
Camping—Arizona—History—20th century. I. Swanson,
Frederick H. (Frederick Harold), 1952– II. Title.
F826.F836 2005
917.9204′31—dc22
2004018012

Publication of this book is made possible in part by a
publication grant from the Charles Redd Center for Western
Studies at Brigham Young University.

Contents

Figures

Foreword

Hal K. Rothman

One facet of tourism at the turn of the twentieth century was a dimension that included affirmation of American culture but thoroughly eschewed the opulence that the luxury set demanded. Undertaken in part as a cure for physical or psychosomatic ailment, in part as homage to a mythic way of life passing from the industrial stage, this form appealed to specific segments of people within the market for travel. These were expeditions for the hardy, those who wanted more than a train trip dotted with stops at interesting places. The consumers of this kind of heritage and cultural tourism were a small specialty niche, the more adventurous, the more serious, the aficionados, those who did more than pose their distance from the mainstream. These were the people who recognized that when they pierced through the facade of the staged setting in places such as archaeological entrepreneur Edgar L. Hewett's Santa Fe, they first encountered not what they deemed real experience, but instead a second facade designed for their comfort. Tearing through this construction that so many of their peers accepted offered sheer pleasure to such people, proof of their difference from even the most sophisticated and adventurous of their kind. While their neighbors and friends settled for the fabricated and diluted Santa Fe, these adventurers believed beyond that last cloak was genuine experience, untempered by the amenities of the industrial world.

The people who made up this small but important group were similar to the wealthy travelers who stayed within the constraints of organized travel. They, too, were typically well-off beneficiaries of industrialization, most likely to originate in the Northeast, and often had access to the corridors of power. They differed from their brothers and sisters, cousins and friends in the way they understood the world; out of step and leaning toward the odd, most evinced the traits of the antimoderns, who played such an important role in the rise of American reform and the transformation of American culture as the twentieth century approached. These out-of-sync individuals were even more conscious of the discord that lay beneath the surface of industrialization, even more repulsed by the official banality of fin de siècle society than were their peers. They were also truth seekers, individuals who believed that in some instance of authenticity, they could seize the meaning of life and convey it to others.

Before the 1930s, two traditions, the visit to the archaeological site and the trip to the dude ranch, dominated such tourism. These two distinctly different events shared innumerable characteristics. Both required physical travel from the main rail lines to remote places, and, in both, participants lived in less than luxurious circumstances. Neither contained the purported authenticity laden with amenity that so characterized the development of tourism. Here were activities, the structure and organization of an archaeological camp or a dude ranch seemed to shout, that truly pitted individuals against themselves, people against the rough, cold realities of the American West in a genuine quest for experience and understanding. The fulfillment people experienced served as a direct counter to the public and private crisis of cultural authority, the slipping and increasingly slippery legitimacy of the mainstream. In experience aimed at truth was the opportunity for individual salvation, redemption, and transformation in an industrial society.

Their authenticity was relative, based in the sense of what was real in the antimodern consciousness. These travelers craved experience but preferred it without the filtering of the lens of the railroad—although most were not adverse to luxury hotel accommodations when possible. They wanted to touch and feel as part of understanding the mythic West and the human past; this unfiltered proximity to what they regarded as nature and the natural world, human as well as physical, made their experience "real" in their own terms. Their understanding of the world shaped their authenticity. They required a filter, but one different from those who accepted the railroad's visions and definitions. This crowd needed to be close to the experts, the scientists, paleontologists, archaeologists, anthropologists, linguists, and others who, in the understanding of the antimodern world, possessed the credentials and the knowledge that held the key to truth.

Even more telling, they spread out across the landscape in a fashion that served as precursor of later forms of travel. They rejected the parameters of railroad travel; eschewed the limitations of the "West from a Car Window," as renowned journalist Richard Harding Davis so aptly titled his travel narrative; and used whatever transportation necessary to reach into remote corners of the region. They carried their own baggage, occasionally hunted their own food, and generally scoured up sustenance in distant places. In the form of their travel, although not necessarily in its purpose, they mirrored the automobile tourists who followed them much more than the railroad passengers who preceded them. The only boundaries to the experience of these travelers were self-imposed; the limits they experienced came from within and not from railroad brochures and amenities or tour syndicates.

In this respect, these denizens of cultural and heritage tourism initiated the context in which its hegemony collapsed. Although they constructed their reality against the form and function of railroad travel, their very method moved beyond its limitations. When they rode in automobiles, camped, hunted, broke cattle, or dug in the dirt, they extended the limits of tourist endeavor into experiences that were far more idiosyncratic than anything offered along the rails. Paradoxically, such visitors typically sought a hegemonic result. The truth they craved affirmed the intellectual ethos of fin de siècle American society even as their means of seeking it seemed to refute the dominant notions of the time. In their search, they created a context in which tourism became a pastime for a broader swath of the American public. By the early 1900s, these seeming eccentrics were sufficiently wealthy and existed in large enough numbers to sustain divergent forms of mainstream tourism. They stood among those who sought more than a temporary release from the feeling of overcivilization that seemed omnipresent in American society, who craved a preindustrial reality closer to nature and tied to village roots of the human species. These, too, were questers, people who sought not only escape but also reconstitution as a new whole as they extended the space between themselves and Pittsburgh, Chicago, and even the Grand Canyon and Santa Fe.

George C. Fraser almost perfectly mirrored this type of turn-of-the-twentieth-century person. He had all the advantages his society had to offer: wealth, access to power, and, most important to later generations, time. A curious man, he seemed interested in almost everything. He traveled widely as a young man, carrying that passion into his adult life and passing his love of the road on to his children. Fraser talked with people incessantly, serving as a participant/ethnographer in the best of the tradition in late nineteenth- and early-twentieth-century America. He listened and learned, thought, and later spoke. His adventures mean more today as a result.

Fraser was heir to the tradition of taxonomy in natural science, the citizen-observer who observed the natural world and, using the intellectual tools of the age, sought to combine the empirical and the sublime, laced with the articulation of science and progress, that defined nineteenth-century thought. Fraser's embrace of this ideal followed on the heels of Clarence Dutton and the other founders of the age; his explorations in a small way mirrored those of John Wesley Powell, progenitor of the second great age of exploration. In this meshing of seemingly disparate ideals, Fraser reached for the highest traditions of his class and time.

Today travel is different. Not only is the activity so common and the people along the way so heavily visited that they tell the same story over and over again, but the idea of heading off the beaten path is a cliché regurgitated in car commercials. In some ways, this new idiom is testimony to the desires of people like Fraser, to the democratization of experience, and to a world where all things are in reach to most Americans. The iconography of this kind of travel, this tourism of the self and the outside world simultaneously, remains fraught with meaning. George C. Fraser would seem naive today in his sense that he can get to the bottom of it all with discussion; his journals are also a memoir of a time as well as of his experience, an expression of a simpler world, where truth and knowing were within the grasp of ordinary people who made the effort to get beyond the limits of their world.

Despite their decidedly fin de siècle intellectual objectives, Fraser and his kind were antecedents of a physical revolution in tourism made possible by Henry Ford and the assembly line and made real by the construction of roads on which to drive. The devotees of archaeology first recognized this freedom; the automobile took them from the locales overwhelmed by tourism, the railroad depots, the plazas, the towns and places that seemed inauthentic and corrupted even to naive turn-of-the-century eyes, and transported them to places where the intrusions of the modern world were limited to these drivers and the vehicles they piloted. The technology permitted, even encouraged, the manufacture of the distance that archaeology aficionados craved. Personal wheels gave choices that even the most affluent railroad tourists could not purchase. They allowed travelers to burst the bubble of the corridor of transformation that the steel rails created, to move beyond a world that catered to the whims of industrial society. Sometimes that distance could be real; at others, it could be in the eyes of the travelers, certain that the landscape they viewed remained unchanged from a moment in the far-off past. In the eyes of tourists who assumed they defined every scene into which they wandered, any presence became part of a past. In the process, they made travelers like Fraser first ordinary and then anachronistic. Yet the words remain and they tell a story of a different age, when listening mattered and when people truly thought they could reach truth through experience.

Acknowledgments

The path that led me to George Fraser's journals was as circuitous as a sandstone tributary to Glen Canyon, and every bit as delightful to follow. In studying the career of Dave Rust, southern Utah's preeminent backcountry guide, I noticed he often mentioned a favorite client, a man he credited with opening his eyes to the possibility of deeper study of the Southwest's landscapes. Not until I read Stephen C. Jett's 1974 article on George Fraser's journals, however, was I aware of this hidden alcove containing some marvelous travel writing.

The Shields Library at the University of California, Davis, generously loaned me their microfilm copies of Fraser's journals for transcription. William W. Slaughter and his colleagues at the Latter-day Saints Church Historical Department made available Fraser's letters and photographs in their David D. Rust collection. Margaret Rich of the Princeton University Library arranged for me to read Fraser's original journals. The Special Collections staff at the Marriott Library, University of Utah, helped me locate materials related to tourism of the period, and Scott Reiter researched the maps of the day, finding some of the same editions Fraser and Rust may have used. Marriott's Digital Technologies staff, led by Kenning Arlitsch, deserve mention for their prodigious efforts to place Utah's historical newspapers, Dutton's *High Plateaus,* and other important works on the World Wide Web—an invaluable aid to researchers.

Sarah Fraser Robbins shared delightful recollections of her father; George Fraser III, Myra Mathers, and Dorothy Shore helped bring their grandfather's memory to life and painstakingly bundled up precious albums of photographs to send to me. Leighton Coleman III, Ian Fraser, and Hanson Robbins provided helpful information about the Fraser family. Blanche Rust Rasmussen generously shared her father's photographs for use in this book.

My deep appreciation goes to Dr. Hal K. Rothman for contributing the foreword to this book. His insights, based on long experience studying tourism in the West, provide a valuable perspective to George Fraser's travels.

Patti Hartmann of the University of Arizona Press guided the manuscript through review and publication, and copy editor Monica Phillips gave it needed polish. Any factual errors, of course, are my own.

Two individuals stand out for their unceasing encouragement: Dave Schleicher, my longtime colleague in the editing game, and my wife, Bessann Swanson, who patiently listened to my enthusiasms and helped me understand that this book was not such a far-fetched idea.

Introduction

On Sunday, July 5, 1914, the Union Pacific's San Pedro No. 1 train slowed to a stop in the sun-struck Great Basin town of Lund, Utah. George Corning Fraser, who had boarded the train with his seventeen-year-old son in Salt Lake City the previous night, noted the time (9:38 a.m.) in his journal. Already he had filled several pages with his observations of the route west from his home in Morristown, New Jersey, including remarks on the geology of the mountains they had just crossed.

The Frasers bypassed the gleaming white-stuccoed station depot and stepped into a warehouse run by H. J. Doolittle, a local businessman. Here they exchanged their jackets, starched collars, and pressed shirts for more rugged attire. Lund was frequented by teamsters picking up freight destined for the towns and settlements of southwestern Utah, but Doolittle had received instructions from Salt Lake City to watch for a tourist party, a rarity here. He had arranged for an auto to take the Frasers to Toquerville, sixty miles to the south, at the end of the drivable road. There they would meet their guide, David D. Rust, who was familiar with the country they were about to enter. For the next four weeks the three men would be climbing barren cinder cones in hundred-degree heat, wading rivers locked within rock-walled canyons, and negotiating crude trails favored more by deer and wild burros than by travelers from back East. Two hundred miles to the south of Lund, by road, wagon track, and trail, lay their destination: the North Rim of the Grand Canyon.

The Frasers were entering a domain of sinuous sandstone gorges and piñon-covered mesas whose inhabitants were still struggling to make a living under near-frontier conditions. This was the "Plateau Province," explored, mapped, and named by Maj. John Wesley Powell and his men only four decades earlier, and it contained geologic and scenic wonders that had sparked the designation of some of America's first national monuments. Among these were Mukuntuweap (now Zion National

George C. Fraser.

Park), enclosing the soaring canyon walls of the Virgin River; Rainbow Bridge in the nearly inaccessible slickrock north of Navajo Mountain; Natural Bridges in the head of remote White Canyon; and, of course, the Grand Canyon. Tourists rarely probed these canyons, except for the latter. Even at the Grand Canyon, most visitors ended their scenic quest at the canyon's South Rim, where the Santa Fe Railroad had opened the El Tovar Hotel in 1905.

The Frasers (George Sr. and Jr.) had been to the South Rim in 1911 and had ridden mules down the steep switchbacks of the Bright Angel Trail to the Colorado River. But the elder Fraser knew that the canyon's North Rim offered a superior perch from which to study the myriad towers and amphitheaters that made the canyon the geologic wonder of the world. A northern approach through the hinterlands of Utah beckoned to Fraser, for it would also allow him to see the great canyon of the upper Virgin River—a place settlers called Little Zion—and to detour westward out onto the distant Uinkaret Plateau, home to a marvelous display of geologically recent volcanic cones and lava flows. Only after these preliminaries would the Frasers climb up into the pine forests of

The Frasers at Morristown Station, June 24, 1916,
headed for Arizona and the Navajo country.

the Kaibab Plateau, make a long traverse of the North Rim, and finally
cross the canyon to the Santa Fe station at the South Rim.

When the Frasers emerged from the Grand Canyon on August 1,
after a harrowing crossing of the canyon via the Bass Trail, they had
covered hundreds of miles of some of the most scenic and geologically
interesting backcountry to be found in the American West. Despite
having completed a journey that most travelers would never experience
in a lifetime, Fraser was far from finished. Over the next sixteen years, he
would make five more lengthy excursions into the canyon lands by
horseback, wagon, and boat, accompanied by various members of his

Dave Rust, the Frasers' guide.

family. On four of his excursions he kept a detailed journal, recording his observations not only of geologic phenomena but also of the unusual people he met on the trail. The result is a delightful recounting of life in a region that was about to be transformed by the arrival of the automobile.

In Search of the Southwest and Its Inhabitants

Although he had traveled widely from his youth onward, George Fraser was hardly the model of a heroic adventurer. He was a partner in a New York City law firm and invested in land and ranch properties in the South and Southwest. He served on the boards of railroads and other corporations and belonged to some of the city's most prestigious clubs. Though trim, and familiar enough around horses, he spent much of his time behind a desk. It was his love of geology, not physical challenge, that drew him to the canyons of the Southwest. More than anything else, he wanted to study the magnificently exposed landscape of the Colorado Plateau—a region brilliantly described in the writings of John Wesley Powell, Capt. Clarence Dutton, and geologist Grove Karl Gilbert.

Fraser, an avid book collector, purchased these authors' works to help him plan his perambulations through canyon and plateau. He sought to stand at the same vantage points used by Major Powell's men when they had gazed at unknown mountains and rivers and began to map out one of America's last frontiers. He craved an intimate under-standing of the landscape—not just a tourist's glance—and each year took the four or five weeks he felt he needed to witness the region's expansive landforms from as many perspectives as possible.

Fraser's law partners found his fascination with the Southwest a little mystifying; it was customary for the well-to-do to escape New York's summer heat by spending a month at the shore. Such idleness bored Fraser. He found release in the even more punishing heat of the Utah and Arizona deserts, indulging his passion for studying the bare-bones geology of the canyon and plateau country.

George Fraser was born in 1872 in New York City, the only child of George Smith Fraser, a second-generation Scottish American, and Anna Maria Corning. As a boy, Fraser traveled extensively in Europe, North Africa, and the Middle East, accompanying his peripatetic father, who visited spas throughout Europe. At times Fraser's mother and various cousins joined these travels, which included horseback rides through biblical landscapes, a visit to the pyramids, and sojourns in the Swiss Alps. Sometime in his adolescent years Fraser took up the then-common practice of keeping a journal of his travels. Under the eye of his Swiss tutor, a Dr. Merrill, he began to jot down everything that interested him, which in his case turned out to be a great deal. His adolescent journals recorded varieties of wildflowers seen, the details of paintings and gems displayed in museums, and—in what would become a lifelong habit—the arrival and departure times of the trains he rode. Visiting a mine in Spain when he was sixteen, Fraser took copious notes on its workings and machinery, the strata exposed, and the method of extracting and con-centrating the ore.

Studies at Princeton, from which he graduated in 1893 with a ma-jor in geology, undoubtedly exposed him to the accounts of western landscapes published by the various government surveys, including the pioneering works of Major Powell and his associates. While at Princeton he also displayed his engaging ability to seek out people unlike himself: as manager of the football team, he roamed rural New Jersey, scouting for athletic-looking young miners and farmhands and persuading them to try out for the team.

He chose to pursue a career in law, however, receiving his LL.B. degree from George Washington University (then Columbian University) in 1895 and practicing in Washington, D.C. In 1900 he became a partner in the firm of Martin, Fraser and Speir, located at 20 Exchange Place in Manhattan's Wall Street district. Commercial law was his specialty, including matters pertaining to oil companies (he served as a director of Texaco), but he was also known for his ability to write an airtight will. One of his later colleagues, H. Maynard Kidder, wrote that "Mr. Fraser combined to an extraordinary degree a capacity for rapid and decisive judgment with the thoroughness and precision in detail which are generally accounted the essence of a lawyer's genius."[1] His legal training undoubtedly influenced his meticulous journal keeping; however, his strong sense of order may have drawn him to the law.

His years of travel as a young man sharpened his attention to the world around him. As historian Stephen Jett noted, Fraser "seems to have been fascinated by nearly everything."[2] Rare is the amateur enthusiast who is as mindful of the geologic record on display in the Southwest. Even while riding trains, Fraser would peruse the literature, such as Nelson H. Darton's geologic field guide to the Santa Fe route. He would spend hours on the trains' observation platforms, noting the passage of cliff lines, buttes, and other eminences and checking out agriculture and irrigation works. Once a conductor took him for a spy sent by eastern railroad financiers, believing no well-dressed person could have such an interest in mere scenery.

As it happened, George Fraser relished human contact almost as much as he enjoyed geologizing. He sought close acquaintance with those he met along the trail and had a gift for drawing out their stories. He could converse late into the night with young herders on a wind-blown Henry Mountain hillside or discuss Forest Service politics with a Kaibab Plateau ranger. At a time when Mormons were still widely distrusted, he made many friends among the villagers and ranchers of southern Utah. Although his speech was correct and his bearing could be quite formal, local people found him to be an unprejudiced and interested listener. Social rank meant little to him; he was comfortable chatting in the local bishop's drawing room or sitting with cowhands around a campfire. About all he required of company was a willingness to talk; over and over he would get people to tell him their life histories. He seemed bemused only by those who would not open up to him. Most people, however, were eager to talk with this dignified gentleman who took such an interest in their lives. They and their parents had built a new society in Utah and Arizona, and they were proud of their accomplishments. The historian Earl Pomeroy has remarked that "the Western resident himself smarted under the stigma of backwardness, and striving to hide the raw edges of what he built, hoped for the compliments and the assistance that visitors and investors might give."[3]

Fraser never outgrew his interest in rocks or in people. His grandson, George Fraser III, recalls taking an automobile trip (with a hired driver; Fraser never learned to drive) through the New Jersey and New York countryside in the 1930s to study rock outcrops. Visiting a quarry, the elder Fraser fell into discussion with the Italian quarrymen about Mussolini. At a roadside orchard, the Frasers helped themselves to fresh peaches, occasioning friendly conversation when the owner came over to investigate.[4]

George Fraser married Jane Gardener Tutt of St. Louis, Missouri, in 1895. Their first child, George C. Fraser Jr., was born in 1897. Four daughters, Myra, Jane, Ann, and Sarah, followed. George Jr. went on his father's first three trips to Utah from 1914 to 1916; his sisters were each given the opportunity to accompany their father on his later western trips. Sarah Fraser recalls her jealousy watching her older sisters pack for these excursions. Her turn came in 1930, on the last wilderness trip George Fraser would make: a canoe voyage down the Colorado River in Glen Canyon with his longtime guide and friend, Dave Rust, accompanied by legendary Colorado River boatman Bert Loper.

Fraser's Journals

Fraser kept detailed journals on four of his canyon country trips: Zion and the Grand Canyon in 1914, the High Plateaus of Utah in 1915, Lees Ferry and the Navajo country in 1916, and an overland journey to Glen Canyon on the Colorado River in 1922.[5] Included in these journals are many photographs that, although of amateur quality, record numerous geologic and scenic features.[6] On two additional trips, a family excursion to Bryce Canyon and the Kolob Canyons of Utah in 1921 and the Glen Canyon trip in 1930, he took photographs but did not keep a journal.

Fraser's travels also took him elsewhere in the Southwest, visiting geological and archaeological sites in New Mexico and Arizona, as well as touring the Navajo and Hopi Indian reservations by automobile. He kept journals on several of those excursions, and these also make fascinating reading. The accounts presented here, however, concern the three trips he made from 1914 through 1916 within the region commonly known as the "canyon lands."[7] These journals present a remarkable overview of this intriguing geological and cultural landscape.

Writing in a spare, dispassionate style, Fraser nonetheless succeeded in conveying his deep appreciation of the landscape. Though he was not writing for popular consumption, he employed thorough description and the apt metaphor to bring scenic features to life. His journals describe riding across the Aquarius at a gallop in order to reach the next viewpoint early in the afternoon; his constant clock-watching documents the hours he spent at each "lookoff," maps and books spread out on the ground. One feels his excitement at getting up with the dawn to peer off the edge of Pine Valley Mountain and later, after hours of landscape study, his reluctance at having to pack up and leave.

He was modest about his physical abilities, and it takes some familiarity with the country—such as wading the narrows of the Virgin River or bushwhacking down Muav Canyon—to realize how hard he must have pushed himself. Dave Rust admired his willingness to tackle physical challenges, and Rust was not known to coddle his clients. Still, when Fraser faced the hardships of traversing this country, such as winching a dilapidated cable car across the flood-swollen Colorado at the end of his 1914 trip, he did not minimize the danger.

The journals often display Fraser's dry, almost cryptic wit, most in evidence when he felt put upon. Trying to find a quiet spot to read in a St. George hostelry, he observes good-naturedly the family life swirling about him. When the desk clerk at El Tovar tells him he is "unlikely to be robbed" on the other side of the Colorado, Fraser merely notes the size of his hotel bill. He comments on Rust's frequent attempts during their 1915 High Plateaus excursion to trade one of their pack string for a "live horse." And throughout the journals we see his continual and sometimes comic efforts to get a bath.

His open-minded temperament contributed much to his enjoyment. Traveling through the remote villages and outposts of Mormon country, Fraser found himself immersed in an unusual culture. Although he was Presbyterian, Fraser saw much that was exemplary among the Latter-day Saints. Time and again he marveled at meeting some well-read and articulate person in an impoverished hamlet far out in the wilderness. His descriptions of Mormon life in the Utah and Arizona outback are sometimes amusing, sometimes poignant, and consistently enlightening.

Fraser's method of keeping a journal was to write down field notes, review them when he returned home, and then dictate an expanded version to his secretary. He typically sent a rough draft to Dave Rust, who would add a few notes and corrections. George Fraser Jr. also provided some details.

The typewritten journals contain numerous photographs, unfortunately of generally poor quality, mounted among the typed pages. George Fraser Jr. kept the journals following his father's death in 1935 and donated them to the Princeton University Library in 1965. Included in the journals are a few letters from his guide, Dave Rust, recalling the trips. He and Rust corresponded for years and became good friends. Many of Fraser's letters to Rust are found in the David D. Rust collection at the LDS Church History archives in Salt Lake City.

Fraser kept notes as he rode from camp to camp, and while he described these as "very brief and rough," he had an extraordinary eye for detail. Expanded after each trip into more than two hundred typewritten pages each, his journals noted the temperature of every body of water, the time of day he reached viewpoints, and similar minutiae.[8] His penchant for detail sometimes amused his colleagues. As a preface to his 1914 journal, Fraser attached a bit of parody by his law partner Newell Martin, titled "Adventures in the desert of the Painted Mountains." It exaggerates, but not by much:

> July 22, 5 a.m. Got up. 5:30 did not wash. Thermometer 52. Barometer 7726. Rust rustled horses, 2 hour 27 minutes. He wore new pedometer, cost $3.82 at McAllister's. Pedometer registered 23 kilometers.
>
> 11:35 View from Point Sublimity. Consulted Frith's Cyclopedia of colors and compared four sections of landscape with descriptions by Dutton. Identified 36 shades of color. By clinometer 18 slopes 3° sharper than Brenva face of Blanc, 82 cliffs more than 4% sharper than Italian front of Cervin.
>
> 12:30 By diary and chronometer, 37 hours since last wash, 82 since last shave.

1:28 Met Boston man. He did not speak and did not offer food.

*Note: Let George avoid Harvard. Harvard men have bad manners.[9]

*Second note: July 23. Must be just to Boston men. Rust suggests Boston men may have been terrified.

Fortunately, Fraser turned his penchant for observation onto more interesting matters, including not only the geology and scenery of this wild, little-known landscape, but on the human culture he found there as well. His journals thus provide a detailed and insightful look into a region that was still largely embedded in rural, preindustrial ways.

An Evolving Tourist Mecca:
The Plateau Province, 1900–1930

In the early part of the twentieth century, the Grand Canyon was everyone's emblem of the Plateau Province. And for nearly all of the canyon's visitors, the South Rim was the point at which they made contact with its immense and sometimes bewildering landforms. The South Rim was incomparably better equipped than anywhere else in the region to cater to the needs of tourists. When the Frasers first came in 1911, they found an impressive assemblage of buildings sprawled over nearly half a mile of the rim. These included the Bright Angel Hotel, built in 1896 during the initial period of tourist development at the rim, as well as the luxurious El Tovar, the Santa Fe's showpiece attraction.[10] In addition, there were tent camps, a post office, the Mary Colter–designed Hopi House (the canyon's first curio shop), the Kolb Brothers' photography studio, a second dining hall, various ancillary stables, shops, and even a schoolhouse for employees' children. Anything the visitor might need was available, from fine dining to souvenir purchases to evening entertainment. While many arrivals at El Tovar were content to view the canyon from the nearby rim-side walkway, never doffing their elegant traveling clothes, the more adventurous, of whom the Frasers counted themselves, took the guided mule ride down the Bright Angel Trail to Indian Gardens and onward to the canyon bottom. Trail rides were also available to Hermit Camp, another Santa Fe project offering well-maintained overnight cabins within the canyon.

The typical visitor's encounter with the canyon occurred only a few hundred feet from the depot of the Grand Canyon Railway, where travelers disembarked after a sixty-five-mile trip from the Atchison, Topeka

& Santa Fe's main line at Williams, Arizona. George Wharton James, one of the chroniclers of life and scenery at the Grand Canyon during its early tourist period, wrote of the shock and astonishment that many first-time viewers felt upon reaching the canyon rim. "To see women burst into tears and in a tremble of ecstatic fear is a common sight," he wrote in his book *In and Around the Grand Canyon*, published at the turn of the century.[11] Such reactions fell into the concept of "the sublime" or "the awful," the frame through which educated travelers were inclined to view grand scenery. Even James was not immune to the spell of grandeur, recounting an incident when he happened upon a South Rim viewpoint and "experienced for a moment an indescribable terror of nature, a confusion of mind, a fear to be alone in such a presence."[12]

James knew the canyon intimately, having ridden its trails and camped in its depths with William Wallace Bass on numerous occasions. For casual visitors, though, some of the disorientation they experienced must have come from having arrived so abruptly at the canyon. Stepping down from an elegant railway car, adjusting their hats against the Arizona sun, they walked along a gentle path to an abyss heretofore hidden from view. They could be excused for experiencing a bit of vertigo. Fortunately, visitors could retreat to the comfortable environment of the El Tovar. There they could enjoy an evening meal in an atmosphere of "quiet dignity and unassuming luxury" and later perhaps take in a lecture or music recital provided by the Fred Harvey Company.[13]

Nor did Grand Canyon Village offer the only tourist accommodation on the South Rim. To the east, at Grandview Point, canyon pioneer Pete Berry had built the Grandview Hotel during the 1890s, offering tourists arriving by stage from Flagstaff "meals prepared by a European chef, surrey tours along the rim for a dollar, and saddle trips along the Hance, Tanner, and Grandview Trails for about three dollars."[14] And farther west from the main village, William Bass, who, like Berry, had come to the canyon as a prospector, had built a tourist camp and hotel to complement his trail guiding business. By 1914, in an effort to stay competitive with the Santa Fe's operation, he had built a hotel at a flag stop a mile from Grand Canyon station and was offering automobile rides along the rim.[15] That these enterprises were soon outclassed by the development at Grand Canyon Village shows how willing early-twentieth-century tourists were to pay for their western experience. By 1914 the canyon, at least from its South Rim viewpoints, was high on the list of important American destinations. President Theodore Roosevelt had visited it twice and in 1903 named it "one of the great sights which every American, if he can travel at all, should see."[16] Authors as famous as John Muir, and many others less well known, visited the canyon and urged Americans to take in its glories.[17]

Having spent a week at the canyon during his initial visit in 1911, George Fraser was already more thoroughly engaged with its scenic and geologic features than the average tourist. But he was not tethered to the elegant facilities at the South Rim and thus was able to broaden his experience to include the expansive region north of the river. A few tourists reached the North Rim by making difficult cross-canyon traverses, using trails initially scratched out by prospectors but rebuilt and extended in the early 1900s. William Bass had laboriously constructed a trail from his camp at Bass Rapids up to the rim at Muav Saddle and occasionally took sightseers as far along the rim as Point Sublime.[18] In 1906–7, a group of Kanab, Utah, promoters led by Edwin D. ("Uncle Dee") Woolley Jr. built a trail down Bright Angel Creek to the Colorado River, erected a 400-foot-long cable tramway to ferry visitors across the river, then constructed more trail up through the cliffs on the other side, connecting with the Bright Angel Trail below Indian Gardens.[19]

While the canyon traverse offered the shortest route to the North Rim, it was by no means easy, and most visitors still required a guide and pack string. Until the Forest Service completed the first passable auto road across the plateau in 1916, most North Rim visitors were sportsmen who came to hunt mountain lions. "Uncle Jim" Owens, the Forest Service ranger for the Kaibab district, made most of his living guiding hunting parties, including Zane Grey in 1908 and Theodore Roosevelt in 1913. Owens's little cabin near Bright Angel Point was one of only two on the entire Kaibab that catered to visitors; the other was Dee Woolley's, located a few miles to the east at Cattalo Spring. Dave Rust, who operated out of his father-in-law's cabin, often brought clients to Owens for a day or two of hunting. Neither outfit offered much to the traveler except a cot, a hot meal, and, significantly, a jumping-off point for guided adventure along the plateau's spectacular rim and through its towering pine forest. As Fraser's 1914 journal attests, it took an experienced horseman to thread the Kaibab's maze of shallow but steep-walled canyons, which with its lack of prominent mountain peaks made it a curiously featureless terrain—excepting, of course, the great look-offs at its southern rim.

A handful of Mormon pioneers in southern Utah and along the Arizona Strip had known for decades that the Kaibab and the Grand Canyon offered a potential way to supplement their livelihood by guiding tourists. Not long after settling their southern Utah outposts, the Mormons had contact with Major Powell and his team of explorers and scientists who were mapping the region north of the Colorado. It was Powell who urged a French journalist named Albert Tissandier to explore the Uinkaret and Kaibab plateaus in 1885.[20] Tissandier employed a Kanab cowboy named Nathan Adams, who had guided for Powell, to conduct him across the northern Arizona plateaus. Thus began the long association of the experienced Mormon plainsmen of the region with visitors needing an expert hand with their travels.

These guides set their sights higher in 1891, when Dan Seegmiller of Kanab and other local cowboys shepherded Buffalo Bill Cody and a party of English noblemen from Flagstaff to the Kaibab as part of John W. Young's unsuccessful plan to set up a hunting preserve on the plateau.[21] Dee Woolley, a friend of Seegmiller, was among those involved and here launched his long career in promoting North Rim tourism. Woolley, having seen the reaction of these privileged Englishmen to the endless dusty tracks of the region, understood that the key to promoting travel to the Grand Canyon via Utah lay in improving the road system. His and Dave Rust's Grand Canyon trail and tramway, completed in 1907 and only lightly used thereafter, needed connection to adequate transportation from the north. Woolley and his nephew, E. G. Woolley, organized an automobile jaunt from Salt Lake City to the North Rim in 1909 to demonstrate the feasibility of this new mode of travel, but this and several subsequent ventures by other enthusiasts over the next five years succeeded only in demonstrating how difficult the journey could be.

Businessmen in southern Utah worked strenuously to extend roads south from Cedar City and Panguitch to their communities, and by 1914 automobiles could get as far as Toquerville (in Washington County) and Panguitch (in Garfield County). South of these points, however, things deteriorated rapidly. The wagon road leading from Toquerville east to Rockville and into the Mukuntuweap National Monument in Little Zion Canyon was too rutted and prone to mud holes to be passable to autos. To the south, a fearsome hill ascending the Hurricane escarpment challenged motorists, and beyond Short Creek, on the road to Pipe Springs, lay miles of sand traps punctuated by steep-sided gullies. From Panguitch, along the route of present-day Highway 89, the motorist faced high country where frequent rains and snowstorms rendered the soils a quagmire, and upon reaching the uplands between Mt. Carmel and Kanab, one encountered miles of dunes that defied the road builders' efforts. In 1911 a friend of Dee Woolley's, Wesley King of the Salt Lake Commercial Club, attempted the Panguitch-Kanab route in a horse-drawn buggy and got lost in the dune field, requiring Woolley to dispatch "a posse of Indian scouts" to the rescue.[22]

Officials in Washington County vied with Kane and Garfield counties for the advantage of hosting the proposed "Grand Canyon Highway" that would link Yellowstone National Park with the North Rim. Both routes to the North Rim—via Hurricane or Kanab—underwent improvements, and various touring parties organized by the Union Pacific and the Salt Lake Commercial Club publicized the trip. The *Salt Lake Tribune* sponsored an exploratory auto trip to Zion and the North Rim in 1916 that included railroad representatives as well as Utah governor William Spry; this was followed by more semiofficial trips consisting of railroad and highway boosters that were designed to promote the region as a tourist destination and to obtain funds for road improvements.[23] Utah newspapers of the period trumpeted their belief that tens, even hundreds of thousands, of visitors would soon be arriving in autos, headed for Zion and the North Rim.[24]

The road improvements, aided by sporadic federal funds starting in 1916, turned the trick. By the early 1920s, the North Rim was hosting nearly three thousand visitors a year.[25] Little Zion Canyon saw its first autos run up a newly graded road in 1917. That same year W. W. Wylie, originator of the tent-camping concept at Yellowstone, opened permanent tourist camps at both locations. In Cedar City, Utah, Chauncey and Gronway Parry started a bus touring venture that offered all three of the major scenic destinations in the region—Zion Canyon, the North Rim, and Bryce Canyon—linked together in a ten-day loop tour. By 1923, the Union Pacific had set up a tour service called the Utah Parks Company to ferry tourists from the rail station at Lund to a new hotel at Cedar City, and it bought out the Parry brothers' bus tour operation.[26] With the completion of Grand Canyon Lodge at the North Rim in 1928, the remote northern shore of the canyon entered the modern age.

As tour operators began to supplant one-on-one service, Dave Rust, and discerning travelers like George Fraser, retreated to the inner fastness of the Plateau Province—to Glen Canyon and other hidden wonders that resisted the advance of roads. The two men visited the Crossing of the Fathers in Glen Canyon in 1922 and floated Glen in Rust's canvas canoes in 1930. This southeastern section of the canyon lands was where Dave Rust's compatriots in the guiding business, Zeke Johnson of Blanding and John Wetherill of Kayenta, led most of their trips.

Wetherill was well known for guiding the Theodore Roosevelt and Zane Grey parties to Rainbow Bridge in 1913; he had been appointed custodian of the monument in 1910. Johnson specialized in trips to the natural bridges in White Canyon, which had become a National Monument in 1908, and was appointed custodian there in 1921. As early as 1918 Rust started exploring the Paunsaugunt Plateau, where Bryce Canyon National Monument would be designated in 1923. He also began outfitting the first regular boat trips in Glen Canyon in that year.[27]

George Fraser knew all along that the days of quiet wanderings in the isolated park lands were numbered; he was, after all, an investor who helped direct railroad and ranch development in the Southwest. Still, he lamented the coming of democratic tourism. In 1918 he wrote to Rust, "Of course I thought about running a railway into the Kaibab and was deterred from doing so by purely selfish motives. I cannot bear to have that eden desecrated by the multitude."[28] In 1921 he returned to this theme, telling Rust, "I hope you will let me ride with you again not a few times before the Grand Canyon is turned into a lake and there is an airplane station on Powell's Plateau."[29] Years later, in a letter to his friend J. Cecil Alter, he expressed disgust at automobiles reaching the tip of Point Sublime. Alter, for his part, objected to Fraser's elitism, pointing out that not everyone could afford to hire horses and a guide for weeks on end. This tension between mass tourism and individual adventuring would be played out for the rest of the century, with the automobile (and those favoring easy access) mostly winning.

A handful of avid explorers such as Charles Bernheimer, Neil Judd, and Clyde Kluckhohn kept up the tradition into the 1930s, launching expeditions across the Navajo reservation to Rainbow Bridge, the San Juan River outback, and the Kaiparowits Plateau. Development was encroaching even in this wilderness stronghold, though. The first motorists to traverse Monument Valley and the northern Navajo reservation—south of where Fraser and Rust got lost in 1916—were W. H. Hopkins of Salt Lake City and Dolph Andrus of Bluff, Utah, who took a Maxwell auto from Bluff to Kanab in the spring of 1917.[30] They reported stretches of sand and difficult cut banks, in one case requiring John Wetherill's team to pull them out of Laguna Wash, but they envisioned the track through Kayenta and Tuba City as a great tourist route. Monument Valley soon became a regular destination for auto wayfarers.[31] At Navajo Mountain the Richardson brothers opened Rainbow Lodge in 1924, welcoming visitors arriving by auto on a newly constructed track and guiding them on horseback to Rainbow Bridge.

The bridge itself would remain difficult to reach until Lake Powell offered access by motorboat.[32]

Although isolated by today's standards, the plateau and canyon country of George Fraser's travels was by no means uninhabited. Sheepherders and cattlemen ranged into every canyon and plateau, and homesteaders were staking out almost every mountain valley outside the forest reserves.[33] But these people, as well as most villagers, were dealing with their own challenges and were not exactly anticipating tourists. There were few inns or stores outside of towns such as Hurricane or Kanab. Nor were Park Service officials present to help; the national monuments in Utah were entirely unmanned at least through 1916. If a wagon axle broke or a horse went lame, the traveler had to hope that whoever was living nearby would be able to help. Since such upsets almost always occurred even to the best prepared, the traveler was often forced into negotiations with the people of the region. Most of the people Fraser and Rust met, however, displayed a wonderful generosity. When they showed up at some herder's or ranger's isolated cabin, they often were invited to spend the night, have a meal, pasture their horses, and share a story. Their hosts would insist on sending them off with loaves of fresh bread, fruit from their trees, a leg of mutton, and a promise to write. In those days travelers were few and were a welcome source of news and entertainment. What visitor today would be invited to return with his family and spend the next summer, as Ranger Walter Hanks's wife offered at Wildcat Station on the Aquarius in 1915?

As the Southwest's parks and monuments became more accessible, some of this intimate immersion in the culture was lost. Rare is the visitor today who will strike up a conversation with a cowboy met on the trail or sit down to dinner with a family in Fredonia and talk about the drought or the price of beef. Most of us lack the time to spend day after day in a leisurely examination of the landscape as Fraser insisted on doing.

While the canyon country of today may be thoroughly mapped and understood, it still captivates us with the glow of its sandstone cliffs, the mystic wonder of its abandoned pueblos, the limitless allure of its winding gorges. With a little care, it is still possible to string together a four-week adventure of discovery, even if one is never more than a day's hike from a road. George Fraser's journals encourage us to slow down and savor these landscapes, to treat them as worthy of careful study. We might venture some of the same curiosity and openness that led him to his instructive encounters with the residents of this wild region, many of whose families still live there. Though the bedrock of Fraser's beloved landscape has changed little, there are new stories to hear that mark the continuing evolution of man's relation to a wondrous part of the earth.

Notes on the Journals

Fraser took notes on a great variety of natural and cultural phenomena, many of which may interest the modern reader but some that could only be described as arcane. In an effort to make three of his canyon lands journals available in one volume, I omitted many of his more mundane observations of rock outcrops and soil conditions. As Stephen Jett notes, the geologic features of the canyon lands are not ephemeral and have been thoroughly described elsewhere.[34] I retained many more of Fraser's observations of local people and culture. These cannot be revisited and provide much of the interest of these journals.

Where Fraser was traveling through unremarkable country (or where for other reasons his journal did not seem especially lively), I dropped whole days from the journal and substituted a synopsis.

Much of the journals, the first especially, are written in a telegraphic style ("Left camp Nixon Ranger Station 5 p.m."); this is mostly left intact to keep the flavor of contemporaneous field notes. He also shifts tense repeatedly, even within paragraphs; this may reflect notes written at different times of the day as well as after the trip when he dictated the manuscript. With some reluctance, I have changed most verbs to past tense for consistency's sake, except where he is describing some permanent physiographic or cultural feature. The historian may fault this liberty; I can only argue that the journals do not have the supreme significance of Lewis and Clark's or some other preeminent explorer's, within which scholars can find meaning in every line. The facts as Fraser states them are left unchanged.

Obvious errors of spelling have been corrected, as Fraser no doubt would have done had he prepared the journals for publication (again, the typos in his dictated account do not have the charm of Clark's "Ocian in view!"). Words that we compound today were often hyphenated or split in Fraser's time ("to-day; up hill"), and these are retained. The spelling of geographic names is standardized with modern usage unless a historical appellation was being used. I have retained his lowercase use of geologic ages ("jura," "eocene") to emphasize their provisional status at the time.

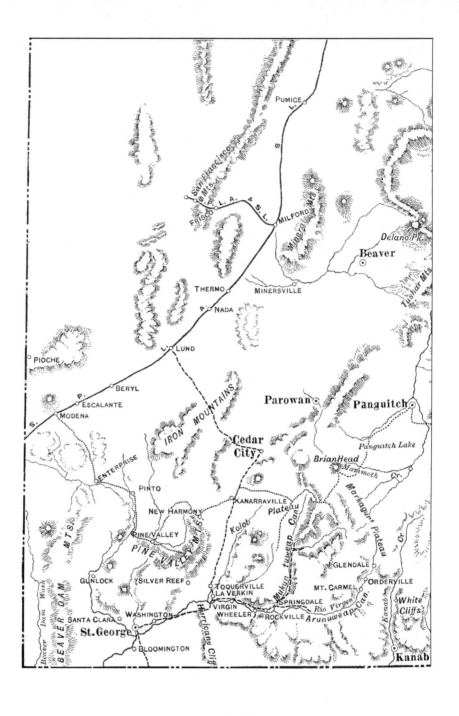

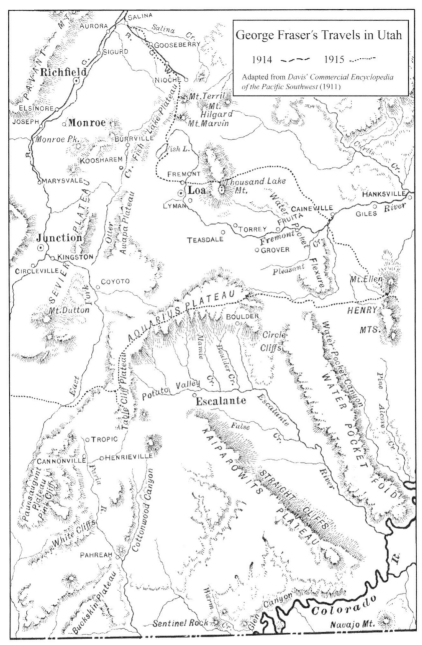

George Fraser's Travels in Utah

1914 ~ ~ ~   1915 ......

Adapted from *Davis' Commercial Encyclopedia of the Pacific Southwest* (1911)

Base map courtesy Special Collections, Marriott Library, University of Utah

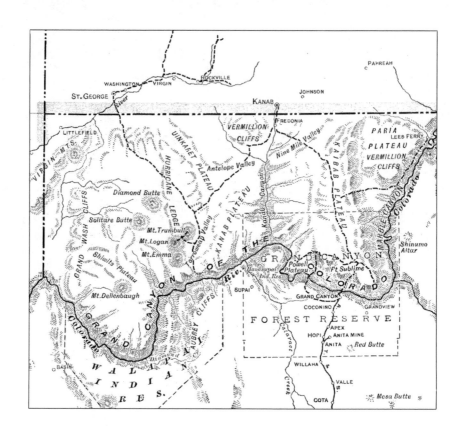

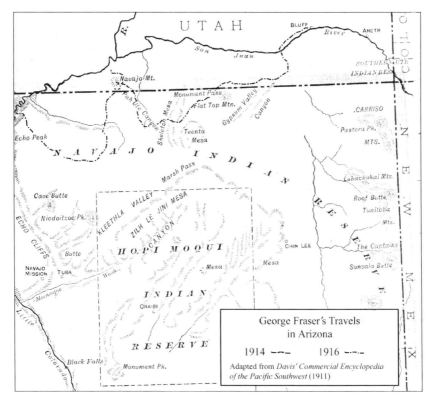

Base map courtesy Special Collections, Marriott Library, University of Utah

Many of his barometer readings, times of day, and temperatures are omitted, but some are retained where they help give the flavor of the day's activities.

Fraser used a scattering of terms to describe the rock layers found in the canyon country. Some of these are from Dutton, others are from Gilbert, Powell, or later works.[35] In an addendum to his 1914 journal, he tried to update these terms to accord with then-current usage, but some of these would still be foreign to the modern reader. Briefly, the rock strata he describes correlate as follows:

Granite: The Precambrian Vishnu Schist and Zoroaster Granite found in the depths of the Grand Canyon.

Algonkian: An older term for the Proterozoic Era (Late Precambrian), represented by various formations within the Grand Canyon Supergroup.

Cross-bedded sandstone: Fraser sometimes uses this to denote the Navajo Sandstone north and east of the Grand Canyon; within the canyon, he seems to use it interchangeably to denote the Esplanade Sandstone and the Coconino Sandstone (both Permian).

Kaibab Limestone: The Kaibab and Toroweap Formations (Permian) forming the rim of the Grand Canyon.

Shinarump: The Shinarump conglomerate, the basal member of the Triassic Chinle Formation.

Trias: Generally the Wingate Sandstone or Moenave Formation. Debate continues over the age of these formations; many publications assign them to the Jurassic, others maintain they are Late Triassic. Occasionally, Fraser uses this term to refer to what appear to be the red beds of the Moenkopi Formation.

Jura: Generally the Navajo Sandstone (Jurassic), the white, cross-bedded sandstone found throughout the canyon country. Fraser includes the underlying Kayenta Formation in this.

Despite the many revisions geologists have made to the stratigraphy and formation of the Colorado Plateau, Fraser's understanding of this region, based on his careful reading of the literature of the day, is much the same as we would know today. As Stephen Pyne observed, "After a hundred years, the larger interpretation of the plateau country is still the one which Powell, Dutton, and Gilbert collectively gave it."[36]

Journeys in the Canyon Lands of Utah and Arizona

Chapter 1

From Zion to the Grand Canyon, 1914

The roar of the river was not soothing; perhaps one would become accustomed to it in time, but I was never a moment unconscious of it. This roar seemed to speak of force, fierce and destructive, ready for immediate application, and the canyon walls seemed to bear silent witness to the speaker's power.
—George Fraser's journal, Bass Crossing, July 31, 1914

By early 1914, three years after his visit to the South Rim, George Fraser had worked up his wish list for an excursion to the North Rim of the Grand Canyon. Besides traversing forty miles of the rim from its east-ernmost edge to Powell's Plateau, he wanted to explore the Uinkaret Plateau and the Toroweap Valley to the west, where dramatic cliff lines and recent volcanism were on display. In addition, he wanted to ride up the Virgin River in Utah, where a great sandstone canyon known as Little Zion had been designated as Mukuntuweap National Monument just five years earlier.

It was an ambitious foray for an Easterner with little experience in the backcountry of the Southwest. The nearest rail stop—a branch of the Union Pacific—was at Lund, Utah, two hundred miles to the north of Bright Angel Point. Much of the route from Lund to the canyon consisted of successively worse dirt roads and wagon tracks that led through a harsh, windswept desert and up onto the confusing pine forest of the Kaibab Plateau. The few tourists who attempted the route usually went by horse or wagon.

Fraser wrote to the Union Pacific for information. The railroad's pas-senger agent in Salt Lake City, J. H. Manderfield, sent Fraser an account of a 1913 trip to the North Rim that had appeared in the *Salt Lake Tribune*. Fraser promptly wrote to its author, J. Cecil Alter, who was a Weather Bureau official in Salt Lake City, outlining his proposed trip.

For such an undertaking, Fraser asked, was a guide necessary? "Guides?" Alter replied. "They are usually good animals to have around, in theory, at least, though my guide consisted chiefly in a map, some knowledge of the stars, and plenty of faith in Good [sic]. But, if you want a guide, I happen to know there is only one, and he is D. D. Rust of Kanab, Utah. He was with us several days, as company, as well as guide at the Canyon rim. He was a cowboy a long time and knows Arizona north of the Gash like a book—says he has walked over most of it."[1]

Alter's advice proved fortuitous, for it led Fraser to the man who would not only guide him to the North Rim but also pilot him on four subsequent expeditions covering thousands of miles by horseback, wagon, and canoe through the most remote reaches of southern Utah and northern Arizona.

As it turned out, David Dexter Rust was a good deal more than a cowboy. He had been elected superintendent of schools in Kanab, published the local newspaper, and was a prominent tourism promoter. From 1906 to 1909 he had been in charge of a crew building a cable-tram crossing of the Colorado at the mouth of Bright Angel Creek in the Grand Canyon, where he also opened a tent camp for tourists. He knew J. H. Manderfield through his contacts in the Salt Lake Commercial Club, and Manderfield was happy to make arrangements for Rust to guide the Frasers on their journey. They were to meet at the little town of Toquerville, Utah, and head up the Virgin River to explore Little Zion.

Fraser's route would visit most of the terrain described in Capt. Clarence E. Dutton's *Tertiary History of the Grand Cañon District* (1882), the masterful overview of the so-called Grand Staircase of cliffs and plateaus stretching a hundred miles north from the Colorado River to the high Markagunt and Paunsaugunt Plateaus in Utah. Fraser brought a copy of this work along to study at the canyon overlooks. In four strenuous weeks of travel he and his son would get a sense of a huge swath of territory—a landscape sculpture created in what Dutton called the "Great Denudation," wherein thousands of cubic miles of stratified sedimentary rock had been stripped away, leaving a sequence of scenic promontories rising nine thousand feet above the base level cut by the Colorado.

Dutton's works (including his *Report on the Geology of the High Plateaus of Utah*, published in 1880) continue to interest readers today, long after his contemporaries' work has faded. Part of their timelessness stems from the excitement they convey, so unusual for government reports. Wallace Stegner, in his introduction to the 1977 Peregrine Smith reprint of *Tertiary History*, ascribes the immediacy of Dutton's work to his use of a "narrative frame," in which the reader travels with Dutton and W. H. Holmes, his illustrator, watching stone temples and parapets slowly emerge as they ride across the desert. "Dutton," Stegner wrote, "not only taught geologists how to explain the chasm [of the Colorado], but taught all sorts of visitors how to see it."[2] George Fraser was quite willing to be instructed. A noteworthy instance occurred near Grafton, Utah, at the end of a long day that had included an exploration of Parunuweap Canyon. Reaching camp, Fraser and his son did not even dismount, but rode up a steep wagon road to the south, hoping to catch a late afternoon view across the Virgin River valley from Grafton Mesa. He was in search of a viewpoint Dutton memorably described on page 57 of *Tertiary History*; whether he reached it is not clear, but the weather indulged him in a brilliant display of a double rainbow arching over Zion. His description of this event echoes Dutton, and it is clear that his reading prepared him for an unforgettable experience.

More marvels awaited as the party continued into Arizona. At dozens of canyon viewpoints, his maps and atlases spread out over the ground, binoculars in hand, Fraser passed along his appreciation of Dutton, Powell, and the canyon scene to Dave Rust. Rust already had a keen sense for the wonders of the canyon lands, but years later he would credit Fraser for completing his education. Fraser, ever appreciative of his guide, would return the compliment.

Their journey concluded with an arduous descent of the Grand Canyon from Muav Saddle to William W. Bass's cable crossing near Bass Rapids. Fraser's account of the night they spent in the depths of the gorge—their food gone, uncertain of the next day's crossing, and listening in awe to the flooding river, ranks as some of the most evocative of Grand Canyon writing.

The Frasers left the East Coast on June 28, 1914, riding the Denver & Rio Grande into Salt Lake City on July 3 (this portion of the journal is omitted). They stayed at the Hotel Utah ("in equipment, service and cuisine, one of the best hotels I ever stopped at"). That evening they visited a downtown market, where Fraser bought two pounds of cherries for fifteen cents, and called on Mrs. J. Cecil Alter to view her husband's photographs from their trip the year before. They observed a "safe and sane" Fourth of July in Salt Lake City, noting the absence of firecrackers and noise in the streets. After calling on Manderfield to finalize arrangements, the Frasers took a tour of Temple Square (listening to the obligatory whisper and pin drop in the Tabernacle) and visited the Bingham copper mine. Heavy rains throughout the day were a harbinger of the wet weather they would experience for much of the trip. At 11:50 that evening they boarded the San Pedro, Los Angeles, and Salt Lake train for Lund, Utah, and the start of their canyon adventure.

George Fraser's Journal

Sunday, July 5, 1914

Up 6:30 a.m.; temperature in car 62, clear; running through Sevier desert. High mountains on the east still showing snow; mud-holes in the desert and water standing in some depressions. Much of the surface bare, with growth of sage and low shrubs. Except for three large birds like crows and numerous gopher holes, we saw no signs of life. About half-way between Milford and Lund, George saw a Ford motor stuck in the mud, with a broken axle, and some horses being attached to pull it out. We subsequently learned that this car had been hired for our use to take us to Toquerville for $15, but the driver had gone to Milford to spend the Fourth, gotten drunk, and in the night ran himself into trouble.

Arrived Lund 9:38 on time. Grouchy young fellow named "Jim" greeted us with the inquiry as to whether we were the parties going to Toquerville and told us to hurry up and get our luggage on the automobile. I demurred and inquired for Doolittle and found him. He pacified Jim for a few minutes and we went into Doolittle's storeroom, changed our clothes, packed the stuff we were not going to take and threw into the duffle bags what we thought we needed, all in a great hurry, under repeated urgings and threats from Jim, who backed up his own insistence with messages from an old lady that was in a hurry to get to Cedar City.

Lund is in the midst of the desert and most unattractive. Manderfield said the less time we spent in Lund the better we would like it, which completely describes the place.

Left Lund 10:40 in a Cadillac motor. In the back seat was an elderly man, his wife and a silent person. On the front seat an old lady, a girl of about 22, named Edna, and Jim, the driver. George and I on the little seats in the middle. Our luggage and everybody else's strapped on the running board or anywhere it would hold.

Jim announced that he had been in Milford to spend the Fourth and had not gone to bed all night and was very tired. Edna kept him awake as long as she stayed with us. She went most of the way across the desert and was dropped at a dry farm operated as an experiment by a Nebraska man. In every depression the recent rains had made havoc with the road. We ran through many puddles and mudholes and in places had to leave the road altogether, which, after all, did not make much difference.

Our course lay about southeast to a gap in the hills near Iron Springs, where we struck the road from Modena to Cedar. Across Cedar Valley we looked up the canyon of Coal Creek to the high Markagunt Plateau and vaguely, through the misty atmosphere, could descry the vermilion, white and pink of the outcropping rocks terraced in accordance with the several formations.

After Edna got out, Jim told us to beat him over the head if we saw him going to sleep.

Distance Lund to Cedar City 35 miles. Arrived 1 p.m.

We were taken to a hotel and told to eat lunch, after which Jim would call for us. Hot, filthy dirty and lunch vile. Had to work hard not to eat flies. Two Harvard men at hotel. They were part of a party of six who planned to hunt for 2½ months with Uncle Jim Owens on the high plateaus in an effort to capture alive a cougar. The larger of the Harvard men very fresh. Came from Groton and turned out to be the same fellow that irritated Alter on the Kaibab last year. He had blood-poisoning in his foot and was compelled to lay up. His friend was keeping him company.

While in the middle of lunch the owner of the automobile, B. F. Knell, a large man with a black mustache and loud voice and an aroma of whiskey, burst in and told me he would not take us to Toquerville. He asked what arrangements had been made. I told him Doolittle had arranged with Jim to take us to Toquerville for $20. Knell refused to go beyond Belleview. Considerable argument ensued. Finally Knell got the manager of the telephone office to open up the wire (telephone service is suspended most of Sunday) and we got Doolittle. A compromise was ultimately effected, whereby Knell agreed to take us within 2½ miles of Toquerville, and arranged with Anderson, who had a ranch there, to take us into Toquerville for $2. Left Cedar City 2:45 p.m. Sun out and hot. Knell drove. Jim was sent to bed.

Followed south down the valley along Shirtz Creek, crossing numerous side canyons. Beginning south of where we entered Cedar Valley the Pine Valley mountains rise steadily in height. They form the dominant feature of the landscape until the sheer face of Hurricane Cliff comes into view.

The road was substantially level for the first 12 or 13 miles and everything went well enough. Then we got into the basalt. The valley narrowed and the road ran along the mountain on the east side over a gorge cut by the river. It was winding, with a steep fall of 60–75 feet on the right and descended at a fairly heavy grade. Knell tried to put on the brake and it would not hold. He asked me to take the wheel while he pulled the brake with both hands, which, of course, had no result, as the brake was entirely burnt out. George, sitting behind, took direction of affairs and instructed Knell how to brake with his engine so that we negotiated this stretch of road in safety. A few miles further down, after passing Belleview, another steep down grade was encountered. Here Knell lost his head, turned white, broke out in a cold sweat and said "Boys, she's off." George was sitting in the front seat and tried to get Knell to put the engine in low speed, but Knell was too frightened to do anything. I urged George to jump, but we all stayed in the car, except one of the bags, which fell off and was run over. We ended by running into a dry wash at the bottom of the descent, going part way up the other side and settling back again. Right here Anderson met us.

We paid Knell and sent him about his business. This was at 5:40 p.m.

Anderson had a two-seated buggy with the back seat out and the rear filled up with apricots and peaches. George got out a shotgun and killed two cotton-tails on the way down to Toquerville. Distance 2½ miles. Arrived Toquerville 6:30.

We were taken to the house of Mrs. Naegle, on the northerly edge of town. About the house is a vegetable garden and numerous fruit trees. Mrs. Naegle is a widow. She was married before to a man named Klineman, and her daughter, age about 25, lives with her. Miss Klineman taught school at Enterprise last winter. She played the piano for us very well during supper.

Mrs. Naegle's husband was the son of one of the original settlers, a German, who built a large stone house at Toquerville, back in the 50's. He had seven wives, the only survivor of whom we saw living across the street from Mrs. Naegle.

Naegle's principal occupation was making wine. He made about 2500 gallons a year. He constructed large cellars to keep it in. The old house is now deserted.[3]

Toquerville lies about two miles north of the Virgin River,[4] on the southerly slope of a basalt flow running across the Hurricane Valley. Its water comes from a spring a mile and a half away bursting from the mountain-side. It has the best water in the whole Dixie country and plenty of it. The water flows from the spring to the town in an open ditch and is carried through the town in deep gutters. To get a drink of water for cooking purposes, you walk into the street, stand on a board bridging the gutter, and help yourself. Its name is of Indian derivation, "Toquer" meaning black and indicating the color of the rock thereabouts. Its soil is wonderfully fertile.

We had fresh figs, apricots, cherries, peaches, tomatoes, and various kinds of vegetables. In addition they grow quantities of almonds and grapes. Roses bloom for nine months in the year.

We found D. D. Rust waiting for us and spent part of the evening planning out the trip. To bed about 9:30, G.C.F., Jr. and Rust sleeping on cots on the porch and I in a room.

Monday, July 6, 1914

Up 5:45 a.m., temp. 66, temp. of water in the ditch 58. Miss Klineman tried hard to get us some Dixie wine or at least grape juice, but none was to be had. The wine industry flourished until about three years ago, when a temperance wave struck Dixie, since which time very little wine has been made and none is to be had except on the quiet.

Last night Rust had arranged with a Mr. Duffin to drive us to Hurricane at 6 o'clock. He turned up at 7 and we left at 7:15. Rust had with him two horses and saddles. Duffin provided a side-spring buggy, with one seat, and we filled the back with our luggage and supplies.

From Toquerville we proceeded generally east of south, over a rough road, steep in places, and along a creek. For about four miles and until reaching La Verkin Creek, the way was over lava. There seemed to be flows of different ages, the youngest evidently very recent, because I saw a contact by the road where lava lay over river gravel and had baked the upper surface.[5]

8:15 a.m. arrived at La Verkin, four miles from Toquerville. A small town with little land under cultivation. Floods in the Virgin have created havoc with the old farms. There was growing some grain, many peaches and apricots and grapes. Got some ripe apples here.

La Verkin Creek and the Virgin both flow in deep canyons. We forded the former and crossed the latter on a good iron bridge right by the Hot Sulphur Spring.[6] This spring rises on the south bank of the Virgin, about 25 feet above the river in a limestone. It deposits sinter and a green fungus grows where the waters flow, creating a bright stream of color. Temp. of spring 104 degrees. Sulphurous odor apparent 200 yards away. Taste bitter.

9:20 arrived at Hurricane. While Rust shopped, Duffin drove us one mile to the west, to foot of a volcanic cone. We had to walk up. Arrived at the top at 10:15. Temp. in the sun 117; shade 99. There is a distinct crater at the summit, which is worn off toward the north. Duffin has been familiar with this mountain since the early 70's and he called attention to the obscuring, within that time, of the basalt at the summit. Beside the cone we were on, there were three others in the immediate vicinity, one of them with an even more distinct crater than that we inspected. There was every evidence of recency of volcanic action. I found a perfect volcanic bomb and the ground was covered with pumice, scoriae and clinkers.

Returning from the volcano, arrived at Hurricane 11:50. Hotel kept by Mrs. Ira Bradshaw of English parentage. Husband soft-looking and has reputation of taking things easy. Conspicuous on the parlor table was a large and handsome book, entitled "The Curse of Drink." Except for this, the entire parlor was filled with a patchwork quilt spread out on a frame. Mrs. Bradshaw said she was not expecting any boarders so she had arranged to do a quilting. Soon after lunch one of the neighbors came in to help quilt. House clean; lunch very good. Great many flies, but the house screened, so the dining-room was comfortable. Temp. in the house, 2 p.m., 88; in wagon, 3 p.m., 96. Lots of fruit and fresh vegetables.

We had expected to hire another team at Hurricane, but Duffin wanted to go with us, in spite of the fact that he had no luggage and had not even brought his coat. So we loaded supplies and started at 3 p.m., retracing our steps across the bridge over the Virgin by the Sulphur Spring and to LaVerkin.

Near LaVerkin we turned northeast, ascended a steep and very rough hill and followed along its side above the canyon of the Virgin River to Virgin City. From the crest of the hill above LaVerkin had fine view up the Virgin, showing the towers. Approaching the crossing of North Creek, fine view to the north over the permian and trias, with white beehive shaped peaks of the jura in the distance.

Virgin City is poor, with little land under cultivation. The houses in the town are surrounded by fruit trees. I asked the privilege of purchasing some apricots of the lady who kept the post office. She instructed me to climb an apricot tree and gave me a basket, which I filled. In the meanwhile, she gathered some apples and presented us with all the fruit, and some water thrown in.

The Virgin water is so muddy it must be allowed to settle before being put to household use. As far as possible rain water is preserved, but precipitation here is so slight that there is not a great supply from this source. Each householder consequently takes water from the river in barrels and allows the mud to settle before drawing off the top for drinking and culinary purposes.

From Virgin City we continued up the valley, mostly along the north

Approaching the Western Temple of Zion (then Mukuntuweap
National Monument), near Rockville, Utah, 1913.
Photograph by J. Cecil Alter.

bank of the river, but several times fording the stream, to Grafton (formerly Wheeler). The last five miles of the way the road was very rough
and ran under cliffs of basalt, showing in places fine columnar structure. Camped at Rockville under a tree at river's edge. Barometer
showed rise of 550 feet from Hurricane. Cooked supper; slept on the
ground; to bed 10 p.m. Thirty miles today.

Tuesday, July 7, 1914
Up 4:15; temp. 10 p.m. to 4:30 a.m., minimum 66, maximum 72. Strong
breeze; comfortable night. Rust developed sore throat. Told of tendency
to quinsy and scared us; doctored him with Dioxogen.[7]

Rockville lies about 1½ miles to the west of the forks of the Virgin.
The peaches here were especially fine and we saw many mulberry trees.
The berries are used as hog feed. Years ago silk worms were raised, but
the market for the silk is so poor it does not pay now.

Between Rockville and Springdale we skirted the permian slopes
forming the base from which rose in dignified majesty the Western
Temple of the Virgin, disrespectfully (even if with some degree of veri-
similitude) dubbed the Steamboat.

Arrived Springdale 8:45. Stopped at store kept by J. J. Ruesch, native,
of St. Galleri Switzerland, here since 1874. Has forgotten most of his
German. Here met a party of Salt Lake school teachers—five women and

three men, one of the latter McNeisch, Princeton, '97. These people knew the Alters and had heard of our coming. Their outfit consisted of two riding horses, a big pioneer's wagon driven by Jim Emmet and a buggy driven by a young man. Jim Emmet formerly lived at Lee's Ferry. He is a pioneer. He was driven out of Lee's Ferry by the Grand Canyon Cattle Company people, with whose superintendent he had quarreled. The two men had guns out for each other for some time. Emmett was accused of stealing cattle up in that country and of various irregularities, with what justice I could not learn.

Near Springdale numerous black thorny locusts; flowers—roses, daisies, poppies and single carnations. Lunched by the river, just below Crawfords,[8] near a ford. Bathed in the river, temp. 68. Just as we were going in a wagon-load of women crossed ford. Rust saved the day by covering us with horse blankets.

Fine view up amphitheater running back of the Steamboat. White sandstone walls are discolored by the dripping from the red cap of the mountain, which supports rich vegetation of large yellow pine and Douglas fir trees. This presents the finest view we have seen yet. The Crawfords have fine apricots and peaches. We bought some eggs from them. The river is rapid, carrying gray mud.[9]

Left Crawfords 1:30, arrived at camp, 1½ miles above foot of cableway, 5 p.m. Up 525 feet from Springdale and 900 feet from Rockville. Temp. 5 p.m., 84.

Whole afternoon followed up deep canyon with precipitous walls in most places and the bottom not to exceed half or possibly three-quarters of a mile at its widest points. At cable tramway valley bends toward west for a little way and then north again. We camped in a widening of the valley, between two narrow gateways. Here the walls are so high that at 5 o'clock the entire valley bottom was in the shade. After supper climbed over talus at foot of westerly wall of canyon. Clouds obscured the moon. To bed 9 o'clock, when the stars began to come out and breeze arose from the north.

Wednesday, July 8, 1914
At 2:45 a.m. clear with very bright, nearly full, moon. Up 5 a.m. River down perceptibly since last night. At 7 a.m. started on horseback; rode about a mile and a half up canyon; left horses 7:40. After ten minutes' walking on dry land we had to ford the river and from this point were almost continuously in the water until our return.

About a mile and a half above where we left the horses, the canyon

Little Zion Canyon in Mukuntuweap National Monument, July 8, 1914. Before its designation as Zion National Park in 1919, few tourists took the trouble to come here. Photograph by George C. Fraser.

closed in so that the stream filled the entire bottom and it continued practically this way as far as we went. It was impossible to swim against the current and we had to wade over the rocks, chest deep. About a mile above this point we struck a side canyon of equal depth and narrowness with Zion Canyon, coming in from the southeast. The water was very muddy, of gray color. Rust guessed and afterward confirmed that this was the Orderville Gulch. Up to this point there had been no sun to warm us. The canyon was in places less than 20 feet wide. The walls looked to be 1000, perhaps 1500 feet high, rising sheer and in several places concave, so that the sky overhead was obscured. We were cold from the water and very wet. Here we found some drift-wood, built a fire, took off our clothes, dried them on the rocks and warmed ourselves in the sun. About two miles above where we left the horses, the trias seemed to dip under. From there on we were in the cross-bedded sandstone. The finest and most striking cliffs of this appear on the side walls of the Orderville Gulch.

At 1 p.m. we started up Orderville Gulch and followed it until 2:45. Our progress was slow because of the roughness of the walking and

Dave Rust *(left)* and George Fraser Jr. wading the narrows of the Virgin
River, Zion Canyon, July 8, 1914. Photograph by George C. Fraser.

although there was not a great deal of water in the stream, we kept
pretty wet. We encountered three waterfalls, one of them 20 feet high,
which we had to climb. The Orderville Gulch Canyon is narrower than
the Zion Canyon and apparently equally deep. In five places—perhaps
more—the sky is shut out overhead. We estimated that we walked 2½ to
3 miles up this canyon. Left for return down canyon 2:50; arrived lunch
place 3:55; ate remains of lunch and left 4:30 and followed up Zion

George Fraser Jr. atop the lumber cable headworks
on Cable Mountain, East Rim of Zion Canyon.
Photograph by George C. Fraser.

Canyon until 4:55. The sky was overcast, a few drops of rain fell, and we heard the rumblings of thunder. The canyon was as dark as an hour after sunset. Overhanging walls obscured the sky. Reluctantly we turned back and hurried down the canyon as fast as we could, reaching the horses at 6:25 and arriving at camp at 7:10. We estimated that we walked and waded up Zion 5 miles and up Orderville Gulch 2½ miles, a total of 15 miles, plus 3 miles more on horseback from and to the camp.

While the day was hard and fatiguing and at times we suffered from the cold, none of us were any the worse for it. As a matter of precaution we each took two grains of quinine and some raw whiskey before supper.

Thursday, July 9–Friday, July 10. The Frasers and Rust climbed up a treacherous trail to the top of Cable Mountain, visiting a primitive sawmill and spending the night with Orin Ruesch, grandson of the storekeeper they had met in Springdale, and his wife. On July 10 they inspected the headworks of the 2,500-foot-long cableway that was used to lower logs to the bottom of Zion Canyon, the remains of which are still visible above the Weeping Rock pull-off in the national park. Rust related stories of people who had ridden the cable. Fraser noted that "there is nothing terrifying in the trip up or down by itself, but for anyone to risk his life on the wire in its present condition is foolhardy beyond justification." The party returned on foot to the valley bottom, where Isaac Duffin was waiting to take them down the canyon. They made camp at Shunesburg, a deserted town a short distance up the East Fork of the Virgin River.

Saturday, July 11, 1914

A cloudless night; moon still up at sunrise. Up 6:15; cool. Heavy dew during the night for the first time. Somewhat troubled by flies and mosquitoes, owing to the proximity of the corral.

Ascended hill to west; fine view down Virgin Valley and up Shunesburg Creek. Left camp 8:30. Took Rust's two horses and Maude out of Duffin's team. Rode up Parunuweap eight miles until 11:20.[10] Brilliant sun overhead. Horses could go no further. Instead of the sheer cliffs characteristic of Zion Valley, the Parunuweap is bounded by steep naked slopes, save for the bush-covered talus, and the valley bottom is relatively wide. Though tempted to proceed up the creek to a waterfall that lies about four miles beyond where we stopped, the heat and fatigue and the difficulty of threading the underbrush made us turn back. Left on return 1 p.m., arrived in camp, riding hard, 3 p.m. George, riding bareback, had his saddle blanket slip and fall off. Took bath in Shunesburg Creek. Very hot sun. A little relief around two o'clock when it clouded over and a few drops of rain fell.

Shunesburg was one of the first places settled in the upper Virgin Valley. Its grave yard contains the remains of many of the old settlers; old timers are buried there even now. Outside of the corral and the alfalfa fields about it, the only sign of habitation is a great stone house standing on the hill slope south of the Virgin. This was built by the original DeMills prior to 1874. It is in three sections, each with a door, the center for the old man and two wings for each of his wives.

Left Shunesburg about 4. Arrived Rockville, six miles, about 5:30.

Found eight young men in two groups sitting in the road outside the post office, playing High-Low Jack and waiting for the mail.

Arrived Grafton, via the same road we took on the trip up, 6:30 p.m. Camped in the center of town on the basketball field of the school-house. George and I did not dismount, but proceeded at once up the cliff to the south of Grafton over a new road lately constructed. Rise from Grafton to summit of this hill 800 feet by barometer. On the way up, overtaken by a shower, but before this struck us, stopped and pho-tographed panorama of the towers of the Virgin. As we ascended the hill, the shower left us and passed over the Virgin Valley to the north; to the southeast in the direction of Short Creek another shower appeared, creating a rain-bow. As we neared the summit, the rain-bow spread and arched completely over the Virgin Valley to the east of us. Soon a double rain-bow appeared, the outside bow not quite complete, but the inside one rising at the north from the summit of the Steamboat, and ending at the south in and near the head of a side canyon coming into the Virgin Valley from the south. To the west the Pine Valley Mtns. stood up as a high wall and to the east the entire upper Virgin Valley was spread before us with all the temples brought out in sharp relief by the light of the setting sun; the colors of the rocks of every shade, from the light shales at the base of the permian through the chocolate at the summit, the vermilion cliffs above and the brilliant white of the jura, capped and streaked by the gypsiferous layers above, were accentuated and changed chameleon-like, as the sun moved down, and finally its light reflected from the clouds struck them. In the maze of color and sculpture, inter-est in and appreciation of details was lost. We were not tempted to have recourse to our glasses. This view was a picture framed by nature in the rain-bow, that only disappeared when the sun's rays passed. Whether this view was more beautiful than any other I have ever seen is not subject to determination; it is, however, one of a very few to be remem-bered as the most magnificent.

We lingered on the summit until dusk had well set in, and reached camp after dark—about 9:15. Three men living in Grafton sat about while we had supper, and gave us considerable information.

Grafton was formerly called "Wheeler," and as such appears on the old maps.

To bed 10:30.

Sunday, July 12. The party returned down the Virgin River valley to Hurri-cane, taking lunch at Mrs. Bradshaw's home. On the way, Rust noticed a stray sheep and roped it. Finding it badly injured, presumably by coyotes, Rust dispatched it, lashed it onto the wagon, and gave it to Mrs. Bradshaw. Back in Hurricane, they "regretfully" said goodbye to Mr. Duffin. Fraser provides this description:

Isaac Duffin is 58 years old. His home has been in Toquerville since 1862. When a boy he helped build the fort and stockade between La-Verkin and Hurricane and had experiences with the Indians, then rampant in these regions. For years he covered the country, prospecting as far north as Wyoming and west as California. He devoted much time to the Grand Canyon and the canyon of the Little Colorado. For some years he operated a ranch near Flagstaff, Arizona. At other times he operated sawmills and worked as a teamster, driving as many as 18 horses in a team, hauling lumber. Born and brought up a Mormon, he lapsed from orthodoxy, for years was a cigarette fiend, and according to gossip neglected his family and their interests in favor of the rum bottle. He neither drinks nor smokes now. He is a fine shot and an interesting, square old fellow. A brother of Duffin's was prominent in the Mormon church, for several years being president of the Southern State Mission.

During the lunch hour we laid in some supplies and made connections with our new driver, Dalton, who claimed to know thoroughly the Trumbull country. He had a buggy similar to Duffin's and a span of mules.

We left Hurricane at 2:45 p.m., and proceeded southwesterly on the east side of the Virgin River, across the Hurricane Valley. There is little grass and without water no prospect of improvement. A portion of it is appropriately called "Purgatory Flats." A noticeable feature to the west of the Hurricane Fault is the steep dip of the strata (60 to 70 degrees) toward the east. About eight miles from Hurricane we crossed the Virgin and soon connected with the road from St. George to Toquerville, a fine highway for this part of the country. Washington (four miles from St. George) has a cotton mill, built in the '50's by Brigham Young. It was used in the early days of settlement to supply cotton goods to the entire Mormon community and more recently for the Dixie country alone. When transportation facilities were provided 14 or 15 years ago, its operation was discontinued, except in a small way for the purpose of making cotton-batting for quilts, which is still carried on at some seasons of the year.

Arrived St. George 7:15 p.m. Put up the horses in a corral and camped in yard. After cooking supper we went to the soda fountain, but were refused any refreshments because of a curfew law that shut everything down on Sunday night at 8:30. We then went to the Dixie Hotel kept by Samuel Judd, who is Postmaster. In the office or parlor we found two girls, age from 20 to 25. They were the Misses Judd, and received and entertained us as though we were paying a formal call. Pretty soon a young man appeared in the hall and the older of the girls became agitated, arose and left. By and by a fresh boy of 12, the younger brother of the girls, came in. He asked every question he could think of and then began to tell me about the family. He said that his older sister's young man had come and they were sitting around the corner in the dark and invited me to come out and look at them. He became interested in my spectacles, never having seen such large ones, and called his sister's attention to them. I took them off to show him and his sister took off her glasses, which were of the patent clip variety, and stuck them on my nose, greatly to Rust's edification. Pretty soon a little girl came in, by name Phyllis (who I subsequently learned was a sort of granddaughter of Judd's), and the small boy took her on for trouble. Rust and I had come here on account of the light to write and read quietly.

Presently Judd appeared, age about 55, weight about 255. He looked as though he had never done a day's work. He makes up the mail at five in the evening, to go out at four the next morning, and some days he makes it up at noon and will not open the bag to put in anything deposited later.

In a little while we were joined by a frowsy-looking girl named Annie. She addressed our host as "Brother Judd," from which I assumed she was a sister-in-law. But I find that this form of address is customary among the Mormons and that she was brought in from near Enterprise to help with the work of the hotel. It was a very hot night. We slept on straw near the corral and fought ants and flies.

Monday, July 13, 1914

Up at 5:15. Washed and had breakfast at Hotel Dixie. We had ordered our breakfast at six, but it was quarter of seven before the dining-room opened. Then Annie appeared with her hair down, her clothes more messy than they were last night, and, as she subsequently advised us, with her shoes unbuttoned—she had been so hurried she had not had time to fix herself up. The breakfast was to match, except for the hot cakes. Annie had never seen a railway, though coming from a town 20 miles from Modena—this was Enterprise!

The morning was clear; a few fleecy clouds in the sky and intense heat in the sun. None of the stores opened before 8 o'clock and then it took much talk and patience to make our necessary purchases. Rust bought some meat and canned goods, while George and I each bought a flannel shirt for 60 cents.

Left 9:45 a.m., proceeding southeasterly, passing near the temple, which is constructed of white stone, and crossed the Virgin River, and at 11:30 arrived at the State Agricultural Station and met Ray Smith, Director in charge. Smith entertained us very lavishly. He supplied alfalfa and grain for the horses and took us into the garden, where he loaded us up with everything that was ripe. Among the products of the Agricultural Station are cantaloupes, tomatoes, corn, alfalfa, grapes (especially the seedless for raisins), mulberries, apples, peaches, figs, cotton, sugar-cane, sorghum, plums (Samoan), bees and trumpet vine. 12:30 temp. shade 85 degrees; sun 124 degrees. We had lunch with Smith, partly on what we had, but mostly on what he supplied. He had just received a consignment of lemons from home and gave us half of them to take along.

Left Agricultural Station 2:30 p.m. Thunder storm to the southwest in the distance. Sky overcast; cool all afternoon. Course generally to the south, over flats toward apparent mountains, but really a plateau. About a mile beyond the Agricultural Station we passed the last farm and met its owner, a Mr. Segmueller, who greeted us with enthusiasm and lavish hospitality. He not only gave us all the peaches we could eat, but insisted on our taking a soap box full of peaches, apricots and plums to eat on the road. The plums were of a variety strange to us. In size and shape they were similar to the large claret colored California plums on the New York market. They are less juicy than our Eastern plums but more tasty and have some of the flavor of a musk-melon. They are known here as Samoan plums.

On approaching the plateau which lay before us in the distance as we left the Agricultural Station, we followed up a long draw. In the streambeds some signs of recent rains were apparent; but otherwise everything was dry. We followed up this canyon to near its head and made a dry camp, arriving at 8:15 p.m., having covered about 25 miles. It was cool, pleasant breeze blowing, and we had no flies to bother us. George shot two rabbits which we ate for supper. We had crossed the Arizona line.

On the way up the canyon we had a view of the Steamboat in the distant east. From the Agricultural Station we brought a barrel of water (32 gals.) for the stock and a keg (8 gals.) for ourselves, and a quantity of alfalfa. We estimated the load, exclusive of wagon, up to this point, weighed about 1300 pounds.

Tuesday, July 14–Wednesday, July 15. The Frasers, Rust, and Dalton made their way south into the remote tract known as the Arizona Strip, slowly ascending onto the Uinkaret Plateau. Water was scarce; Fraser abstained from bathing, to his discomfort. They followed poor roads, crossing many washes, and at one point Dalton got lost and managed to get the wagon stuck on a steep hill. Crossing the Hurricane Ledge escarpment, they drew a bead on Mount Trumbull, the high point of the Uinkaret Mountains, where there were pine forests and the promise of relief from the desert heat. They camped at Nixon Spring the afternoon of July 15, enjoying the good mountain water and meeting forest ranger Alexander MacFarlane and cattleman John Findlay.

Thursday, July 16, 1914

Up 4:45 a.m. Cooked a little coffee; ate some crackers, and leaving George and Dalton asleep, Rust and I set out at 5:45 a.m. (barometer 7200) for the top of Trumbull. Followed along pipe line leading from Nixon Spring with a faint trail for 30 minutes, and then straight up over basalt cliffs, steep and showing columnar structure, to the surface of the plateau sloping up to form the summit of Mt. Trumbull. Until reaching the basalt cliffs, the way led over sedimentary rocks—probably permian—obscured by the vegetation and talus from above.

Arrived summit 7 a.m.; barometer 8600; rise 1400 feet from camp. Fine timber on top. View from summit very extended. The plateau forming the top of the mountain breaks off steeply to the north. Its slope for a long way down overgrown with timber, much of which is good yellow pine. Northwest, north and northeast within a radius extending probably 10 miles from the mountain, there are a quantity of volcanic cones, a few, with the aid of glasses, showing distinct craters. In several instances it is apparent that some of these cones lie in straight lines as if formed by eruptions at various points along a single crack.

Beyond the volcanic field in the same direction lies an extension of the Kanab desert with little or no visible vegetation, sloping down to its boundary below the Chocolate Cliffs. Above these stand out the Vermilion Cliffs towering high and rugged in the vicinity of Short Creek and to the east of that over by Pipe Spring, forming a long low tongue on the plain. Back of them are visible the Towers of the Virgin to the north and to the northwest the Pine Valley Mountains, and east of Pipe Spring the White Cliffs stand out. As a back-ground beyond all, rise the Pink Cliffs, this morning, because of the haze, dim and colorless.

To the west we overlooked the Hurricane Valley and saw into the Shivwits surmounted by Mt. Dellenbaugh, and beyond, a little to the north over Solitaire and Diamond Buttes, looked into the face of the Virgin and Beaver Mountains. To the east we saw the upper reaches of the Toroweap and beyond the Kanab plateau a desert similar to that between the Trumbull lava field and the Chocolate Cliffs. From the summit of Mt. Trumbull, the view to the south is obscured by heavy growth on the plateau which we had ascended.

Leaving Mount Trumbull, Fraser and his companions returned to camp and then set out at once to climb Mount Logan, directly to the south, reaching the top around noon. Although Fraser liked to linger at view-points, often spending hours studying the panorama and its geologic features, he typically rode at a breakneck pace between high points. His haste to take in every possible vantage point was characteristic of his first two trips particularly. Reaching the summit of Logan, Fraser was im-pressed with a "naked, desolate, barren valley" to the west:

Wholly without vegetation and rough to exaggeration even in this country, it is happily called "Hell Hole" by the cattle-men, apropos both its infernal temperature (it being wholly shut in and the rocks absorb-ing and radiating intense heat) and it being a well nigh impossible place to get wandering cattle out of.

Unpleasant as this valley may be on close acquaintance, it forms the most beautiful foreground. The entire permian series is here displayed, its brilliant colors shading from light blue gray to blue, red, yellow, orange and deep chocolate. Probably Dutton has stated with scientific correctness the coloring and shades of this formation. To me, every time I saw a full exposure the shades and colors seemed to vary from the last, and even as one looked at a single view, the changing lights induced by clouds and the sun's movement gave rise to different color schemes.

11:30 a.m. Left summit of Logan and proceeded by another route back to camp. Except for a mile or so near camp, when we followed lumber roads, we rode through the woods without a trail, most of the time among tall pines, widely separated with clear spaces in between and only occasionally in flats through dense groves of quaking-aspen or on breaks of shallow canyons in undergrowth of oak.

Findlay being here for business to brand his father's cattle, was supposed to be working while guiding us about. He had an eye for every calf he saw, and pretty soon spotted one with a mother bearing his brand. We had a good exhibition of riding through the wood and driving the calf into an open space large enough to permit of throwing a rope. Directly he caught the calf by the hind legs, dismounted, put the noose about the calf's neck, tied it to a tree, lit a fire, heated his branding iron, which took less than five minutes, drew in the calf, threw him down, marked its ears, branded and cut it, the whole operation not consuming 20 minutes.

After descending from the slopes of Logan and traversing a mile or two of flats, we came upon a sawmill operated by a gentleman well named John Stout. As soon as we hove in sight, Stout quit his job, all his men stopped working, and the engineer let off steam, nearly causing all the horses to run away. Dalton used to work for Stout, who we found is an easy going genial pleasant soul, always in debt, and intensely agitated about his troubles. He is said to be a fine man to work for, because when his men want to go to work early in the morning, Stout says to them "It is a fine day, boys, let's take it easy for a couple of hours," and when they want to finish up their job toward evening, he says "It is a pity to go on working when we can do this all to-morrow just as well." He had nothing to say to us, but wish us luck.

Between Stout's saw-mill and the camp, about a half a mile from the latter, we passed the edge of the black lava flow conspicuous from the east cone of Trumbull. This flow rises sheer about 15 feet above the level of the plain, the vegetation growing right up to its edge and beyond everything barren, except for an occasional tree growing in a bed of ashes. It reminds one of the pictures of lava flows of recent eruptions of Vesuvius terminating in the cultivated gardens of the small towns near Naples.

Arrived camp 3:10, down 1275 feet from summit of Logan. MacFarlane and Findlay entertained us until we left, and the latter gave us a supply of jerkie (strips of beef dried in the sun), the product of the steer killed last week, part of whose remains discommoded us by smelling bad and breeding flies. MacFarlane a week ago had taken his wife and two little girls (both aged under six) down the Toroweap, and was himself obliged to leave for the Shivwits (locally known as Parashont) to look over some lumber which is to be sawed there; otherwise he would have gone with us. After lunch we unpacked all the supplies we did not want or need, principally cans of pork and beans and peanut butter, which nobody would touch. These we gracefully presented to MacFarlane. But

Colorado River from Toroweap Overlook, Grand Canyon, 1930. Sarah
Fraser is perched on the cliff at left. George Fraser first visited here
in 1914. One of the great lookoff points in the Plateau Province.
Photograph by George C. Fraser.

first all hands took a shot at a can of beans with a revolver at a distance
of 20 yards. When everybody had failed to hit it, I tried my luck and
knocked over the can and so created for myself an undeserved reputation, which I took care not to spoil by shooting any more.

We estimated the walk up Trumbull and back to have been about
4 miles, and the ride up Logan and back 13 miles. Much of the day the
sun was under cloud, so we did not suffer from the heat.

Left camp Nixon Ranger Station 5 p.m. We traveled about due east, keeping on the flat along the base of Trumbull for one or two miles over fairly decent road, and then over lava flows with great boulders of lava down a steep descent to the bottom of the Toroweap, occasionally for short distances being spared the intense roughness by driving over streaks of ashes or clinkers of more recent eruptions.

The floor of the Toroweap is so level that it is difficult to tell how it would drain, whether north or south. It is of hard fine clay or loam and carries a good growth of sage brush and grass supporting quantities of cattle and horses. In the winter the Toroweap is used to graze sheep, which lately have been driven off the desert onto the Kolob and the adjoining plateaus. For this stock two large reservoirs have been constructed, one about three miles below where we entered the valley, and the other near its foot at the base of Vulcan's Throne.

We proceeded down the valley until darkness fell, and having plenty of water for the stock and ourselves, camped dry at 8:30 12 miles from Nixon and about 7 miles from where we entered the Toroweap.

Friday, July 17, 1914

Up 4:15. Started 5:30. Arrived reservoir at foot of Vulcan's Throne marking the end of the Toroweap 7:30 and made camp; barometer 4800+; down 400 feet in 6 miles from last night's camp and down 1200 feet from Nixon.

As we proceeded down the valley, the lava falls over the west cliff came into closer view and were better shown in the eastern sun.

We made camp at the edge of the reservoir lying right at the foot of Vulcan's Throne. The reservoir was too dirty to tempt one to wash, so again we dispensed with the conventionalities. While moving my coat off the ground, I found a scorpion—length about an inch and a half—but otherwise saw no harmful vermin.

8:45. Left camp and walked up Vulcan's Throne. Cloudy but still very hot. Rust said we may congratulate ourselves that the sun is not out, because of all the hot places in the universe, this is it. Before starting we divided the stuff to be carried, each man selecting his allotment, the large camera falling to Rust. On arrival at the top, found Rust had forgotten the camera. Over my protest he insisted on going back for it, treating the double climb as a joke in perfect good humor. Dalton accompanied us by preference, not because we wanted him.

Vulcan's Throne is a pure cinder cone covered with scoriae, cinders, clinkers and peperino lying loose on the surface, with a slope, as near as

I could measure, from 28° to 31°. A little sage, many cacti and perhaps some other similar low plants grow on it, but otherwise nothing. Climbing it was like ascending a sand-dune. Every step forward involved slipping half way back and boots were soon filled with painful bits of stone.

The interval before Rust's arrival I occupied in ascending the west and south summits and walking down and skirting the three cones near their tops. The view up the Toroweap discloses signs of volcanic activity; cones and dikes rise in substantially a straight line through the center of the valley, quite distinct from the lava flows originating on the Trumbull platform.

Down the Grand Canyon the view from here is fine, extending through the entire Uinkaret across the Hurricane Valley, the break of which can be plainly seen, and well into the Shivwits, but not so far as the Grand Wash. The principal interest lies to the south, however, across the Grand Canyon where the Toroweap seems to be extending indefinitely with the same striking difference in the altitude of its bounding walls. Directly on the rim of the inner gorge stands a volcanic cone similar to Vulcan's Throne, but smaller, with its east half cut away. It was only the work of a moment with glasses to find the lava neck in the cliff beneath leading up to this cone, and on the face of the south wall of the inner gorge, further to the west, to find three lava dikes in and projecting above the sedimentary rocks forming the canyon wall—all as portrayed and clearly described by Dutton. (Lest we miss something I carried Dutton's *Tertiary History* with me all day and read his description of this country to George and Dalton while Rust was off after the camera; Rust read it when he came up).

At 12 M.,[11] after a bite of lunch on the summit, left top of Vulcan's Throne and proceeded due south down slope into the canyon. The slope seemed very steep, but clinometer measurement indicated an angle of not over 31°. We made for the rim of the inner gorge across the lava cliff. This involved walking along the southerly slopes of Vulcan's Throne, climbing the lava cliffs and then ascending the sheer wall of red (Supai) sandstone.

After crossing the lava cliff, Rust and I discovered a break in the cliff where it was practicable to descend some distance into the inner gorge. While George and Dalton rested under a rock, we went down, as we estimated it, about a third of the way to the river, that is, to within 1,700 feet of it. This brought us to the summit of the Redwall east of the fault. From here we obtained a closer and better view of the dissected volcano on the south side and of the fault in the cliff marked by the deep gorge which cut off the volcano. From here also the direct effect of the fault-ing was apparent and comprehensible. The south wall of the inner gorge to the east of the fault shows beneath the Redwall a talus slope 300 feet or more in height, while to the west of the fault the river laps the base of the Redwall without any intervening talus. The Redwall has been dropped away from above the river east of the fault down to the level of the river, and perhaps considerably below, west of the fault.

Ascending from the summit of the Redwall we reached a sort of terrace formed by the lava flow spoken of, and from this climbed a very steep cliff of red sandstone to the rim of the inner gorge. Arrived 4:30 p.m. By this time our water bag and canteen were empty and our tongues were hanging out. The surface of the red sandstone weathers into cups or pockets and we were very hopeful that the rains, which we were informed had fallen here within the last week, might have left some still standing water.

Pretty soon Rust found a pool. It was full of small active animals ("wigglers") like diminutive pollywogs, and smelt some, but we drank it with relief if not satisfaction. Later we found a number of other and larger pools, all, however, more or less dirty and similarly inhabited.

Back of the rim of the inner gorge the red sandstone forms a plateau rising at intervals in steps or terraces 10 to 20 feet high to the foot of the outer wall of the canyon. On this plateau along the rim we walked to the east, stopping at every promontory to view the inner gorge, the river and the vista up the canyon to the east.

A conspicuous object in the river about two miles east of the fault is a great black block of lava directly in midstream, probably a fragment fallen from the terrace which we had climbed over on our ascent from the summit of the Redwall.

Immediately west of the fault are heavy rapids, referred to in Powell's account of his exploration as the lava falls. The run-off through the gorge, leading down to the river on the south wall of the canyon below the dissected volcano, has formed a delta which dams up the waters of the river, as is the case at the mouth of every tributary canyon and is the occasion of rapids. With a glass these rapids appear as very rough and they seem to extend for nearly half a mile.

In the mid-afternoon the sun broke through the clouds and tried both George and myself considerably. On a ledge 12 feet below the rim, where a projection overhung the river, we found a large crack in the red sandstone affording shade. There we rested in enjoyment of the view, while Rust and Dalton returned to camp for horses and food. After the sun had pretty well gone down, George and I walked farther east along the rim to a point about four miles from Vulcan's Throne. Rust returned with the horses and food at 7:15. We ate supper on the rim and saw a magnificent sun-set behind clouds. In the course of the day we saw several rain storms pass over the canyon, and as we were about to return, a few drops fell, but not enough to wet.

8:30 p.m. Left rim and rode to camp. Arrived pretty tired and very hot. As it was then dark, and we could not see the water in the cow tank, we ventured to take a bath, and then slept without covers save for the tent to keep off the moisture. During the night I was twice awakened by animals crawling over our covering, but could not see what they were. We guessed them to be mice or lizards.

Saturday, July 18, 1914

Up 5:15 a.m. Temp. 58°. It turned cold in the night and we had to cover up. Clear with fleecy clouds. Left 7:20 a.m. We were much tempted to spend another day here following the rim of the inner gorge to the west over a lava flow which there descends into the canyon, and perhaps yielding to the allurements of the Indian trail described by Powell and Dutton as such a fierce climb. Rust advised against it, however, probably wisely, on the score that time was valuable and we had achieved so many points of vantage yesterday that in a further excursion we must look for details rather then general effects.

We retraced our steps up the Toroweap and in three hours passed the point where we entered the valley on our descent from Trumbull. The morning light on the lava flows over the west wall near the foot of the Toroweap accentuated their appearance of recency which is in no wise exaggerated in Holmes' pictures.

Just before stopping for lunch, we began to cross a lava flow which had descended into the valley from the east. It felt pretty hot in spite of actual temperatures, shade 82°, sun 100°.

Left lunch place 1:15. For four miles we drove over the rough lava flow mentioned and then struck the Wonsits Plain, a wide flat depression with hard clay bottom—sage, brush and good grass. Soon we saw a band of five wild horses and then numerous others.

At 5:15 we arrived at a large tank near Clay Holes; barometer 5475, up 600 feet from the foot of Vulcan's Throne. I did not have the nerve in the face of the sun to wash in the cow tank before breaking camp, so started to wash in the tank here. The muck that the first handful of water brought up was too much for me, however. Nevertheless, George and Rust each took a bath, while I climbed the bounding cliffs on both sides of the valley and enjoyed the sunset. The view embraced the Chocolate, Vermilion and White Cliffs with the Steamboat and the Temples of the Virgin conspicuous.

We made good distance to-day—30 miles in spite of the hot sun, which I must admit having felt. To bed early. The tank by which we were camped was constructed not only to water the cattle which graze here-abouts in large quantities, but for the purpose of catching the wild horses. We are in what is described on the maps as the "Valley of the Wild Band," apropos of the bands of wild horses. In times of drought the clay pockets dry up and the wild horses naturally seek a permanent reservoir such as the tank in question. The horse wranglers, therefore, have surrounded this tank with an ingenious layout of wire fencing so contrived that the entire enclosure may be controlled by a single gate, worked at a distance from the water. When a band of wild horses has gone to the tank to drink, the gate is closed and they are imprisoned. The one thing left to be done to make them salable is the simple job of breaking them. This is said to be quite feasible and comparatively easy in the case of horses not over three years old. One of Rust's horses was caught in this country at the age of two years; a quieter or gentler animal could not be found. Beside the wild horses, we saw a wild ass. There is said to be a considerable number of wild mules on these plains.

In normal times, when there is a reasonable rain-fall and some dew, these wild horses will go for many days, and sometimes even weeks, without a real drink of water. Ordinarily they can find in the clay pockets enough water to sustain them. The present season has been a very wet one. John Findlay, who combines horses with his cattle, had planned to catch some wild horses on his present trip; the rains of the last two weeks, however, put the kibosh on this business for the present.

Sunday, July 19, 1914

Up 4:15. Quite cold at awakening. Heavy dew. Clear all night, but fleecy clouds at and after sunrise. Heard coyotes barking in the night. More wild horses. Started at 6 a.m. Followed east by north[12] through the shallow canyon or valley by which we had come yesterday and in which we had camped. Then we went up a draw to a level sandy plain. Fine view to the north, due to the trough-like depression mentioned yesterday.

Up to the tank where we camped the road was fairly distinct, that is to say, we followed somebody's wagon tracks. After going out of the canyon on to the level plain, we lost these wagon tracks. I was in the wagon with Dalton while George and Rust were riding. Leaving camp they went north by west or perhaps even northwest in search of a direct road from Trumbull to Pipe Spring. Dalton was quite at sea until about 9:30, when we saw Rust and George in the distance to the northwest.

At 10:15, half a mile from the southeast extremity of the Chocolate Cliffs, we struck the road from Trumbull to Pipe Spring. Stopped to rest until 11:45. The sun was scorching and it was clear overhead, though cloudy on the horizon. In the distance to the east the Kaibab rose like a wall. The significance of the Indian derivative of its name becomes apparent—"the mountain lying down." Between us and the Kaibab were visible the breaks of Kanab Canyon cutting into the desert like a great ditch.

Two hours straight away over the desert down a very gentle grade brought us to Pipe Spring at 1:45.

The spring flows out of the triassic sandstone at the foot of the Vermilion Cliffs and is piped into a large watering trough for stock, the over-flow going to fill a reservoir below. Over the spring proper is an old fashioned spring house. The water is fine and cold and the best we have had since Shunesburg. A single house and the ruins of another are the only habitations. The house is built of large blocks of red sandstone in thick walls and with the ruined house and joining walls formed a rectangular enclosure or stockade. All the windows of the house open on this enclosure. The only openings outside of that are loop-holes. These habitations were constructed during Indian days and used as a fort and place of refuge for people in the vicinity.

When the Federal officers undertook to enforce the Edmunds law, a number of Kanab people brought their junior wives to Pipe Spring and here maintained them. Among them was Mr. E. D. Woolley,[13] who formally entertained here the U.S. Marshal for Arizona, wife No. 2 cooking the dinner, while across the border in Utah he would entertain the U.S. Marshal for Utah on wife No. 1's cooking.

Some people by the name of Colvin live here. Rust had promised us good food with piano playing by Miss Colvin. Unfortunately the whole family had gone to Fredonia to spend Sunday. Rust entered the house (which was not locked) and telephoned to his brother's wife at Short Creek, where we had originally expected to turn up to-night. It developed that in anticipation of our coming Rust's brother was returning from his goat pasture and bringing with him a kid slaughtered for our benefit. To miss this is a severe disappointment—the only one we have had so far.

Left Pipe Spring 2 p.m. Over-cast; raining hard in the vicinity of Trumbull. Turned very cool and had to put on a sweater, a strong breeze springing up because of a light rain.

Since his strenuous day climbing about on the rim of the canyon at the foot of the Toroweap, Dalton has not been fit. This morning he complained of stomach and head aches and has refused all food. He is more reticent than ever and quite bad-tempered with the beasts.

About five miles from Fredonia we passed close to the foot of a permian butte, an outlier of the Chocolate Cliffs, which I recognized from Dutton's picture and photograph [Dutton 1882, 52]. Still nearer Fredonia, as we crossed a wash, we passed under the lee of another butte known as the Battle-ship. I have found imaginative likenesses fixed upon rocks all over the world, but never one as apropos as this. The deck and hull of the battle-ship are a chocolate brown, its prow and stern are accurately delineated and the joints in the rock answer very well for port-holes and gun apertures, but most remarkable of all, the vessel sits with the correct nautical tip and on its sides break blue green waves formed by the disintegration of the lower permian members (shales) washed into gulleys by the rains.

About this point we met a solitary horse-man, a boy of about 19. He hailed Dalton with intimacy and turned out to be his nephew. He had been working in the vicinity of Kanab and was on his way to Hurricane. He asked us what we were doing and if by chance we had a load of fruit from the Dixie country. I saw his tongue hanging out as he said it. If there had been time I would have told him the story about working that side of the street ourselves.

Fredonia lies on the east side of Kanab Creek, the floods of which have played sad havoc with the road and even with the surrounding country. In the bed of the wash, at the bottom of which the creek runs, are the most extraordinary relics of a flood which occurred about three years ago. Great masses of alluvium torn from the valley bottom in which the stream flows along its upper courses have been transported in solid blocks and here deposited in and near the river-bed in all sorts of fantastic shapes, including columns running quite to 12 feet in height. They have the appearance of solidified out-pourings of a mud volcano.

Kanab Creek, where we crossed it, carried scarcely any water. Above Kanab is a reservoir feeding irrigation ditches, from which the run-off is extremely slight, except in time of flood. Some of the water used for irrigation drains back into the creek and this in turn is ditched onto the arable land about Fredonia, so that below this point the creek is entirely dry under normal weather conditions.

Arrived Fredonia 6 p.m.; barometer 5025 feet; down 375 feet from our camp at Clay-Hole.

We put up at the house of a Mr. Jensen, a Dane, with Uncle Sam-like chin whiskers, whose wife and daughter cooked and served a capital dinner. It is the custom at all these houses of entertainment for the men, including host as well as strangers, to sit at the table and eat heartily while the ladies of the family, themselves enjoying a barmecide feast,[14] wait on and entertain them. Everything was clean and the meal was thoroughly good.

The water problem at Fredonia is a serious one. The town is entirely dependent upon Kanab Creek, the flow of which is depleted by the demands of Kanab. All water for household use has to be carted in barrels from a point above the town. As in the Virgin Valley, it is necessary to settle the mud out of the water before using it.

Rust tried to induce Woolley to send his automobile for us, but the machine was busy. We found out why when we struck the road. Failing in this, Rust arranged for a team to drive us to Kanab in Dalton's wagon and return with the wagon in time for Dalton to leave to-morrow morning.

Here we parted from Dalton, not at all sorry.

7:30 p.m. Left Fredonia, Lewis, a Welsh Mormon convert, driving me in the wagon, while George rode with Rust. The team was unique, consisting of a mare age 19, and her son age 9, one of which galloped and the other trotted. It had rained heavily in the afternoon and the road, poor at best, was a perfect bog. Nevertheless, we covered the 7½ miles at a break-neck speed in an hour and a half and the wagon held together.

It was over-cast when we started and so nearly dark that we could see little of the country. One thing impressing was the fact that some one had arbitrarily run a barb-wire fence across the road, enclosing part of it in his pasture, compelling travelers to take to the open country and rendering driving in the dark extremely dangerous, because the road ran right on through the barb-wire fence.

Arrived Kanab 9 p.m.; barometer 5300; altitude 4925 feet. Rust took us to the house of a Mrs. McAllister, who, we thought, was a widow. She is an aunt of Alexander MacFarlane, the ranger on Trumbull, his mother, but not Bishop Macfarlane's mother, being her sister. As fellow guests we had Professor Horne, late of the High School in Salt Lake, the new Principal of the Kanab High School, and Stockbridge, a U.S. Forest

Ranger. I was given a room to myself on the ground floor, while George slept upstairs in a room with three beds, one of which Professor Horne occupied.

Monday, July 20, 1914

Up 7:15 a.m. Breakfast 8 a.m. It was impossible to get a bath either last night or this morning, because the water works were out of business and the household supply, pending repairs, was mostly in the bathtub.

After breakfast, walked down the street and met Rust in new boots and a clean shirt, minus his beard. I took my first shave—all but my upper lip. Rust introduced us to E. D. Woolley, his father-in-law, age about 70, with an Irish cast of countenance, clean shaven, stockily built, and very young-looking.

Mrs. McAllister is 64 years old, looks about 48, and has four great-grandchildren beside eight grown children and an infinity of grand-children. She came to St. George in 1861 and had many stories to tell about the early days. Apropos the remoteness of the place and the sim-plicity of its occupants, she told of one of the leading women there, in the early days of telegraph service, receiving a wire from her husband to the effect that he would be home at 6 p.m. The wife was much troubled by the letters "p.m.," and in telling the telegraph operator about it, said that after a while their meaning dawned on her; her husband was fond of mush, so she had ready for him against his arrival a dish of plain mush.

By this time we had learned that it was up to paying guests to lend a hand in the kitchen and dining room, so George turned in and did chores by way of helping get dinner ready. Before dinner time, the water works were put in operation, and to the inconvenience of everybody, after much labor and fuss, George and I got baths. The bath-tub, a very nice zinc unenclosed affair, stood well out in the middle of Mrs. McAllister's room and was fed by running cold water. If hot were re-quired, it could be obtained from the stove. After receiving numerous instructions from Mrs. McAllister what to do if her granddaughters tried to enter while I was bathing, I was allowed to get washed.

Just before lunch, Rust succeeded in corralling Woolley's Ford ma-chine, in which he took us a mile up the road to the dam in Kanab Creek, from which the town gets its water for household and irrigation purposes. The road was extra sandy, and, in depressions, a bog, the result of yesterday's rain. Here Kanab Creek is a small affair carrying no more water than the Shunesburg Creek, and very muddy. The dam is of sand, according to Rust, the biggest sand dam in the world. It was constructed by local people on their own lines and contrary to the advice of engineers, but it has held for several years and through pretty heavy floods.

On the way to the dam we stopped at the ice cream saloon, the only saloon in town, were introduced to the lady who ran the soda fountain, and Rust and George consumed the most stomach-spoiling ice cream concoctions—thoroughly up to date. This saloon is run on most orderly lines, no rough talk or smoking being allowed.

At lunch we found Professor Horne very hot and dressed in over-alls. He had come to the house an hour before, and finding Mrs. McAllister's hay cut in the field and a shower threatening, had combined his efforts with those of two boys and succeeded in getting it in the barn.

It took most of the afternoon to buy our supplies for the trip to Buckskin. These we got at one of the general stores, of which there are about four, all owned by different companies, in one of which Mr. Woolley is dominant. The goods were sold to us by a Miss Crosby, who was probably very good looking when she was a few years younger. She snubbed me well when I inadvertently referred to "Force" and the like uncooked cereals as "miserable stuff," telling me they carried no miserable stuff in that store.

In this store was Mrs. Howard, apparently ready to act as sales-lady and keeping general supervision over one of the partners who was buying a large bill of goods for the winter stock from photographs exhibited by a drummer.

Mrs. Howard is about 45 years of age, stout, rosy, and stocky like Mr. Woolley, whose oldest daughter she is. Her mouth is as firm as the rock of Gibraltar, and her face, while we remained there, was as expressionless as that of a friend of mine in a poker game. She said "Good Afternoon" to me twice—on arrival and departure—nothing else.

Mrs. Howard is so far the only woman in this country, except one in Kansas, so they told me, who has acted as Mayor of a town. Three years ago, as the town elections approached, no men stood as candidates for election to the town council. Accordingly, one day, in a spirit of fun, the crowd about the Post Office made up a ticket of women, heading it with Mrs. Howard's name as President of the Council, the duties of that office corresponding with those of Mayor. The women on this ticket were of the best in Kanab and the men concluded, as complaints had come from women about the running of the town, it would be a good scheme to put the women in office, so they were elected. With one exception all of them served; this one withdrew on demand of her husband, who feared she would neglect him, and another woman was substituted in her place. This board ran the town splendidly. No other town, it is said, has ever been controlled by a board entirely composed of women. One of their greatest accomplishments was to pass and enforce an ordinance prohibiting cattle from feeding in the streets, something which had been done from the foundation of the village and a right upon which the cattle-men stood.[15]

The council consists of five; three of the council women gave birth to babies during their term of two years in office.

While walking about town in the late afternoon I ran across a strikingly handsome young man with tough manners and the most profane and obscene vocabulary I have ever encountered, who turned out to be a chauffeur from Flagstaff. Ten days or so ago he started with a Ford car from Flagstaff, having as passengers two or three attaches of the Arizona State Agricultural Department, to come to Kanab and Dixie over the Painted Desert across Lee's Ferry and through House Rock Valley. They negotiated the trip all right into House Rock Valley and there about 70 miles from Kanab, broke a bearing that effactually put their car out of business. They had only stocked up with enough food to carry them through on schedule. Here they met some Harvard men, who refused to help them out further than with a little flour. From the point they broke down, they walked 70 miles into Kanab and would probably have starved to death but for meeting with a Frenchman, a Mormon convert on his way back to the old country, who divided with them what food he had. This chauffeur planned to take Woolley's chauffeur out to the stalled machine, put in new parts, and then drive back to Flagg via Hurricane, the Needles and Williams.

After supper Rust brought us to meet his wife and blew us all to sodas at the saloon. Mrs. Rust is a younger daughter of Mr. Woolley's, large and stout, and, like her sister, Mrs. Howard, quiet and reserved.

8:15 p.m. barometer 5300. Left Kanab and drove through heavy mud, much worse than yesterday. From Kanab we took a light buggy of the regular local type belonging to Rust, or probably Woolley's Grand Canyon Transportation Co., and hitched to it the two riding horses that had accompanied us all the way. George rode a third horse. Food, bedding and the like was piled up in the back of the wagon.

11 p.m. Arrived Fredonia. Down 300 feet. That it took 2¼ hours to cover 7½ miles down hill is fairly indicative of the condition of the road. Fredonia was dark as Egypt and silent as a grave. We drove into Jensen's

yard, as we discovered the next morning without waking anybody, put the horses in the stalls and made our beds on the alfalfa in the barn, enjoying the best night's sleep and the greatest comfort of the whole trip so far.

Tuesday, July 21, 1914
Up 5:30 a.m. Clear and cool. Jensen turned up soon after we got out and seemed not in the least surprised to find strangers occupying his barn. We cooked breakfast in the yard, got a sort of a cat-wash, paid Jensen for what the horses ate, and started at 7:45. Outfit like that of yesterday. Owing to the recent heavy rains for about seven miles over the permian, the road was soft and the wagon wheels were coated with a bluish gray mud. After the first seven miles we got out of the permian onto the carboniferous, making a firm hard road with small stones and chips of flint answering for light gravel. On the wheels the red mud of the Trias overlain by the gray mud of the permian afforded an interesting index to the geology of the country we had been through.

Almost directly as we left Fredonia, we began to ascend and kept on climbing gently, here and there crossing broad depressions with dry washes at the bottom. After 18 days of hard work (2 days with Rust before we met him and 16 days with us) Rust's horses were pretty tired. As I wished to get to Jacob's Lake in time to telephone Kanab before the office closed, at 3:10, I mounted the riding horse and rode hard, covering the intervening 15 miles in 2 hours and 40 minutes. Arrived Jacob's Lake 5:50; barometer 7950, up 2975 feet from Fredonia, distance 30 miles.

The difference between the Kanab plateau and the summit of the Kaibab is quite as marked as one would imagine that of the Earth to be from Mars. Almost immediately on commencing the ascent, the sage and low brush of the plain gives place to bushes and trees—piñon, live oak and the like, in spots forming dense thickets at each side of the road. Ascending, these in turn give place to trees, small at first, but increasing in size as one climbs, until at the summit one finds that by imperceptible degrees a great forest of large trees has been entered.

On the way up I heard sounds of explosions and soon came across a man working on the road dynamiting stumps. This was about 4 o'clock, and after exchanging a few words of greeting, as I started off he called attention to the hour, the fact that I had no pack, and urged me to stop at his shack half a mile up the road and help myself to his grub—just another instance of the hospitality one meets with universally in this country.[16]

As I approached the summit of the plateau, the sounds of a saw-mill in operation became audible from the east in the upper reaches of the valley or canyon to my left. About two miles before reaching Jacob's Lake, there was a high wooden fence with gate (all sorts of offensively imperative signs are affixed by the forest supervisor directing that the gate be closed under penalties a little short of death).

Jacob's Lake is a muddy water hole about 20 yards in diameter, surrounded by a high corral. To the east is the Ranger Station and to the west, 100 yards away, is a cabin maintained by the Grand Canyon Cattle Co., the lessee of the pasturage of all the Kaibab, except a strip on the westerly side. This company is locally known as the Bar-Z outfit from its brand

$$\overline{\text{Z}}$$

The Ranger Station is a one story cabin with a porch in front and two rooms, one kept locked and containing the ranger's personal effects, and the other with the stove and telephone kept open so that travelers can enjoy conveniences. The telephone system out here is maintained by the forest service, a party line affair, with different complicated rings to call various stations. Apprising myself of the Kanab call, I rang the bell until my arm gave out, never raising a soul, except a man at V.T. (De-Motte Park) who wanted to send a telegram. As there were some people at the Bar Z house, I thought they might tell me how to work the telephone, so I went over. They had a fire and were evidently cooking supper. As I neared them, they got together in a group, stood up and looked at me. One man responded to my greeting, and in answer to an inquiry about the telephone, said he knew no more about it than I did. Their response to other remarks from me was equally cordial, so I retired to a seat on the steps of the Ranger cabin.

Pretty soon I was surprised and shocked to see emerging from the forest at a swift pace a Ford car with a genial, stout fellow running it. This turned out to be a mining engineer named Mouat from Denver, who is working on a copper mine a mile or two to the southwest of Jacob's Lake. He too was trying to get Kanab, and through some good fortune succeeded. I thus had an opportunity to make an appointment with Miss Greenough to call me before she left, and in the mean while try to get connection with Panguitch, which had been denied since the day before. Mouat told me that the copper here lies in pockets as if by way of filling up sink-holes (of which Jacob's Lake is one, and Dutton says there are many all over the plateau), by seepage through the formerly overlying permian. Mouat invited me to supper with him, but I declined on the score of sticking by my outfit.

At 7:10 Rust and George arrived in the wagon. All hands slept on the floor of the porch of the Ranger Station and wished for more blankets for it was very cold. At 7:45 Kanab reported over wire nothing for me yet.

Wednesday, July 22, 1914

Up 5:30 a.m. Clear and cold; barometer 7950. Our neighbors were already up and rushing about at a great rate looking for their horses. Rust, pretty wet from walking through the dew laden foliage, brought in our horses about 6:45. At 7:30 our neighbors were still looking for their beasts, and one of them came over to ask if Rust had seen them. It turned out that two of these fellows were from Boston and were seniors at Harvard. They were traveling with an Englishman, who had been resident in Arizona for six or eight years. We attributed their lack of cordiality and inhospitability of last night to the New England atmosphere, which even the heat of the Painted Desert had not been able to thaw out. This party came from Flagstaff via Lee's Ferry and is the one that refused to give food to the strange automobilist we met at Kanab.

8 a.m. Left Jacob's Lake and rode south or a little west of south through the forest—growing more impressive as we progress.

About two miles from Jacobs Lake we ascended a forest ranger's observation tower, a wooden skeleton structure, 75 feet or thereabouts in height, with a ladder fastened along one side, affording a view over the tops of all but the highest trees. The road here runs and this tower stands on the summit of the north and south ridge, affording an extensive view over the forest, but that is all. Higher ground along the near horizon cuts off the distant views. As a forest scene the climb was well worth while.

An hour further on we stopped for lunch. As we were peacefully following our way along a grassy, flower-grown valley bottom, we were surprised to see a man and woman on horseback emerge from the forest on our left. Rust's sharp eyes recognized forest ranger Swapp, and we jumped to the conclusion that the lady was one of the Salt Lake schoolmarms, having heard they were in this vicinity on their way north. The lady acknowledged our greeting by a wave of the hand, but on a word from Swapp started up her horse and they cantered away from us down the valley. Pretty soon, at 2:45, beside a small lagoon or sink-hole, we ran into the whole school-marm outfit and spent half an hour gossiping with them. Swapp was not sociable, but Rust succeeded in getting him aside and conveying the idea that I was intimate with the forest authorities in Washington and had been requested to let them know on my return how the forest rangers seem to be attending to business, and that I had gotten a good snapshot of him and his lady coming out of the woods, which would be entitled "The Hardships of a Ranger's Life."

The school-marms (male and female) looked pretty dilapidated and were extremely dirty. McNiece is thin and haggard and looked worn to the bone. They had been to Bright Angel Point and the Transept and down to the river. When they left the lady who had been riding with Swapp clambered to a seat beside Jim Emmet on the grub wagon and another took her mount. By way of making Swapp thoroughly comfortable, Jim Emmet said "If I am discommoding you in any way, Swapp, by sitting up here, you might take my place and I'll try to ride your horse." As a parting shot, Rust told Swapp he would try to keep the matter from being mentioned, and Swapp went off looking ready to commit murder. We learned afterward that he has a wife and five children somewhere north of Kanab.

At 3:15 left the lake of the school-marms and continued in the same southerly direction, past Crane Lake, through Pleasant Valley, over a divide and down into DeMotte Park, at a point about 2½ miles north of the spring and lake, at which stand the Grand Canyon Cattle Company's main ranch and the Big Park Ranger Station. (DeMotte Park is currently called "V.T.", being the brand of a cattle outfit which formerly controlled this section, and it is designated on some of the maps as "Big Park.") Arrived Ranger Station 6:40 p.m., barometer 8850, and made camp at the edge of the forest, 100 yards from the station.

The whole 25-mile ride today was over a good road, through a succession of vales, glades or parks in the valley bottoms, with intervening forests on the slopes and divides. Except for vistas along these glades, there was not a distant view. In no place was there any underbrush, and except for thick groves of quaking aspen, one could ride at a gallop through the forest anywhere.[17] The parks are carpeted with rich grass and a great variety of wild flowers, yellow tints predominating. The trees are mostly yellow pine[18] and quaking aspen, with some spruce and Douglas fir. The pines grow far apart, with their lowest branches usually over 15 feet above the ground. Beneath them the ground is covered with needles and a sparse growth of grass. Few cattle are in the forest proper, but each park is a well used and sometimes quite crowded pasture. The whole country looks and is well watered, and yet we have not encountered a brook or running stream to-day. Numerous sink-holes—some dry and some holding muddy water—are to be found in each valley bottom.

We found Ranger Stockbridge (who had been our fellow-guest at Mrs. McAllister's in Kanab) occupying the station and invited him to supper with us.

George and I undertook to make our bed out of spruce boughs, which we laboriously cut with an axe and then laid with the butt-ends sticking up. Rust and Stockbridge showed us the error of our ways by turning over the boughs, so that the butt and tip of each branch touched the ground and the natural bend of the wood acted as a spring—a first lesson in woodsman's comfort.

Bed 10:30; clear and cold.

Thursday, July 23, 1914
Up 5:30; clear and cold, with a white frost. Reciprocating our entertainment of last night, Stockbridge got breakfast ready in the station.[19]

In the Z Bar pasture on the Kaibab there are now about 10,000 head. Last month a large number of cattle were driven over to Lund and shipped to another ranch in California, owned by the same people. Even with these gone, the range is overstocked.

Stockbridge is here to inspect and improve the road. Not having been beyond V.T., he selected to-day to make an inspection further south and rode along with us. He is a curious character; born and brought up in west central Texas, he punched cows, etc., throughout the state, more particularly the southern part. I take his age to be about 40. He is baldheaded, clear-eyed, a reckless and voluble talker, frightfully profane and offensively obscene. In other respects he is a pretty nice fellow. He criticizes Forester Graves as a theorist, but has high respect for Pinchot, whom he describes as a real woodsman.[20] He seriously warned George against Yale because it had graduated both Taft and Graves.

From the station for about six miles our road ran south through DeMotte Park to its southern end. There we ascended a rise of not exceeding 100 feet, passed through a narrow rim of pine forest and descended into Little DeMotte Park—the prototype of V.T. on a smaller scale. This region of forest between the two parks, Dutton poetically terms "the Sylvan Gate."

We passed close to Thompson Spring and in about two miles reached a fork in the road. The right (southwesterly) fork in half a mile reaches

Bright Angel Ranger Station. We took the left fork (southeast) and at 1 p.m. (barometer 8350 feet) arrived Camp Woolley, 20 miles from V.T.

Thus far the road has been very good. Except for blowing out of stumps along the tongue up which we ascended the mountain, and the cutting of trees where it ran through the forest, it has been little worked. In no place is there any real made road. The surface of the Kaibab is a hard, firm loam carrying quantities of chipped flint from the disintegration of the Kaibab limestone, which form a sort of gravel base and make a solid road surface.

Camp Woolley consists of a single room log cabin, with peaked roof, about 16x20, and windowless. It is used for storage of saddles, etc. by the Canyon Transportation Company, composed of Woolley, Rust, and an ex-Attorney General of Arizona and one or two others, which built the trail down Bright Angel and the cable crossing at its foot. It stands in a half acre fenced enclosure on the slope of a small park. Fifty feet above the cabin a very small spring oozes out of a bed of sandy limestone and is gathered in a little pool two or three inches deep and three feet in diameter, from which a pipe carries the water to a horse trough.

After lunch, 2:15 p.m., Stockbridge left us, proceeding to the Bright Angel Ranger Station, and thence back over the road we had taken this morning to V.T.

The Transportation Company has pasturage for horses here. The two riding horses which have been with us from the beginning were quite played out and the little mare brought from Kanab was not good for the hard work ahead, so George and Rust rode these three beasts into the pasture and after two hours returned with five fresh horses. In the meanwhile I read a little Dutton and slept on a canvas-covered cot that felt pretty good.

4:45 p.m., left on fresh mounts for Bright Angel Point, riding along the valley bottom 1½ miles to Bright Angel Ranger Station and thence through the forest, over steep divides, into deep canyons to Bright Angel Point.

The approach to the Grand Canyon was not heralded by any visible signs. We rode through the forest, as we had done for two days past, and suddenly, through the trees ahead, saw hazily the south rim with a multitude of buttes in between. At 5:30 dismounted and followed a rough path along the crest of the point, with precipices on either side, to the bench mark marking the top of Bright Angel Point (8153 feet); barometer 8325 feet (arrived 5:45).

E. D. Woolley's outfitting cabin on the Kaibab Plateau, 1913. Dave
Rust based his guiding operations in the North Rim area from here.
Photograph by J. Cecil Alter.

I was surprised and disappointed at the impression the magnificent
view from here creates. Accustomed to a consideration of the landscape
in its details, the mind at first is probably confused by the myriad of
objects vying with one another to concentrate the gaze. As we first saw
it, the canyon was brilliantly illuminated by the sun still high in the

Southeast from Bright Angel Point, North Rim, Grand Canyon, 1913.
Photograph by J. Cecil Alter.

heavens. As the sun went down, the shadows lengthened and the details were brought out. Perhaps it was due to this that after an hour's study of the view, we began to make something of it.

Perhaps my initial confusion and lack of appreciation resulted from preconceptions of this view, predicated upon my recollection of the Canyon, as seen from the south rim. Here we stood directly opposite El Tovar, viewing the same scene as is there disclosed, but yet one irreconcilably different. From the south rim one looks off a steep precipice over the wide plateau capping the summit of the inner gorge with the great temples and buttes on the opposite side of the river—none of them nearer than four or five miles. From the points of the north rim, on the other hand, one stands, as it were, among these buttes, as if upon the summit of one of a number of peaks rising in a cluster from the trunk of a mountain range. Oza Butte to the southwest of Bright Angel Point, for instance, is only a mile away, a mere stone's throw, as it seems, across the abyss of the Lower Transept.

The architectural symmetry and regularity of the transept are presented as described and pictured in Dutton's book. He has not exaggerated in any way. The stillness of the evening was broken by the whistling of the wings of an occasional swallow and the deep roar of Roaring Spring emerging from the upper reaches of Bright Angel Canyon to the east.

We reluctantly left the tip of the Point at 8, but managed not to reach the horses until 8:45, tarrying to get last views in different directions. We rode back in the dark at a fast trot or gallop, arriving Camp Woolley at 9:15. Bed 10:45; George and I slept on a bed of boughs left by the schoolmarms and built wrong side up. This was thoroughly uncomfortable and besides full of ants. A red ant bit me in the hand. Neither yesterday nor today has it rained, but on both days we have had some clouds and have seen rainstorms in the distance.

Friday, July 24, 1914

Up 5 a.m. Capturing the horses and apportioning the luggage for the pack outfit took a good deal of time. We found Rust to be an expert packer. By a little before noon Rust had everything in readiness. We ate a light lunch and at 12:30 started for the Walhalla Plateau, locally called "Greenland," proceeding up the road we came in by yesterday.

Within ten minutes of our departure we encountered a young man and woman on horseback and were presented to Miss Jansen, formerly of Fredonia, now of Salt Lake, and Vaughan, a good-looking fellow of about 25, formerly of Texas. After about five minutes' conversation, Vaughan said he had three telegrams for me. It appears that the Kanab operator got Stockbridge on the phone last night after his return to V.T.; that a party of Fredonia people enjoying an "out" were camped by the Ranger Station, ready to leave this morning for Jacob's Lake and home; that Stockbridge had insisted these telegrams should reach me promptly and he represented it was impossible for him to bring them because he only had one horse which had taken him 40 miles, to Bright Angel and back, yesterday, and could not be asked to do the same thing today. Accordingly the entire Fredonia party had agreed to stay over an extra day and Vaughan and Miss Jansen had undertaken a 40-mile ride for my accommodation.

I was profuse in my expressions of appreciation of their consideration and somewhat embarrassed to know how to set about offering some return. I was afraid of insulting Vaughan by tendering him money as if he were a messenger, so hinted along, invited them to help themselves to our reserve stock of food at Camp Woolley, as the best thing I could think of, and generously gave Vaughan a five-cent sack of "Bull." Pretty soon, however, Vaughan, also somewhat embarrassed, said the Kanab operator had given assurance that I would make proper payment to anybody who brought me these messages, which I promptly confirmed. I asked what it was worth and Vaughan said he did not know but would leave it to Rust, who, of course, declined to arbitrate. Finally Vaughan suggested $7.50 as a sum which would fairly compensate for the expense entailed in keeping the whole party over a extra day. I was glad enough to pay this, but I resolved to pray every morning hereafter that nobody would think of telegraphing me any more.

Leaving our friends and the main road, we took a trail passable for wagons toward the east, through the forest, over a rougher country than any we have yet traversed, on the summit of the Kaibab. A little before 2 we reached a spring in the bottom of a canyon tributary to and near the head of Bright Angel Creek—a mere ooze of water into mud-holes. Here we gave the stock their last drink until to-morrow.

At 2:15 daylight suddenly showed through the trees ahead of us and in a moment we were on the rim, looking out over the Marble Canyon platform near the head of Nankoweap Valley. To this place it is possible to take a wagon. While infinitely more extended, this view is free of the complications that confuse the one from Bright Angel Point. Assurance of better things beyond and fear that something might be lost by tarry-ing, dragged me away much sooner than I wanted to go, so we followed down the plateau in a substantially southeasterly direction to Cape Final, only touching the rim once at the head of Chuar Creek, which presents a similar view to that just mentioned. On this ride for the first time we saw the indigenous flying squirrel, said to be found nowhere but on the Kaibab. It is about the size of our gray squirrel, with a glossy black body and a snow-white tail. Deer, of which we had seen some yesterday, appeared with great frequency.

Although most of the time we followed no trail, the trees in the forest grow so far apart that we were able to make good speed, galloping when the surface was sufficiently level.

From 3 to 4 we rode through heavy rain and at 5 p.m. arrived at Cape Final—a 17 mile ride. An attempted description of the view from Final would be futile. To the north and east the country is spread out like a map. With glasses one can follow the Vermilion and Echo Cliffs dis-tinctly and way beyond discern the outlines of the cretaceous mesa country in northeastern Arizona. Shortly after arrival a heavy wind was blowing across the Painted Desert and the resulting sandstorm tinged the atmosphere yellow. The greatest butte in the view lies to the south-west, where Vishnu's Temple stands in unsurpassed grandeur. This is evidently the point from which Holmes made his very accurate drawing [Dutton 1882, 176].

At several points seen from here the real constitution of the Redwall becomes apparent in the landscape for the first time. For example, at the southerly tip of Jupiter's temple, a great tongue of Redwall limestone extends beyond the overlying Supai sandstone, and, deprived of the coloring matter of the latter, presents a bluish gray face. Wherever this limestone is overlain by the sandstone, its face is colored red (perhaps more accurately vermilion).

We made our camp on the tip of the point and slept within 15 feet of the precipice. Thus we could watch the changing lights as the sun went down and after until the canyon was lost in darkness, and on awakening catch the first light of the dawn and see the canyon spring into life. Temperature 8:15 72 degrees. Bed 10:15. Rained in the night from 4 to 5, but not enough to awaken anyone but me, or to tempt one to pitch a tent.

Saturday, July 25, 1914

Up 5:15. Much overcast, but clearing to the east. While Rust spent two hours wrangling the horses, George cooked breakfast with but little assistance from me, for I was too much engaged in studying the landscape.

With the Topographic Sheets and especially Walcott's Geologic Map[21] of that part of the canyon spread before us in the marvelous clearness of the atmosphere, bereft of its moisture by yesterday's and last night's rains, the structure of most of the abyss before us could be read like an open book. I would have thought it incredible that an untrained observer could unmistakably see and locate a fault a mile below him and six miles away, or that the unconformity between the Algonkian and the overlying Cambrian would force itself upon his observation. But so it is and must be for anyone with open eyes.

Perhaps the first thing to strike one on studying the prospect with a good glass is the black lava outcropping at numerous points but most impressively in the shape of a large butte due east of Final, and just west of the river. To the naked eye the river looks like a gleam of light coming through a crack. With the glass it is in places seen to be very rapid. Here and elsewhere these rapids occur at and below the inflow of tributary canyons. They are evidently occasioned by the piling up in the Colorado's bed of the detritus brought down the side canyons by floods.

Navajo Peak, probably 100 miles away, stands out more clearly than do the Orange Mountains from back of Madison.[22] To the south rise the San Francisco Mountains and way to the southwest in the dim distance other (apparently volcanic) mountains, probably from the maps the Santa Maria Mountains.

11:10, with real regret we left Final, but only because the horses have had no water since 2 p.m. yesterday. Really they were not badly off because they had wet grass last night.

Final is the end of a quite level stretch of the plateau. This we followed for some distance, then cut down into a steep canyon, up, over and down a ridge into another canyon, along which we proceeded to Dripping Spring at the head of Clear Creek. The spring is well named. Water oozes out of a sandy stratum of the Kaibab limestone. The flow of the spring is so slight than in no place on the rock wall is there a real run of water, only innumerable points from which the water drops. A few of these drops we ran together with the aid of a stick, and laboriously filled the water bags a cupful at a time. Each bag held 50 cupfuls and the canteen 20. On the lower ledge a little pool has been formed by means of a miniature earthen dam. From this the horses drank and in it we washed for the first time to-day. From the spring there is a view due south, down Clear Creek Canyon to the rear of Wotan's Throne—a magnificent prospect. Stopping at Dripping Spring only long enough to water and wash, we retraced our steps one-quarter of a mile and then ascended steeply what would seem to be a hill but is really a continuation or outlier of the main Greenland Plateau, constituting Cape Royal, where we arrived at 1 p.m.

We find Royal to be cut off from Greenland on the west by the upper branches of Clear Creek Canyon, where we have just been, and on the south by the beginning of one of the tributaries of Unkar Creek. Thus Royal is in the process of becoming disassociated from the north rim and turning into a canyon butte.

Beside the main promontory marked as Royal, other points jut into the canyon near by, all terminating precipitously. In one of them the limestone along the joint planes beneath the plateau surface has been weathered out, leaving a hole clean through and presenting the appearance of a natural bridge.

We arrived in brilliant sunshine and it was pretty hot, but showers were visible across the canyon to the southeast. It was interesting to watch these showers cross the canyon. Their extent was clearly marked and every now and again the play of sunshine on them brought out the colors of the prism, sometimes full rainbows.

One such storm we watched for two hours, first along the south rim and then gradually creeping over the canyon to a point a little across the river, where the wind took it and blew it eastwardly. From Royal the view to the northwest is obscured; Vishnu is too close to permit of its tremendous size being appreciated. The view across the river to the east and a little north of it is complementary to that from Final, but the finest outlook is to the west, where the great buttes visible from El Tovar are seen at a new angle. To the artist perhaps Royal presents more attraction than Final, but to one not possessed of the artistic instinct the great scope of Final must be given preference.

At 4:45 we left Royal and descended to Dripping Spring; arrived 5:15. Temperature of water 51; barometer 7725. Here we again filled the water bags, watered the stock and washed. At 5:50 left for what Rust called Naji Point, but which I subsequently made out to be what the maps called Atoko Point.

On the way here we saw numerous deer, usually in groups of two or three, sufficiently tame to let us approach at times within 75 yards of them.[23] The wild flowers—mostly in small parks on the valley bottoms—grow in great profusion and variety. Among them I recognized Indian paint-brush, wild roses, Scotch thistle, yarrow, wild peas, buttercups and gentian-like blue flowers.

Sunday, July 26. More views awaited as the party traveled north along the eastern rim of the Kaibab to Atoko Point and then returned to Woolley's cabin. After repacking for the final leg of their journey, they took in the sunset from the head of the Transept, northwest of Bright Angel Point:

Here we saw in a way the most gorgeous sight, next to that from the hill above Grafton, on the trip so far. The clouds had begun to break through the west, so that the light of the fast sinking sun fell on the easterly wall of the Transept and some of the buttes in the Canyon. In the lower reaches of the Canyon there was a small shower, creating a rainbow, and hovering about Zoroaster's Temple and adjoining buttes were sheets of filmy cloud condensed by the high cold air as the sun raised the moisture from the depths of Bright Angel Canyon.

The sun set clear, illuminating the summits of all the temples and buttes and the south rim, bringing their details into the sharpest relief, plainly visible, the distance being eliminated by the rain's clearing of the atmosphere. In the background of the picture stood the San Francisco Mountains, clear to the tip—almost the first time we have seen them so, for their extreme altitude seems to breed clouds.

The architectural features of the easterly side of the Transept were accentuated by the lights, and I am more than ever impressed with the truthfulness and the literal accuracy of Dutton's verbal descriptions [Dutton 1882, 172]. We stayed until darkness fell upon us and I had trouble saving my glasses in riding back through the forest.

It was too wet to sleep out comfortably, so I lay on the cot, with George and Rust filling up the floor.

Monday, July 27, 1914

For the first time Rust beat me in waking up. He was off at 5:30, wrangling the horses, and returned pretty wet, tired and hungry, at 8:30. I never woke until 7. Rust baked bread; we washed dishes, and finally (10:20) in bright sun left Camp Woolley. Striking northwest, we passed Bright Angel Ranger Station, and kept on a faint trail to a canyon leading from Milk Creek. Most of the ride thus far was along the summit of the divides, through heavy timber, with little underbrush except in the breaks of the canyons and creeks.

Milk Creek is a very tiny pool of disagreeably warm water trickling along the muddy bottom of a treeless park-like canyon. Nowhere was it deep enough to give the horses a good chance to drink. As they were not thirsty, they declined to drink.

1 p.m. left Milk Spring and followed generally west, the trail growing extremely faint. Probably much of the time we lost it altogether. In the valley bottoms were many flowers—yellow daisies and white snowdrops predominating. The rains of yesterday brought out mushrooms and toadstools in places forming perfect mystic circles. Again we passed numerous sinkholes, some no more than three feet in diameter, others large like craters.

2 p.m. reached the rim at the head of Crystal Creek, being the west fork of the Hindoo Amphitheater. For ¼ mile we followed the rim toward the west, where we could look down the center axis of Crystal Creek due south into the Hermit Amphitheater.

Leaving the rim we went back into the forest toward the west and then turned south, heading straight for Point Sublime. The tip of the Point is bare of large timber but supports sage, mountain mahogany, cedar, yucca and live oak. Here we encountered many horns and bones of deer. One-quarter of a mile from its tip was an excavation—a sort of quarry—5 to 10 feet deep and 20 by 30 feet in area—the Point Sublime Copper Mine. A pile of ore on the side yielded specimens of malachite and azurite.

Arrived Point Sublime 4:30 p.m. We camped on the end of the Point, as far out as we could get.[24] On arrival it was cloudy, but, according to local custom, the sun set clear, giving a grand view and fine coloring. With Holmes's diagrammatic panorama of this view [Dutton 1882, pl. XXVIII], an analysis of the scenery was relatively easy. It was extraordinary how objects of first magnitude were lost in the immensity of the canyon and then suddenly, by changing light, revealed with such distinctiveness that to think of overlooking them seemed an absurdity.

The general impression of the view from Sublime is, like that from Bright Angel, one of confusion. There are too many buttes and mountains on either hand to permit of seeing anything clearly and well. One is too near the nearest and too far from the farthest.

The sunset was grand. Heavy clouds covered the western sky, except at the horizon, and brilliant color tinged the lower clouds and the eastern sky as the sun went down directly behind and a little to the north of Mt. Trumbull, silhouetting the entire Uinkaret Plateau.

George and I fixed our bed closer than ever to the edge of the Point and sat there long after the rays of the sun had gone, seeing very dimly in the light of a young moon some of the closer objects in the Canyon. The clouds disappeared after sunset, leaving a perfectly clear starlit sky.

Almost equally impressive with the view was the absolute silence on the rim. Before sundown the whirring of an occasional swallow flying by was all one heard; afterward crickets and the whistling in the wind of flying bats' wings.

Tuesday, July 28, 1914
Up 5:15; overcast, the light just showing in the Canyon. It was easy this morning to follow the north rim of the Canyon down river west as far as the Uinkaret. The Toroweap fault stood out plainly when viewed with a glass.

By 8 o'clock showers began to fall (east and southeast) across the Canyon, in the direction of the San Francisco Mountains. Soon one of them reached us.

Directly beneath Point Sublime, on the east face of what Dutton calls the West Cloister (which is mapped as Sagittarius Ridge) were magnificent examples of alcoves in the Redwall, each shaped and proportioned like a niche built by an architect, ready to receive a statue. I had observed these niches at various places in the Canyon, some more perfect than others—some deep, some shallow. In one instance the niche seemed to recede into the rock a considerable portion of its height, as it were, a shallow cave without a bottom ledge. In every case the niche appears beneath a water runway or draw. But for the fact that Dutton failed to find a satisfactory solution of how these alcoves are formed [Dutton 1882, 260], I should have entertained a very distinct theory as to their occurrence. It would seem to me that their formation results directly from the flow of water from these draws. When it rains, each of these draws is filled with water carrying its full load of sand, picked up on the relatively gentle slope of the Supai sandstone. The torrent of muddy water flows down the draw over this slope, drops over the Redwall and proceeds as a waterfall. The back throw of the water, heavily loaded with sand, corrodes the face of the Redwall precipice and at the same time acts chemically upon the limestone by taking up its lime content in solution. The precipice of the Redwall is so steep that the stream spreads over its face, giving a large scope for the chemical action. Naturally, the greater action—both corrosive and chemical—will be beneath the point of flow; such action will lessen the further one gets away from that central point. The result must be a deepening of the niche to a center beneath the point of flow and a gradual progressive shallowing of the niche away from that point of flow on each side.[25]

Left Sublime 10 a.m. Most conspicuous of all the plants on the barren tip of the point were the tall Spanish bayonets or yants, as they are called here. The stalks of some of the biggest must rise as high as 12 feet.

We followed yesterday's trail back for about five miles to the head of Crystal Creek, then turned west through the forest and after six miles reached the lower Kanabonits (meaning little water and willows) Spring. The horses were glad to get here for they have had no water since leaving Camp Woolley yesterday noon.

On the way here George shot two blue grouse, which we ate for lunch. Rust cleaned one bird by way of giving George a lesson and George cleaned the second. When he had gotten it all but ready, he brought the bird over to Rust, showing him a worm-like appendage hanging from the bird's neck, where the head had been severed. He said "See how curious; this bird must have been swallowing a worm when he was killed." Rust suggested it would be a good scheme to cut out the bird's esophagus.

On the way out here Red Wing got shoved off the trail by Jake and caught the rope on his pack on a projecting branch of an aspen. In his efforts to get loose, he circled the tree, tied himself up tighter and tighter and finally pulled the tree up by the roots—a good sized one at that, being four inches in diameter.

All afternoon we rode hard. From 4:15 to 8 it rained gently, but firmly and steadily. Soon after leaving the spring we gave up the trail in search of a shorter way westward in the direction of the Saddle between the Kaibab and Powell's Plateau, and threaded the forest without any trail until we made camp. Our course lay at right angles to the drainage, involving the crossing of very many canyons, mostly V-shaped, some with very steep sides, 150 and even 200 feet high. In the absence of sun it seemed impossible Rust could rely on his sense of direction. On a few occasions he called for compass readings. While we undoubtedly wandered somewhat out of the way and lost a little time, in spite of adverse conditions Rust was never seriously out of his reckoning.

At 7:30 we reached the rim near the head of Shinumo Creek, above the Merlin Abyss and here made camp in the woods, about 50 yards from the rim; barometer 8100 feet. For the first time on the whole trip, in anticipation of threatened rain, George and I set up the tent. We built a modest camp-fire back from the rim in the trees and were surprised very soon after it was lighted to see two fires close together on the south rim, near Bass camp. The question at once arose whether this was a signal, and I got out my telegram sent to Bass from Kanab and his letter of instructions to me. Both were plain to the effect that we should build two fires on Swamp Point. All hands were rather worried by these fires. For my part I was extremely doubtful whether there was more than one fire.

To bed 9:30, George and I under the tent. Rust preferred to stay outside so that he could get after the horses if they made a break for water. The wind was cold and damp but not really troublesome.

Wednesday, July 29, 1914
Up 6:15; still cloudy. The rocks on the rim are weathered into shallow basins. In these each of us enjoyed a good wash, in spite of the wrigglers that inhabited them. Left camp at head of Shinumo Creek above Merlin Abyss 9:30. For a mile or two we followed north our trail of last night, then bore west, crossed two steep ravines and at 10:30 arrived at Castle Lake, a large sinkhole in a very deep canyon, with outcrops of Kaibab limestone on its upper slopes and summit. Here we watered the horses and at once proceeded westward. Cattle grazed in every glade and

we encountered them even in the forest. Near one sink-hole carrying water we found two bulls fighting but unhappily the weaker one gave up the contest.

At 12 o'clock we arrived at the head of the trail leading down into the Saddle. Views both east and west—the former down Muav and the latter down Tapeats canyons—very fine.

The trail down is excessively steep and very rough. It has evidently been little worked and much abused by cattle and horses climbing independently. It zigzags continually and most of the way riding was impossible. The Saddle is filled with heavy undergrowth. Here we lunched and repacked, leaving our surplus luggage to be picked up when we returned from Powell's.

Rust informed us there was a spring down the Muav canyon trail ¼ of a mile, the exact location of which he did not know, because whenever he has been here, he has let some other fellow fetch the water. Not to break his rule, George and I undertook that errand. The trail was very faint on an extremely steep side slope and in places wholly obliterated where it threaded almost impassably thorny locust and oak.

We located the spring by the bright coloring of willows in the thicket below the precipice. We thought Dripping Spring a poor apology for a spring but this one was worse. Exposed to the full strength of the sun, intensified by heat radiated from the cliff, and with every breath of air cut off by the underbrush, it was a literally infernal job to fill the water-bags. There was not enough flow of water to run into the bags, so we had to fill them from a pocket drinking-cup—the slowest kind of job. On our return we advised Rust always to let the other man get the water at this spring.

3 p.m. left the Saddle and climbed up to Powell's. A wonderful array of pinnacles adorns the rim on both sides of Muav Creek—to the east on the Kaibab and to the west, where we were, on Powell's. In making the ascent to Powell's we followed a trail along the precipice falling off into Muav Canyon, enjoying fine views down to the river all the way. On the way down to the Saddle we saw distinctly a cougar's footprint.

Our food had gotten pretty low and George was constantly looking for grouse. A moment after we reached the summit of Powell's two fine grouse rose near and flew into the Canyon. George hunted for two hours and never saw another bird. Deer were tremendously plentiful, also horses and mules. A lonely mare grazing near the head of the trail from the Saddle joined our party, coming as close as she dared, like a

View east from Dutton Point, North Rim, Grand Canyon, July 29, 1914. Point Sublime in the distance, across Muav Canyon and the Shinumo Amphitheater. Photograph by George C. Fraser.

tame animal, and stayed by us until we ran into a drove of other horses, which she joined. The whole of Powell's is a horse pasture run by Uncle Jim Owens, Vaughan and Uncle Jim's other boy. Arrived Dutton's Point 5 p.m.

From here there is incomparably the best view of the river. At six points is the river visible.

Most of the day it had been cloudy. Only while we were engaged in getting water at the spring was the sun out in full force, but as usual, the sunset was clear, throwing fine lights on the clouds in the eastern sky and over the buttes in the Canyon.

The glass revealed a fault in Mystic Spring Creek, the canyon leading toward and close to Bass's Camp, with a downthrow to the east. For amusement, for advertisement and for the benefit of Bass in case he was disposed to consider our fire of last night as having any meaning, George and Rust built an enormous fire on the very tip of Dutton Point. Immediately this was answered with two fires at Bass's Camp, and we were thrown into renewed speculations. Again we slept on the rim. Bed 9:30. Clear moon and the brightest stars one ever saw.

Thursday, July 30, 1914

At 5 a.m. light rain started, which continued until 8. Up 5:30. The sun found its way into the Canyon through the clouds in spots, but the Heavens were overcast. Rust wrangled the horses 6 to 8. They were very dry, for their last drink was at 10:30 yesterday morning at Castle Lake.

Our breakfast menu was limited to one box of crackers, a little bacon and the toughest of the tough end (now quite high enough) of a beef donated to us at V.T. seven days ago, some salt and coffee.

We had a little more bacon and some flour cached at the Saddle. After breakfast but half a water-bag of water was left. We again dispensed with washing, practically for the second day because Castle Lake was not a very inviting washstand, and the spring below the Saddle had too small a run-off to really wet.

The ants were troublesome again—this time I had both hands stung, the third finger and entire back of my left hand was much swollen and a bit tender. The effects of the previous bite passed off in two days. I expected these would also.

In the hopes of a good lunch, George tramped through the wood for an hour, with a shotgun, but did not get sight of a grouse. The shade the clouds afforded gave a good light for detailed study of the Canyon. Of all the views within the Kaibab division of the canyon, this one is the most appealing. It combines with great range distant glimpses of the buttes and temples east of Point Sublime, and at close range (within five to seven miles) the details of the canyon sculpture, here in some respects more graceful than that of the eastern part of the division, though not on so grand a scale.

10 a.m. left Dutton Point and retraced our steps about four miles past the mud hole mentioned yesterday. At 11:30 we took off the packs and tied the pack horses and rode northwest across the shank of the plateau until 12:10, when we reached the rim at a point apparently nameless, jutting into the Tapeats amphitheater toward the west. By this time it had cleared and the sun was dazzling.

By 1 o'clock, however, tremendous heavy thunder clouds had gathered over the Kaibab. The sun was obscured and we were disturbed by distant rumblings of thunder coming nearer and much lightning. After studying the view from this point we moved half a mile to the north, keeping along the rim, to another point which from our first position somewhat obscured the view toward the north. As we reached this point, we and the entire foreground of our vision were in the shade, but beyond the sun had broken through the clouds and shined like a spotlight directly upon the towers of the Virgin, rising high above the Vermilion Cliffs. This view is complementary to that from Final and Atoko. We were on the line of the upthrow side of the West Kaibab Fault and looked down into the immense amphitheater bounded by the outer walls of the Canyon, where the Colorado made its big bend north, west and south, past its junction with Kanab Creek.

We had, as it were, a birdseye view of all our journeying up to the point where we crossed the desert for the Kaibab. In the far background was Mt. Dellenbaugh, behind and a little to the south of the Canyon and of the Uinkaret. The entire Trumbull platform stood out in relief, and with a glass we could distinguish Vulcan's Throne, and, by the difference in altitude between its east and west walls, the Toroweap. To the northwest, across what looked like a wide ditch and was the Kanab Creek, rose the Chocolate and Vermilion Cliffs and the Pine Valley Mountains. The Pipe Spring promontory lay like a great lizard on the surface of the desert and almost over it, in unmistakable and characteristic contour, the Steamboat, the great western temple of the Virgin, stood as a sentinel charged to guard the scene.

While looking at the view, the shower that had been deluging the Kaibab reached us about 1:30. We wanted to spend another day or two or three skirting the rim of Powell's, and I earnestly coveted an opportunity of viewing the Canyon from Ives and Wheeler Points at the southwest and south extremities of the Plateau. But we had begun to get thirsty, the water was all gone and the horses had stood their limit of thirst, so at 1:50, in the rain, we turned our backs on this great north and west view, wondering whether it really was finer than any of the others, as at the moment it seemed to be.

Left northwest point of Powell's Plateau 1:50 and rode back east to a point above the Saddle, near where our trail of yesterday came up. We had left the gun with the pack horse, and of course had two fine shots which surely would have produced a fine supper. Rust left us to go back for the horses, suggesting we might proceed down to the Saddle. We soon picked up a trail. There was no such thing as a real worked and well used trail on Powell's or leading up to it. The horses pastured here make trails for themselves.

Following what appeared to be a trail, George and I started down the steep slope of Powell's toward the Saddle. The trail, such as it was, constantly branched and lost itself through the wanderings of the stock, which evidently used it as a route to and from water. We had to walk the whole way, sliding and stumbling over rocks, wading through underbrush soaked by the rain, tearing ourselves and our shirts on live oak, locust and such like thorny things.

During our progress over the Kaibab limestone there was a constant temptation to stop and load up with fossils, but I kept my resolution, made at the outset of the trip, to collect no specimens (this was only broken a very little bit at the copper mine at Point Sublime).

Eleven hundred feet down by the barometer we struck the cross-bedded sandstone and were still in it when we reached the bottom of the canyon on the westerly side of Tapeats Creek, down 1300 feet. Crossing the creek, we struck a fairly well-marked trail running parallel with the stream-bed, which, needless to say, here was perfectly dry. Confident that the spring of which we had heard could not be far beyond, we turned left, down the valley, and in five minutes sighted willows and knew we were at water.[26]

The spring came out of the red Supai sandstone on the north side of the canyon in fair volume, forming a large pool and creating a slight but perceptible run-off. It was all we could do to get the bridles off the horses so they might drink. Their 30 hours of abstinence had told on them pretty hard. As all hands had drunk and we had washed (of course without soap) for the first time in over two days, we mounted the horses and rode hard to the Saddle.

Thunder storms are very frequent in the Kaibab and we encountered a surprisingly large number of trees that had been struck by lightning. On the summit of the plateau, near the saw-mill above Little Zion, we found on the ground some slabs and splinters of pine, apparently freshly broken off. How they got there was a mystery until looking into the tall trees above we found one whose bark for several feet had been stripped off and from which there had been gouged great pieces of the trunk.

When we arrived Rust had unpacked and was ready to take the pack horses and his mount to the spring for water. We took account of our larder and Rust instructed George how to bake bread, which he did while Rust at 4 p.m. went to the spring.

At 6 p.m. supper—a light meal except for George's bread, which was very heavy. We ate in haste because we had to build our signal fires on Swamp Point before sunset.

6:40 p.m., left camp. Walked up east slope of Saddle to summit of Swamp Point (leaving horses in pasture). We immediately started two large fires 120 yards apart; as soon as the sun went down two answering fires were lit at Bass Camp. The fires seemed to be very close together and in the same position as those we saw from the point above Merlin Abyss and from Dutton Point.

The rain had passed over and the sky was clear. A moon just entering on its second quarter lighted the Canyon, so we stayed to enjoy the view. 9:15 started down trail by moonlight. Arrived camp 9:30. George made the bed on a stony slope with humps underneath, resulting in an extremely uncomfortable night. Field mice attacked the luggage and ate the rim of my straw hat. A mouse cut scallops in the brim of Rust's felt hat the last night we spent at Camp Woolley. It was very damp under the trees.

Friday, July 31, 1914

Up 5:30; cloudless. Temperature 6:30, 55 degrees. We managed to get a pretty good breakfast; coffee, cream of wheat, bacon and a loaf of George's bread. The only food left was coffee, very little bacon, some flour and baking powder and salt, which we left, and two of George's dough cakes and a pot of raspberry jam, which we took with us.

The horses, having watered late yesterday, were easily caught. We left Rust's horse and Red Wing, taking our two mounts and packing Jake with our three bags and the shotgun. The rifle was left with Rust, so that he might get some food on the return trip. George and I started off riding. Rust walked, leading Jake.

9 a.m. left saddle. The trail was very faint. It followed along the easterly side of Muav Canyon for nearly half a mile, directly under the base of the cross-bedded sandstone, past the little spring where we watered en route up Powell's. This would never be noticed except for the bright green of its sheltering trees. The slope is very steep and much washed, giving little foothold. Rust had never been over this trail, and we began to doubt whether anybody else ever had. The large-scale topographic sheet gave a fair notion of the trail's direction, and after we had gone along the wall about as far as we thought reasonable, Rust began to look for signs of a trail leading down to the bottom of the valley. He found the way but we would never have recognized it.

10:05, passed benchmark 5466 feet. Near here, right in the valley bottom, we found a single magnificent yellow pine growing all alone, with no trees of its species nearer than the Saddle. In the valley bottom vegetation was thick enough, but only undergrowth, locust, live oak, buck brush and some others of the 57 varieties of prickly plants that were encountered during the day. This brush was bad enough near the head of the creek, but nothing compared to what we found lower down.

10:35 passed benchmark 5181. There was not a cloud in the sky and the sun beat furiously upon us and every rock radiated heat. The trail seemed to end at this point. So far we had been able to ride. The heat and hard walking (for we had come very rapidly) had played Rust out a bit, so I clambered along the rock for half an hour, looking for the trail. Temperature in the sun during this time, 112 degrees. We found numerous signs of animals.

At some remote period a trail had been blasted out in spots along one of the ledges in the Redwall precipice. I walked along this in search of a way down. After half an hour Rust joined me. I found a place where we could walk down, but none that looked passable for the horses. Rust, however, soon located where the trail ran or had run. We went back for the horses and got down the very steep cliff by zigzagging, without difficulty. From above the descent looked almost impossible for horses and from below it was hard to find where we had scaled it.

Reached creek at the bottom of the precipice 12:35. Where we left the creek and started over the Redwall it carried no water. Here ran a goodly stream.

It began to cloud over. We were tired, hot and hungry, so we stopped for lunch. Temperature, shade, 12:35, 83 degrees. We found a sort of natural pool in the brook and enjoyed a good cold bath—the first since Kanab. I took this opportunity to change my shirt for the first time since Kanab, saving a clean one for my entrance into El Tovar.

There was absolutely not a spear of grass for the stock. They got watered and had a bit of a rest with saddles and packs off.

We tarried here longer than the exigencies of the journey down warranted, but all of us were tired and the sun was very hot. As we made ready to leave clouds which had been threatening in the distance obscured the sun, bringing some relief and a very little rain.

At 2:35 p.m. we started downward again following along and through the creek. 3 p.m. passed benchmark 3770 feet. From the foot of the Redwall to the head of this canyon the descent had been gradual and the trail fairly easy. Going was bad because of boulders and underbrush. The further we descended the canyon, the more annoying and painful became passage through this undergrowth. There did not seem to be a single variety of bush without thorns of some sort. The locust and live oak were mild compared to the prevalent species realistically called "Cat's Claw." This bush grows to a height of about 10 feet and every branch is armed with innumerable spines in shape and dimension like the extended claws of a sizable Tom cat. These fasten into one's clothes, tear off one's hat and unless skillfully avoided gouge the flesh. George's arms suffered most because of his sleeveless athletic shirt.

At some point in the Tonto sandstone gorge, White Creek (the stream flowing down Muav Canyon) lost itself entirely. When we came upon the stream-bed three miles or more below the head of this canyon and above its junction with Shinumo Creek, we found it dry.

To our left was the deep canyon; to our right the high bounding walls surmounted by Masonic Temple, with Dutton Point above, and ahead of us was a hill sloping very steeply toward the east toward the valley bottom. The trail, faint enough at best, here ran out entirely. We came upon quantities of burros in groups of from two to five, trying to scratch a living out of the rock. Why they were not all starved to death in this place of desolation was a mystery. They must eat cactus and Cat's Claw.

We constantly mistook their trails for the main trail, but Rust's knowledge, derived from previous experience in similar places, aided by the topographic sheets, gave us the general direction to pursue and we never got far from the line of the trail. We came on a precipice falling off into the Shinumo Creek, just below its junction with White Creek. Here the trail seemed to come to an end, and it was some time before Rust found a way down to the stream. Walking along a ledge here Jake's pack hit an overhanging rock and he almost rolled down the precipice. We would have lost him but for the control Rust had through holding the halter short.

It was only a trifling distance from this point to the cleft or crack with the large boulder caught between its narrow sides photographed and exploited by the Kolb Brothers and other canyon specialists.

I noticed Rust looked pretty tired and worn, for he had walked the entire distance. George and I had been compelled to walk a little, but not more than one-quarter of the way. I therefore urged Rust to mount my horse and walked over the hill. The way was so steep, however, that most of the time it was impossible for Rust to ride and when we finally reached Shinumo Creek, 5:10 p.m. I was pretty well used up. The clouds which sheltered us when we left the lunch place were dissipated in less than an hour and the intense heat of the sun, aided by the radiation of the bare rocks, had aggravated the effect of the fatigue upon me, and beside I was awfully hungry. We got out the last of our food—less than half a dough cake—and divided it into three equal portions. On the principle of the economist who ate dried apples for breakfast, drank hot water for lunch and swelled up for tea, I took large draughts of the clear cold water out of Shinumo Creek. This, with a shampoo, revived me, so that I was able to go on strong.

For two or three miles we followed the bed of Shinumo Creek, fording it many times, and always had difficulty in locating the trail on the opposite side of each ford. The descent was steep, the stream rough and rapid, and the bed full of boulders, among them many of black basalt.

We had to make haste to reach the river before dark, and unhappily there was no time to stop. While traveling, the trail absorbed one's entire attention. So down we went, over the Algonkian, almost due south to the summit of the granite, here about 50 feet above the river, and followed that half a mile to Bass's cable crossing, benchmark 2272'. Arrived 6:30. Our disappointment was intense when we found no sign of life. Bass had promised to meet us, and I had his assurance by letter before leaving New York that a man would be down at the river all summer. We hastily unsaddled and took off Jake's pack and George began to investigate the cable. Tacked on one of the supporting posts he found a card of Bass's with the following written on it in ink: "Have wait in vain; no feed; return tomorrow, 31st."

This was the 31st. We made sure of that by looking back over my notes. Bass must have come down either yesterday after seeing our camp fire on Dutton Point, or the day before, after seeing our camp fire on the point above Merlin Abyss. Rust was confident that Bass would appear at any moment, but we wanted to be prepared for eventualities and so investigated the cable crossing device.

This was a primitive contraption, almost on a par with the Little Zion cableway, but safer, in that the towers at each end were anchored by wire cables attached to stakes driven 20 yards or so behind them. At the crossing the granite fell sheer to the river's edge, as we estimated 45 feet. The towers stood at the edge of the precipice on each side of the river. They supported five cables, two on the same horizontal plane about three feet apart and two others (also in an identical horizontal plane) about 18 inches below them. The fifth cable hung slack between the other four, all of which were fairly taut, but of course with quite a sag down midway between the towers. The width of the river here must have been 200 to 250 feet. The distance between the towers was probably 50 feet greater. The cables were all ⅜-inch twisted wire and seemed in fair condition.

Bass had written me something about a wheel being kept at each side of the river so that one could cross in case the cage happened to be on the opposite side. I had no idea what this meant, but Rust explained that it must be a pulley wheel and we looked around for one. Finally we found a wheel about six inches in diameter, grooved to fit a single cable and bearing a steel shank with holes drilled through it to permit of its being fastened by bolts. We hung this wheel on the cable, ran a halter rope through two of the holes and Rust tied it into a painter's swing. George climbed into this swing, used a sweater to protect him from being cut by the rope, put on a pair of gloves and pulled himself across the river, hand before hand, the crossing occupying 10 minutes. We hurried this operation because of the fast falling darkness, in the hope that some food might be found on the other side, and in order to get the cage over before dark and have it available for a crossing in the morning.

Directly beneath the crossing the river was calm, though swift. Both below and above there were rapids. By shouting loud we were able to talk with George across the stream. In the way of food nothing developed but half a can of spoiled salmon. After a thorough search and investigation of the modus operandi of the cage, George started to bring this over. It took 25 minutes for this job and by the time he got back it was quite dark.

The cage is of heavy timber, about five feet long by three feet wide and six feet in height. It is suspended from four pulley wheels, like that on which George crossed, each running on a wire. The fifth and slack wire is wound once around a windlass or drum rigged on top of the cage between the pulley wheels. This windlass is merely a section of a log with a hole drilled through the middle, in which hole there was inserted an iron half-inch bar for an axle. To move this contraption, one sat on a board on top of the cage and turned the windlass by pulling on three rough stakes or handles radiating from each end of the windlass. I could not conceive the reason for George's slow progress until he arrived, bathed in perspiration and winded, and showed us that the windlass was without grease and its axle was either broken or bent into the shape of a parabola.

We secured the cage and resigned ourselves to watchful waiting.

Not a breath of air stirred and save for the roar of the water the canyon was as silent as the grave. We lit a large fire for light and Rust and I settled up accounts. I filled out two Travelers' Cheques in the darkness and had some doubts as to whether they would ever be honored.

Of course we discussed all the reasons for our predicament and speculated upon what would happen to-morrow. I suggested to Rust that he leave his horses to find their way up to the Saddle and himself stay with us and make a trip up the San Francisco Mountains. Very properly Rust pointed out that this could not be done. There was not a particle of feed in the bottom of the canyon and the horses could find nothing short of the Saddle. They would surely starve to death.

We finally decided that Rust should return with the horses in the morning and we should cross the river, leave everything except absolutely necessary clothes, and walk up the trail to Bass Camp. It was very warm and perfectly clear, the moon (now in its second quarter) shining brightly. We had no blankets, but slept comfortably on a horse blanket. Rust took another horse blanket a hundred yards up the canyon to a point where he could cut off the horses in case they were disposed to wander in the wrong direction.

The canyon bottom was sandy and bare of vegetation except prickly cactus. For the last three hours down the trail the variety of prickers increased as we progressed. Prickly pears, Spanish bayonets and every species of painful cactus (except the barrel cactus) seem to thrive.

We lay down at 9:30, but none of us slept much. I found lying on my stomach relieved the feeling of emptiness which was really my only inconvenience, because I had ceased to be hungry.

Saturday, August 1, 1914

We were all more or less wakeful all night; I was figuring how we would make out on the south rim and between times admiring the stars and studying the heavens with the glasses. The roar of the river was not soothing; perhaps one would become accustomed to it in time, but I was never a moment unconscious of it. This roar seemed to speak of force, fierce and destructive, ready for immediate application, and the canyon walls seemed to bear silent witness to the speaker's power. The desolation and ruggedness of the canyon and the sound of the river were depressing and fearful.

At 4:40 a.m. I noticed the stars in the eastern heavens becoming faint and knew dawn was approaching; but the first rays of the sun did not penetrate to these depths until more than an hour later. I aroused George and the wakeful Rust corralled his horses and joined us in a moment. Last evening we had packed all our stuff, including the usual contents of our pockets and every bit of clothing not needed to protect us from the sun, so we were ready to put the luggage on the cage immediately. By the light of a candle and the fire (of drift wood left by some high flood) we looked the ground over for stray possessions—our invariable custom on breaking camp, the observation of which had kept our gross loss down to a single lead pencil—and said a hasty and regretful farewell to Rust.

Rust offered to go with us, but as he would have to return directly and take the horses up to the Saddle we could not permit him to do so, altho' it looked as if he was impaled on the best horn of our dilemma—with three horses to ride over a known trail and the certainty of grub at the top, against our lack of mounts, ignorance of the trail and conditions ahead and general incompetence, with the possibility that Bass Camp might be deserted. I was grieved at his dejection over our departure and evident worry lest we fall by the way-side.

At 5:15, in darkness, we started the cage across the river, George taking command. Under his direction I pulled up on the lower handles of the west side of the windlass while he pulled down on the upper handles of the east side. For 20 minutes we worked as hard as we could, and at 5:35 reached the south side, both dripping wet with perspiration and blown as if we had run a race. The iron axle of the windlass grew more out of gear with each turn and as the angle of ascent from the sag of the wire toward the south terminus of the cables became more acute, the labor of moving the primitive contraption was severe. There seemed to be a live possibility of the cage disintegrating, which afforded interesting speculation as to what, in that event, would happen to us. We were suspended 45 to 50 feet above the water flowing smoothly—in contrast with rapids commencing at a bend towards the south 300 yards below—but fast, as was evidenced by swirls and eddies. The river's color and consistency is hard to describe—perhaps not quite congealed molasses candy affords a fair comparison. It was unusually high for this season owing to frequent and heavy rains the past month, and so bore its full load of solid matter in suspension. To swim any appreciable distance, with clothes and boots on, in such a stream would be impossible. Our salvation, if immersed, would have been a sandy bar or beach on the north bank 150 yards below the cable.

As Rust would never be far from water, we took the canteen and water bag both nearly full. We left the luggage in the cage without even running the latter to the cable tower, 10 feet back of the rim of the granite, for we felt it important to conserve all our strength for the climb, and after getting our wind, shouted adieu across the river and at 5:40 hit the trail.

For nearly ½ mile we walked up stream along the steep north slope of the Algonkian over the river, Rust keeping abreast of us on the other bank. He urged us to catch a tame-looking burro standing sleepily near by; I tried to do so, but when I approached within 20 yards, the beast made off wild as a hare. By 6 the canyon was in full light and the slopes with eastern exposure were illuminated by the sun. A gradual ascent along the steep slope brought us to a pass through the Algonkian hill which carries the run-off—evidently never very heavy—from the canyon leading to Bass Camp. Here we turned south away from the river, giving Rust a last shout as he turned back toward the horses.

I led the way, a long step to each breath, and we made fine progress. We found the trail obscured by burro tracks, but our past month's education had been sufficient to keep us on the line followed by Bass' horses.

6:50. We stopped five minutes to rest, breathe and drink a swallow each. Well it was we brought water for not a drop did we see from river to rim; all was barren, bare and stony without even the relief of undergrowth such as we encountered yesterday. Not the least of our blessings lay in the fact that the trail ran along the east side of the canyon and consequently in the morning lay in the shade. It was hot but not oppressive except when we got from under the shadow of the easterly canyon wall.

From 1 to 1½ miles back from the river and until about 6:20 we climbed steeply—zig-zagging part of the way—over the Algonkian and then struck the Tonto sloping gently and affording good footing, so that we were able to make excellent time. The reduction in altitude (the Tonto slope is approximately 2800 feet to 3500 feet above sea level) from what we had lately been accustomed to, aided the lung power and the lightness of our equipment and emptiness of our stomachs made for easier walking. Our progress was so good and my strength held so well I began to revise our initial estimate of 12 M. as the hour of our arrival at the summit in favor of 11 and perhaps even 10 a.m. But we were alive to trouble ahead; the Redwall and cross-bedded sandstone would be steep and long and when we climbed the higher reaches, the sun would be full upon us.

At 7:20 as we neared the foot of the Redwall I heard a rock fall and George shouted that a man and a horse were ahead and immediately whipped out his revolver and shot three times in rapid succession. The man yelled and put up his hands and we hurried up to him.

It was the great and unique W. W. Bass with his boy Bill (age about 14), four horses and two photographers (of whom more later). Bass was not delighted to see us, but on request gave us food—a can of salmon and some soda crackers—and immediately started a harangue about the machinations of the Santa Fe road designed to demonstrate that that system is maintained solely to do him injury. Incidentally we learned Zane Grey is a liar and because of his lies no one was spending the summer at Shinumo, and that a burro, which Bass had nurtured and fed as an infant, basely deserted the party on the way down and was not available to pack the luggage to camp. I managed to get in a word about the importance of bringing our luggage from the river and at 8 a.m. we separated, Bill guiding George and me—all three mounted on large horses—and Bass and the two photographers proceeded downward on foot leading the other two horses.

Most of the way through the Redwall we were able to ride. The trail ran along ledges, here and there blasted a little, with a precipitous fall on the right (west). It was not in good condition and would have been somewhat appalling perhaps on our first day out; after yesterday, however, it looked to us like a boulevard.

A steep climb on foot at the apex of the canyon through the Redwall brought us to the slope of the Supai (red) sandstone, talus covered and broken, making hard going, but without difficulty or danger. Here we encountered the full force of the sun, from which we had been shaded while threading under the easterly cliff of the Redwall, and were glad of our mounts.

At 9 a.m. we reached the summit of the red sandstone and entered upon the worst part of the trail.

The cross-bedded sandstone presented a surface that looked impossible of scaling with animals. Along an east-west line on the easterly canyon wall, however, it was broken somewhat and we found a trail worked in zig-zag fashion here, in places blasted a little and in other places built up. The way was steep, beset with broken rocks in large fragments, and where the bed rock formed the surface smooth and slippery; we walked and the horses, all old timers, followed tamely.

In the cross-bedded sandstone and at its summit we passed two cliff dwellings—walls of large angular rock fragments enclosing shallow caves in the precipice.

At the rim where the trail began was a similar wall called by Bass a Spanish fort, but more probably a shelter from which the dwellers among the cliffs below could watch and if need be defend the approach to their homes.

At 10 a.m. we reached the summit of the cross-bedded sandstone and thence rode easily, though the trail was still steep, over the Kaibab limestone to the rim. Arrived 10:30 strong and fit, with good appetites, but by no means starved. The enforced abstinence from food to seemed to have made it easier to endure the sun, which had shone full upon us since we got well up the Redwall, about 8:30. The upper part of the trail was risky; in many places rain wash had weakened the bed, and the horses frequently found their footing insecure and started rocks falling. Yesterday Bass was nearly hit by a large rock while descending the zig-zags in the cross-bedded sandstone.

We were so anxious to eat and rest and get out of the sun that we made more haste up the trail than its interest would otherwise have allowed. I was unable to trace the fault which, as viewed from the north rim, seemed to run down the canyon heading at Bass Camp. This region both north and south of the rim should be slowly traversed—three or four days and plenty of food and fodder should be allowed and provided for the trip from rim to rim.

Bass Camp consists of a four-room cabin, two smaller cabins, a shed, corrals, and two large tents. The runoff from the roof is collected in cis-terns—some, according to Bass, constructed by the cliff dwellers; there is no spring in the vicinity.

Bass had told us to make ourselves at home and Bill had the key to his father's trunk in which was cached two loaves of bread. On arrival we found the kitchen in possession of Dr. and Mrs. W. K. Simpson of Riverside, Calif., who were just cooking breakfast. They gave us some coffee, fresh made, that was delicious—we learned later their supplies had all but given out and hence they could not extend further hospi-tality. George, however, scrambled some eggs and fried plenty of bacon, while I opened a can of peaches, with which, supplemented by plenty of bread and more coffee, we made a 3 in 1 meal.

We were not disposed to seek the sun any more that day, so sat about talking with the Simpsons and investigating Bass' literature—a mess of magazines dating from about 1895, government publications and nov-els, all dilapidated and soiled. I found Powell's *Exploration of the Canyon* and reread parts; also Dutton's *Atlas* to accompany the *Tertiary History of the Canyon*, and had a good chance to fix in mind the broader features of our past route.

Dr. and Mrs. Simpson proved very agreeable and congenial. He is a native of San Francisco, studied medicine at University of Wisconsin and now resides in Riverside. Mrs. Simpson is a native of Detroit, Mich.

After graduating in medicine the Dr.—I judge on account of his health—spent two years wandering on horse-back through Utah with excursions into Arizona and New Mexico. During this time he covered upwards of 10,000 miles. While wandering about the Dr. practiced as opportunity offered, and he told blood-curdling tales of conditions he had found among Indians and even the Whites. Rattlesnake poison he encountered twice, but in each instance preliminary doctoring with whiskey in allopathic doses at homeopathic intervals had induced such acute alcoholism as to obscure the effects of the snake-bite.

At 4 p.m. Bass alone emerged from the depths riding one horse and leading the other, loaded with our three bags. He was in bad humor and made no effort to conceal the fact. A halter rope was missing, as Bill explained, because Bass had told him to leave it on the trail to be picked up on Bass' return from the river. Bass cursed Bill for this, and attempted to hit him with the cinch of a saddle Bass was carrying. Bill skillfully kept out of range—an easy matter on account of the weight and clumsiness of the saddle Bass carried—and replied to his father's epithets, in kind, finally scaling the fence of the corral and making his escape. Old Tex, had he witnessed this scene, would have recommended both father and son to seek culture in Texas.

At 6:30 in company with the Simpsons, we rode two miles east to the rim at Signal Hill on the west wall of Ruby Canyon and thence north to Havasupai Point, whence we saw our last magnificent sunset behind Trumbull. We had not appreciated how long a ride this was to be and were surprised, as we sat on Havasupai Point, to see one, then two, and finally three fires start on Swamp Point—Rust's signal as arranged, telling us he had arrived in safety. We greeted these with sincere satisfaction for all day we had mentally followed his lonely and empty journey. Fearful that his fires would not be answered, we made all haste back to camp, but only arrived at 9 p.m. through missing the way in the dark. Fortunately Bill had given the reply signal, we having told him of our arrangement in that regard.

In the cabin we found Maude and Robinson [the photographers that had accompanied Bass] more dead than alive. Maude[27] is about 60 years old, Robinson about 33. The former has climbed about the Canyon and knows life in the open, but Robinson is of city type, never rode a horse until he came here, and except for going down Bright Angel trail, has had no experience of real walking.

10 p.m. to bed, George and I in the front room of the cabin sleeping on a bed together; sheets and blankets clean but room untidy.

Sunday, August 2, 1914

Up 7 a.m. Dr. and Mrs. Simpson left on horseback at 8. At 9:30 George and I on horse-back started on the 25-mile ride to El Tovar, Bass to follow in a wagon with the Simpsons and our luggage, Maude, Robinson and Bill. Bass has built a very good road, quite passable by motor. At 10:15, six miles from camp, we struck the river at head of Turquoise Canyon and got a good view directly across to Point Sublime. One of the twin temples rose on our right—so colossal it was inconceivable it should have been inconspicuous to the point of being lost in the panorama from Point Sublime. We pushed on rapidly, cantering on all level stretches, and by 11 had covered close to 15 miles.

At 11 George, who was riding ahead, came to a sudden stop and I found him confronted by a man holding an old fashioned .45 army Colt six-shooter; this individual turned out to be Bass's chauffeur and to be engaged in no more desperate occupation than trying to kill birds while waiting for us. In a moment we came upon the motor, Mrs. Bass, her little girl (age about seven) and Dr. and Mrs. Simpson. Mrs. Bass had some melons, pie and other good things, of which George partook.

Mrs. Bass had expected Bass to return two or three days ago and was on her way to camp to ascertain the cause of his detention and bring supplies when she met the Simpsons. At her suggestion the Simpsons and ourselves with the small girl went to El Tovar in the car, leaving her with our four horses and the food to await Bass's coming. At 12:30 we reached El Tovar, or rather the main road below the hotel for the chauffeur refused to drive in the grounds because of the Bass-Santa Fe feud.

When we met Bass in the Canyon he told us of diplomatic strain between Austria and Serbia and severe breaks in the stock market. The chauffeur told us there was talk in the papers of Germany getting into war. At the hotel I found telegrams and Saturday's papers telling of the starting of a great European conflict. Since Kanab, save for the telegrams brought to Camp Woolley, we had been without news; the last newspaper we saw bore the date July 16.

At El Tovar we found our suit cases and were able to dress in normal style, except as to my neck, for all my collars were in the luggage Bass was conveying.

After a good bath I read the news and during lunch we discussed plans. Dr. Simpson invited us to motor to Flagstaff and considered going up the San Francisco Mtns. with us and we were severely tempted to accept. But considering the uncertainties of the business situation and the possibilities of trouble coming on clients from the disturbance of credits, I felt it wrong to prolong this vacation, so I had our tickets validated, greatly disgusted at throwing away transportation from Lund to San Francisco via Los Angeles and back over the Santa Fe to Williams.

About 5:30 we learned Bass had appeared with our luggage but refused to leave it. We then started a hunt for Bass and the bags. George, Dr. Simpson and two Japanese bell-boys raked the town and finally at 7 p.m. found the bags locked up in the station. We had to repack all our stuff and dress in 40 minutes and just made the train.

Left 8 p.m. for Williams. Maude and Robinson left on the same train with us, proceeding from Williams direct to Los Angeles. We spent the two hour trip to Williams listening to their tales of Bass.

George Fraser concluded his journal with an uncomplimentary account of W. W. Bass, based partly on his misadventure crossing the canyon. In his August 2, 1914, entry he concluded that "I should regard it as dangerous and the height of folly to trust myself to Bass's guidance or to place myself in any situation where his judgment might have to be depended on." In fairness to Bass, it appears that when he saw Fraser's and Rust's first fire on July 28, he determined to head for the river the next morning, despite it not being the prearranged two fires on Swamp Point. Such were the exigencies of early canyon communications.

The Frasers returned to Morristown on August 6. George Sr. appended in his journal a full accounting of the trip's cost—about one thousand dollars. The portion of the trip with Rust amounted to $431.[28] In today's world, a backcountry horse trip for two would run in the neighborhood of $200–$400 per day. Still, the adventure the Frasers enjoyed would have been beyond the reach of most Americans at the time.

Dave Rust was at best a sporadic diarist and kept no record of his trips with George Fraser. Fraser, fortunately, made up for this deficiency with his meticulous note taking. If there is anything missing from his journals it is more about Rust; Fraser included a brief description of him following his July 30, 1914, journal entry, in which he remarked on his "clear-cut, regular features and straightforward blue eyes," and his "endless endurance."

Some measure of Fraser's regard for Rust is found in their correspondence, which continued until Fraser's death in 1935. Following their 1914 trip, Rust wrote a long letter to Fraser, expressing his worry at having left him at the bottom of the Grand Canyon. Rust described how he contemplated returning to the river to see if Bass had arrived, but instead he "heeded the pleading of his horses to take them to their feed." He thanked Fraser for his "excellent companionship" and complimented him on his endurance: "from the time you tried to swim the Mukuntuweap till you navigated yourself across the Colorado I thought of you and spoke of you as the best sport I had ever been out with."[29]

Fraser also wrote to Rust, describing his exit from the Grand Canyon and his difficulties with Bass. The two men continued their correspondence that fall and winter, each placing the difficulties of the trip in perspective and recalling humorous moments on the trail. George Jr.'s attempt to bake bread for the group evoked this:[30]

Martin, Fraser & Speir, Counselors at Law
20 Exchange Place
New York City.
November 28, 1914
My dear Mr. Rust:-
The receipt of your very welcome letter of the 18th instant and of the beaver skin and fossil biscuit have given me the very greatest pleasure. . . . If you had not indicated the point at which you found the fossil biscuit I should have concluded, from its specific gravity, hardness and density, that it was one of those baked by George in Muav Saddle. Without having any recourse to my imagination of some supernatural agency, I cannot account for its transportation from that point to Short Creek. I therefore conclude that it is a concretion (probably ferruginous) in the triassic (vermilion cliff) sandstone, which has weathered out and remained intact because of its being harder than the bed in which it originally lay. It stands and will remain on my desk as a paper weight to recall pleasant days with you, mingled, however, with the regret, that I never quite overcame, of our failure to enjoy the fatted kid your brother so considerately provided for our entertainment the day we gave Short Creek the go-by.
Faithfully yours,
G. C. Fraser

One wishes that Fraser had saved Rust's letters, for the two men kept up their correspondence for more than two decades. While Fraser counted many people of high education, wealth, and social standing among his friends, he always seemed to reserve a special place in his heart for Dave Rust, his cowboy guide.

Chapter 2

The High Plateaus, the Henry Mountains, and the Kolob, 1915

I must confess that last night I spent three-quarters of an hour reading Dut-
ton's High Plateaux and planning a trip to the Aquarius Plateau, and thence
along the Pink Cliffs to Cedar City. Later on I shall map out a jaunt of this
kind and write you of it in detail for advice as to its practicability. I shall not be
satisfied until I have touched the Pink Cliffs and seen the Canyon from the foot
of Parashont.
        —George C. Fraser to Dave Rust, August 17, 1914

Upon returning from the Grand Canyon on August 6, 1914, George Fra-
ser wasted little time laying plans for his next adventure, a traverse of
Utah's High Plateaus and their adjoining desert valleys and mountains.
The previous year he had followed the geologic tour de force presented in
Clarence E. Dutton's *Tertiary History of the Grand Cañon District*; this year's
journey would take for its guide Dutton's *Geology of the High Plateaus.*[1]
   For anyone accustomed to the piñon- and juniper-covered plateaus of
the canyon lands, the Utah High Plateaus present a startling contrast.
Formed out of Middle Tertiary volcanic flows, faulted and uplifted into
distinct and lofty platforms,[2] they support extensive forests of spruce and
aspen, grading into alpine tundra, with few prominent peaks. Some, like
the Aquarius, supported an ice cap during the Pleistocene, the leavings of
which melted out to form innumerable small lakes and ponds. The shoul-
ders of most of the plateaus are shaped by recent landslides, creating
hummocky terrain below the high volcanic cliffs. Dutton identified nine
separate plateaus: the Wasatch and Sevier, in the northern portion of the
region; the Fishlake, Awapa, and Thousand Lake, in the east-central; the
Pavant, in the west-central; the Paunsaugunt and Markagunt, overlooking the Paria and Virgin river drainages; and the largest and most famous
of them all, the Aquarius, headwaters for the Escalante and other rivers.
Interesting in themselves, the plateaus are perhaps most notable for their
superb views of the canyon lands to the east and south. Fraser, of course,
wanted to visit as many of those viewpoints as could be crammed into a

five-week adventure. In addition, the group would strike off through the Waterpocket Fold to reach the Henry Mountains.

Dave Rust had been hoping to take the Frasers on a canoe trip down Glen Canyon and suggested so in a letter to Fraser early in 1915, but he readily acceded to his friend's plan. By June, Fraser had mapped out his itinerary and sent it to Rust for approval. As before, George Fraser Jr. came along and Rust served as guide and wrangler. Their ambitious trek took them to most of the viewpoints Dutton described in *High Plateaus*. Beginning at Salina, Utah, they climbed up to the Sevier and Fishlake Plateaus, taking in views from Mount Terrill (11,547 ft.) and Mount Marvine (11,610 ft.). They dropped down to the east from Thousand Lake Mountain to strike off across the nearly barren South Desert to Caineville, encountering the weird erosional remnants of Entrada Sandstone in what is now the Cathedral Valley section of Capitol Reef National Park. Dave Rust had herded his family's livestock in this forbidding desert as a boy and no doubt had seen these striking landmarks.

The party then ascended Mount Ellen (11,522 ft.), the northernmost of the Henry Mountains. Fraser's interest in these desert sentinels was sparked by another classic geology text, G. K. Gilbert's *Geology of the Henry Mountains*, published by the Powell survey in 1877. This work possessed little of the poetic language of Dutton, but Fraser was nonetheless drawn to Gilbert's detailed and innovative exposition of the volcanic intrusions, which he had termed laccolites, that formed the core of the Henrys.

The centerpiece of Dutton's *High Plateaus*, and the subject of his most engaging descriptions, was the Aquarius Plateau. Dutton had famously written that: "the Aquarius should be described in blank verse and illustrated upon canvas. The explorer who sits upon the brink of its parapet looking off into the southern and eastern haze, who skirts its lava-cap or clambers up and down its vast ravines, who builds his camp-fire by the borders of its snow-fed lakes or stretches himself beneath its giant pines and spruces, forgets that he is a geologist and feels himself a poet."[3]

Today the motorist traveling Utah Highway 12 from Torrey to Boulder Town, high on the eastern shoulder of the Aquarius, is treated to some of the most enticing panoramas in the Plateau Province. Fraser and Rust, lacking designated scenic pullouts, chose to climb higher, to the ultimate lookoff platforms of Chokecherry Point and Bowns Point. They had an additional advantage over modern-day tourists: clear air. What they saw is rarely duplicated today.

The Aquarius stretches some thirty miles westward, and it led the Frasers and Rust through trackless spruce forests—perhaps the highest continuous forest in the world—until they reached Johns Valley at the base of Table Cliff Plateau. A long day's ride took them to a remarkable lookoff at Powell Point on the southern end of this plateau, after which they continued west, inexplicably bypassing the Paunsaugunt Plateau and the spires and amphitheaters of Bryce Canyon. Neither Rust nor Fraser evidently knew of Bryce's glories—it was not designated a national monument until 1923—although the view from Powell Point certainly must have hinted at what lay there. Perhaps feeling the press of time, Fraser and Rust headed down Casto Canyon to Panguitch, where the town loafers greeted the entourage as if it were a traveling show.

After a stay in town, during which Rust unsuccessfully tried to prosecute a horse trade, they headed for the Markagunt Plateau, which Fraser found to be well watered and pleasant. From the Markagunt they dropped into the upper canyons of the Virgin River, unfamiliar ground to Rust, and they made a circuitous path around the canyons and beehive spires in what is now the Kolob Section of Zion National Park. Their final high point was the Pine Valley Mountains, seldom visited even today, despite its excellent views of the temples of Zion.

Their journey concluded with a wearisome desert march to the rail station at Modena. At six hundred miles and five weeks, it was the longest backcountry trip George Fraser or Dave Rust ever took.

The Utah portion of Fraser's journal comes to 206 typescript pages. The portions describing the Frasers' rail journey westward, their travels in California (including a visit to the 1915 Panama-Pacific Exposition in San Francisco), and a stopover in Del Rio, Texas, to inspect some of Fraser's landholdings, are omitted. Within the Utah portion of the journal, many descriptions of unremarkable geologic features are also omitted.

The Frasers left Morristown on Thursday, June 24, 1915, riding the Erie, Rock Island, Colorado Midland, and Denver & Rio Grande lines to Utah. The rail journey lasted six days, with hotel stopovers each night. Fraser's interest in railroads is evident in his journal, with mention of the weight of the tracks, the kinds of ballast used, and the conditions of bridges and trestles (Fraser invested in railroads and served on their boards of directors).

West of Grand Junction, the rails passed through Ruby Canyon alongside the Colorado River, a section bypassed by modern highways. Fraser noted "jura trias like the Vermilion Cliffs with white sandstone above, very fine in color and sculpture." They arrived at Thistle, Utah, a town now buried under a 1983 landslide, and spend the night in a boardinghouse run by a retired railroad engineer. In the morning they transferred to the

Marysvale branch of the Denver & Rio Grande for the ride south into the Sanpete Valley. At Manti, where they had an hour's layover, they were met by David Rust's brother-in-law, Dilworth Woolley, and by Rust's father, George Rust. Woolley toured the group around Manti in his motorcar, passing by the local Mormon temple, where George Rust worked. Returning to the station, Fraser was introduced to more of Rust's in-laws, who were returning home to Kanab, Utah. Among them was Mrs. E. D. Woolley, Rust's mother-in-law, whom Fraser found to be "alert, intelligent and quite widely read and perfectly grammatical . . . forceful and physically strong and full of enterprise." Fraser noted that at sixty-nine years of age, Mrs. Woolley was looking forward to a horseback trip to Natural Bridges National Monument with her husband, "Uncle Dee" Woolley.

George Fraser's Journal

Tuesday, June 29, 1915
3:15 p.m. arrived Salina and found [David D.] Rust with a clean shave and a painfully new Abercrombie & Fitch shirt and trousers on the platform.[4] He paid his respects to his mother-in-law, and then we laboriously carried our luggage 200 yards by measurement, but a thousand miles by appearances, to the Robin house, along a horribly dusty street in the full glare of the hottest kind of Utah sun. Here we got a pretty clean room. Assorted and packed our stuff with infinite labor and pains, finally shipping our civilized belongings to H. J. Doolittle, at Lund.

Perhaps we could have gotten a bath at the Robin house. We made a mistake by not trying, expecting to run across a receptive irrigation ditch pretty soon.

At 6:30 we had supper at the boarding house—unsavory, greasy and flavored with flies. There were about six men at the table, no one of whom uttered a word. They were mostly railroaders, and one or two traveling salesmen. After supper a German got into an argument with the rest about the war. By 8 o'clock we got the horses packed and were just about to leave when a curious looking, thin man of about 50, with a scarred face drew up in a buggy drawn by a single small pony. He was Senator Eckersly from Loa. The horse looked a bit tired, but was by no means all in, in spite of having come 60 miles in about 12 hours. The Senator was making a casual trip to Salt Lake for a day, on political business. He invited us to visit him in Loa.

Our outfit consisted of three saddle horses, two pack horses and a pack mule. Rust had the same horse, a big scrawny bay, that was with us on last year's trip from the beginning to Bright Angel Point. George and I had the same ponies we rode on the Kaibab last season—George a little bay called "Indian," and I, the best looking horse, a black with bald face called "Nig." The broad-backed, heavy built, powerful and always reliable bay, "Jake," who packed our stuff over the Kaibab, and nearly fell down a precipice on the way to Bass's crossing last summer, carried the heaviest load. The mule "Jerry" also took a good load. The other pack horse, a yellowish, poor looking beast had to be saved.

Rust had ridden from Kanab to Salina through the Panguitch Hayfield and Grass Valley, at least 200 miles. As far as Richfield, Prof. Horne, principal of the Kanab High School, was his companion.

About 8 o'clock we rode out of the yard in the twilight, across the track to the town where we bought some fishing tackle, chewing gum, etc. and got our last iced drink. Then we proceeded due east up Salina Canyon over a fairly good road, in black darkness. We forded the stream several times and at 3½ miles struck a ranch, the owner of which admitted us to his pasture where we camped. It was very hot. There were a few mosquitoes and more gnats than I ever encountered before. It was an uncomfortable night. To bed 10:30. Clear. A young moon rose at 11.

For our bed, Rust brought a thin, somewhat under sized, double mattress, two double blankets and a quilt. We had the use of another quilt which in the day time served as a saddle blanket on one of the pack horses. Beside, we carried a light tent, about the width of the mattress. Rust had a light, single mattress and a pair of blankets and a waterproof tarpaulin large enough to cover his entire bed. These are typical Mormon beds. The gentiles do not equip themselves so elaborately. It is said one of the ways of recognizing a Mormon in the wilds is by his bed.

Wednesday, June 30, 1915
Up 5 a.m., with the sun just showing over the hills shutting in the canyon to the east. Clear and cool, but turning hot directly. The full force of the sun was felt. No shade.

We found ourselves at the junction of Salina Canyon running east-west, with Soldier Fork coming from the southeast, a few rods above where the Sevier Fault cuts northeast across the canyon. The view west down the canyon showed snow on the Pavant Plateau across Sevier Valley. To reach Fish Lake, we had the option of going up Soldier Fork or following Salina Canyon further, and turning south up Gooseberry Valley. I was anxious to see the unconformity mentioned by Gilbert in his "Henry Mountains," so after breakfast we left our stuff, crossed to the north side of the creek, and first rode up a side gorge, northeast along the line of the Sevier Fault—a barren, red hot canyon filled with lava boulders. In the creek were boulders of a volcanic breccia brought down from upstream, for we found none *in situ*. Leaving the fault line, we rode east up the canyon about 1½ mi. to a small house, close to the opening of a mine tunnel. Here we found the owner, R. E. Ball, with a theodolite, which he hastily put in doors. He then approached us in leisurely fashion, with evident suspicion.

Rust had heard of Ball from the Dr. at Salina, as a queer character who would have nothing to do with anyone unless he happened to be approached just right. Rust broke the ice by reference to the Dr., and I made some inquiries about the geology of the neighborhood. Ball began to warm up. We dismounted, and he was soon drawing diagrams in the sand. After a while, George and Rust became tired of listening to the conversation, and returned to camp and packed up, arranging to meet me in a couple of hours and proceed up Gooseberry Valley, instead of Soldier Fork.

Ball is about 60, a New Yorker, and a graduate of Troy Polytechnic. He has been in mining all his life, and spoke of working in the Franklin Furnace (New Jersey Zinc) mine in 1872. He lives alone in what looks like a one room house (I was not invited to enter). In dress, he is like most people in the country, except that he does not wear high boots. One of his peculiarities is that he does not ride. He told me that not in 20 years has he been on a horse. He walks to town when he has to get mail, etc.

After we had had considerable talk when left alone, he invited me into the mine. How long he has been working here he did not say, but it must be a long while, because he stated single handed he had run about 3,000 yards of tunnel.

Ball has followed the Sevier Fault with care. He claims to have measurements of it which indicate that there is a movement against the direction of throw amounting to about ⅛ inch per year.

To the west of the ranch house, immediately beneath the contact of the tertiary and cretaceous in the gray limestone are five step faults with an upthrow to the northwest of about one foot each. Ball regards this phenomenon with affection. He told me he had repeatedly resolved to run a tunnel at this point and showed me the drill holes above and beneath these faults, but said when he came to the point of shooting the holes, he never could do it.

In the desolation and sordidness of his abode, I was surprised to find just outside the house a number of small, teepee-shaped aggregations of sticks, 8 to 10 inches high. He explained that beneath these he was trying to raise a rare, wild flower from seed.

11 a.m. left Ball's mine and proceeded up canyon about 3½ miles. For half a mile or so, followed graded right-of-way of Denver & Rio Grande which exists intermittently from Salina about 20 miles east, up the canyon to a place that was to be called "Nioche." Before the railway met its large expenditures on the Soldier Summit route, this right of way was obtained, partially graded, and for a few miles laid with light rails. We encountered a few of the rails, mostly washed into the creek.

12:15 p.m. passed ranch house at the junction of Salina Canyon with Gooseberry Valley. Here we turned southeast up the grass covered bottom of Gooseberry Valley, through a fence and passed several small ranches, at one of which, quite deserted, we stopped for lunch. It was exceedingly hot at Ball's and riding up Salina Canyon, but here, under a cottonwood tree, in tall grass, we had protection from the sun and enjoyed a cool breeze from the northwest up Gooseberry Valley. We were lucky to find a cool spring.

On undoing the pack, Rust laid out a rectangular, thin parcel, about 2 feet by 18 inches. I had noticed this when we packed up, but as he volunteered nothing about its contents, I suppressed my curiosity. It was a surprise and gratification to find this contained a cake made by his venerable mother, of the highest degree of excellence.

The day was clear, but the sky showed fleecy clouds. Ball predicts a storm in two days. The break from the dry season is about due.

Left lunch camp 5 p.m. Followed grassy valley bottom for about two miles and then crossed a hill rising in the valley composed of sandy limestone strewn with black boulders. The valley bottom affords fine pasture and is cultivated in small patches, but we found the few ranches we passed deserted. The soil is black, apparently rich, as if decomposed lava. Gooseberry Creek is a fine stream of clear, cold water. We kept close to this and forded it frequently.

Everything went well with the horses until about 7 o'clock, when the yellow pack horse Rust had bought on the way up broke away from the road and lost himself in the thick woods on the opposite side of the stream. His getting away was due to my stupidly chasing him in an effort to head him off. About this time George shot a rabbit with the revolver, and cleaned it while we hunted the horse.

At dusk we came to Gooseberry Ranger Station, a pleasant cottage on a southerly facing hillside in a grove of quaking aspen. Dr. Morse, a botanist, appeared to be in charge of the station and greeted us pleasantly. We declined his cordial invitation to spend the night there, which was probably a mistake. The station is about 17 miles from Salina.

We continued about three miles up the valley beyond the Ranger Station, and at 8:20, it being already fairly dark, made camp beside the creek under quaking aspen and pine trees, for by this time we had gotten up pretty well. Clear, cold, fine sunset. For supper we tried some of Abercrombie & Fitch's prepared bean soup. It was very unsatisfactory. Bed 11 p.m.

Thursday, July 1, 1915

Sunrise clear. Fleecy clouds. Up 5:45, by which time it had clouded over. There was no wind and the clouds had done away with the chill of last night. It took some time to pack up, for Rust had not yet become accustomed to the paraphernalia and George and I were of very little help. The rich grass near the creek was studded with buttercups, yellow daisies and white columbine.

9 a.m. broke camp. Followed up Gooseberry Creek to its junction with Nioche Creek, coming in from the southwest, where we left the road through a gate in the U.S. Forest Service fence. It was a relief to get off the road for the ride all the way from Salina had been exceedingly dusty.

We now proceeded without any trail up Nioche Creek to the east by south, and finally more easterly to the summit of Mt. Terrill ridge. The climbing was steep, mostly over grassy slopes with many wild flowers, wild gooseberries and two kinds of wild currants and occasionally patches of snow.

Near where we struck Nioche Creek we saw a humming bird, the only one we have run across in this country.

Arrived on the summit of the westerly arete of Mt. Terrill 12 M. Followed that to the lower summit of Terrill. Made lunch camp in a cirque on the north side of the peak. The sky became more overcast and the wind grew stronger so that after lunch it was hazy in the distance and cold. I left the outfit and walked alone along the lava arete from the west summit above the lunch camp to the east summit. Arrived 3:15.

We had been able to ride the horses to the lunch camp and there was no trouble in bringing them southerly from the summit of the arete in the general direction of Mt. Marvine, which was our destination, but they could not traverse the bare lava rock at the summit for that was rough and broken by immense cracks. I was glad to take refuge in one of these cracks from the strong southwest wind while I waited for the outfit. It was impossible to take any distant views because of the haze.

At 4:30, after upwards of an hour's observation, left east summit of Terrill. We stayed near the summit of the ridge to the southeast toward Mt. Marvine until the going became too rough and then cut down to the south, crossed an exceedingly rough lava slide and reached the saddle between Terrill and Marvine, which is cut entirely through the lava into the eocene. Here I disgraced myself again by losing my quirt. It took some time and a long walk to find it again. The going was so rough that though freshly shod one of the horses dropped a shoe. This raised a problem I had not thought of, but we discovered later Rust had a complete blacksmith's outfit in the pack.

Along the summit was some stunted spruce and a few quaking aspen just coming into leaf.

From the saddle we cut down south beneath the northerly end of Mt. Marvine's arete and camped in a meadow or park in the spruce timber facing southwesterly across Summit Valley or Seven Mile Flat. Made camp 6 p.m., down 1,350' from summit of Terrill, which meant close to 10,000' altitude. Cold.

Friday, July 2–Saturday, July 3. The Frasers and Rust climbed Mount Marvine, the southerly twin of Mount Terrill. Fraser describes "hard climbing from the first and in many places quite difficult." Since Rust was uncomfortable with the exposure, Fraser led the way, drawing on his modicum of experience in the Alps, and roping up in places. Fraser's descriptions of the view from Marvine are not remarkable, and one may wonder if he was affected by the rapid ascent (he ascribed a headache the next day to eating greasy food, when it appears likely due to altitude sickness).

From Marvine the party rode westerly to the Fishlake Plateau, where they made a high camp at around 11,000 feet. The next day they descended to Fish Lake, passing by a fishing "resort" consisting of "a shack or two, a pavilion for dancing and some tents in a wilderness of tin cans . . . exceedingly unattractive." They camped at the southwest corner of the lake, where Rust caught a three-pound trout for dinner.

Sunday, July 4, 1915
Up 6 a.m. Cloudless, cool but the sun warmed us up very quickly. Over night Rust experimented with dehydro potatoes, one of Abercrombie & Fitch's concoctions, which we found very good. Flies and mosquitoes

exceedingly troublesome. The horses were bothered by them and it took Rust and George some time to round them up. Left Camp 5 at 9:15 a.m.

We avoided the road which ran to the south of us to Loa, looking for a shorter road that would bring us into Fremont. This was the Awapa Plateau, undulating, rough, broken, up and down hill and very dreary. It seemed as though Uncle Sam was joking when in this waste we encountered a post bearing a sign beseeching the traveler to preserve the beauty of this forest.

Our aim was originally to strike the Fremont, i.e. Dirty Devil, river about five miles above Fremont, but we changed our course, intending to go to Fremont direct, so turned southeasterly over a plateau or bench marking a former level of the Fremont River, into which that river has cut a broad canyon about a mile and a half wide. There was some difficulty in getting off this bench into the valley bottom, but we finally negotiated it, striking the Fremont-Loa road at Bryan's Ranch and Creamery. We camped under the portico of the creamery beside a fine, clear, cool brook taking its rise at a spring in the hillside a few rods above us.

Rust's father at one time had been Bishop at Loa and Rust had taught school in Loa. It turned out that Mrs. Bryan was one of Rust's pupils. Bryan, his small boy and a friend of the boy's stood by while we ate lunch. The boys had their pockets full of angle worms and each carried a large branch with a string and an immense fish hook. They retired for about 15 minutes and returned with three trout, which they presented to us. I suggested their hooks were rather large and offered them some small trout hooks. They insisted on paying for these hooks and it was with great difficulty that I got them to understand they cost nothing. They then retired with the new hooks and in 10 minutes returned with more trout. George and I spent a couple of hours fishing the stream. We saw plenty of trout, usually hiding under the overhanging grass banks. George got one fish—a little one. My bait was eaten several times, but I never got a good strike. We had a nice mess of trout for supper.

Rust rode to Fremont with a pack horse to buy supplies and incidentally to interview Senator Eckersly about the prohibition question. George purchased some fresh food from Mrs. Bryan as follows:

18 eggs for 15 c.
24 eggs for 25 c.
1 lb. butter 20 c.
2 loaves of bread for nothing.

After sunset it became overcast and we prepared for a wet night, but scarcely any fell in our vicinity. We were protected under the portico of the creamery. There was much thunder and lightning. Soon after George and I had lain down I heard a step and saw a small boy, who I assumed was the Bryan youngster. I spoke to him and the boy was scared to death. He was Si Tanner's boy and he wanted to know if we had found a horse he was looking for.

Rust returned at 9:45 with a long story to tell about the events in town and preparations for tomorrow's celebration, of the 4th. Bed 10:15.

Monday, July 5. The Frasers and Rust rode into Fremont, crossed the Fremont River, and headed east up the slopes of Thousand Lake Mountain, following primitive roads and lumber trails and entering a pleasant spruce-aspen forest dotted with small openings or parks. Reaching the top of the plateau that afternoon, the party enjoyed far-off views of the Book Cliffs, San Rafael Swell, and Henry Mountains, the latter their next destination. The way ahead involved crossing the forbidding South Desert, which to Fraser looked like "a hard piece of work."

Tuesday, July 6, 1915
A cloudless night. Wind blowing hard, very penetrating and bitterly cold. One-half inch of ice in the water pail on awakening. Up 6:30 a.m. We found what we had supposed to be a spring was the run-off of a large snow-bank, which, of course, froze up in the night, so we had to melt snow in the utensil which we used for every purpose.

Left Camp 7 9:15 a.m. Traveled north about a mile and a half on the flat table and near its center turned east, and with great difficulty followed a sheep trail down the palisade. This was a difficult and dangerous place to make with horses. We were surprised to find that the ranger in charge of this forest did not know the summit could be attained at this point.

Just below the summit of the plateau in a protected spot under a snow drift we found some magenta flowers with leaves like those of the lily of the valley and flowers similar in shape to the jonquil.[5] These flowers we noticed on several occasions at altitudes of close to 11,000'. After safely negotiating the palisade we had to cross a boulder slide—a talus slope on a gigantic scale—and then over more or less grass, still with many lava boulders, we proceeded slowly down the mountain in a northerly direction, so as to strike the trail which crossed the saddle north of Thousand Lake Mountain.

At 12 M. we began to contemplate lunching on canned beef and looked for water. Soon we emerged from the forest into a parklike open space covered with good grass and were astonished to find a fence and inside that a new and not quite finished house readily recognized as a Ranger Station. This turned out to be the Elkhorn Ranger Station established this year and Ranger Adair, of Thurber, was within cooking lunch, to which he invited us. The day before on his rounds he had run across some sheep herders, who presented him with a leg of mutton, some of which we ate for lunch and the remainder of which he gave us, stating in excuse that he was going home that afternoon—a 25 mile ride—and could not carry it.

On leaving the Ranger Station we descended steadily, keeping first to the north and then striking east. After three-quarters of an hour we struck the so-called road from the saddle—a mere wagon track—and followed that eastwardly to the head of the South Desert.

On the descent of the mountain the change in vegetation is most marked. Leaving the quaking aspen we met with a few long leafed yellow pines, old but very poor. We ran across some cattle in fine condition and a band of eight horses. Below the pines we struck a belt of cedars, piñons, mountain mahogany, small prickly pear, cactus, some with yellow and others with red flowers, small Spanish bayonets, Indian paint brush, sego lilies, yellow flowers and some sage brush. On the banks of the creek that the road paralleled there were black birch, box elder and long leafed cotton-woods, all small.

5:45 p.m. arrived at an isthmus between the South Desert running off to the southeast and Middle Desert running off to the northeast. Approximate altitude 6,650. Strong southwest wind. Cool in the shade, although it has been hot riding in the sun.

The South and Middle Deserts are valleys with steep cliffs bounding a flat waterless sandy bottom. Our camp was at the summit of the cliff forming the terminus of the South Desert approximately 400 feet high.

Rust had been familiar with this country when a boy and up to about 25 years ago, but since that time had not been here. Nevertheless, he remembered where water was to be had. While he and George took the water keg and water bags about a quarter mile northerly from the camp, I sat on the brink of the cliff bounding the South Desert and studied the Henry Mountains and the water pocket fold, the latter forming the southerly or southwesterly boundary of the South Desert. After getting water at 6:30 p.m. we walked about three-quarters of a mile to the head of Middle Desert. The coloring and sculpture here is beyond anything

George Fraser *(left)* and George Fraser Jr. viewing the Entrada Sandstone towers of Cathedral Valley, July 6, 1915. Now part of Capitol Reef National Park, Cathedral Valley was unnamed and generally unknown at the time. Photograph by Dave Rust.

we have seen. The cliffs rise precipitously from the flat, barren desert floor 250 feet, perhaps 350 feet. They are bedded horizontally. The top is of white, very soft cross-bedded sandstone, beneath which is a brilliant carmine sandstone or shale. Rising from the desert floor separate from the bounding cliffs are numerous temples. These are wholly of carmine rock, the white bed of the summit having been eroded off. The desert is sandy, cream to yellow, with a few piñons and cedars showing patches of green. On the summit of the cliffs, accentuated and silhouetted as it were, basalt boulders lie on the pure white sandstone.

The sun set clear save for some fleecy clouds to the north. Sitting on the brink of the cliff at the head of the South Desert, the Henry Mountains rose against the sky, appearing in the light of the setting sun first blue, then grayish in the haze of the cloudless sky, and as the sun went below the horizon and still touched them, they appeared burnished with gold which gradually, as the light waned, turned to lilac until their illumination ceased.

The prevailing tone of the foreground was magenta with white and terracotta streaks due to the wash from above. In the desert were patches of piñons and cedar, the distant ones appearing black, those nearby vivid green. The silence was complete save for an occasional bird call and the buzzing of gnats and mosquitoes. These were very troublesome until sun-down, but did not bother us thereafter. The change in temperature this evening from last night was very marked, but the night was comfortably cool.

Wednesday, July 7, 1915
Up 5 a.m. Clear, except for a few clouds to the north. A golden sunrise.

Left Camp 8 7:15 a.m. The horses had poor pickings all night and we had a long ride to go to Caineville over a dry and desolate route. Rust told me that when ten years of age he was once taken over this desert and some time afterward was told to take his horse and a pack animal and make alone the trip we were setting out on. He started early and long after dark found his way back to camp. The pack had turned on his horse. He did not know how to pack the animal himself, he did not know his way and all he could do was to get himself back to the point from which he had started. That is the school in which he was brought up and where he learned the secret of direction and how to fix land-marks.

About four miles down the valley we saw rising from the valley floor a curious three-fingered butte or temple, a remnant of a lava dike that crosses the valley. There are many of these dikes. Some of them can be traced for a mile or more; also some lava flows capping the surface of the plateau on the easterly side. A large butte rises in the center of the valley, and a mile beyond that appears a graceful Temple, the most picturesque feature of the landscape on this trip. This rises about 400′ from the valley floor and is composed of magenta sandstone or shale, the overlying beds having been eroded off.

It was hot and the dust raised by the pack horses which we drove made riding trying. As there was no water between the spring and Caineville, we filled the keg and loaded it on the mule. About 11 o'clock the mule tried to roll, the water barrel having chafed its back, so we stopped for three-quarters of an hour, repacked the mule, drank all the water we could, emptied the barrel and ate a little. The traveling in a southwest wind was hot, but the sun's rays were tempered by a few clouds.

About two miles beyond where we repacked the mule, we turned southeast up a draw and left South Desert, descending into the two-mile wide Blue Flat. The bottom of Blue Flat is a dry, powdery grayish mud sun-dried and in low spots like a quick-sand, very treacherous, so that we were compelled to keep to high ground. It is entirely barren and very dusty.

Ascending the easterly up-dip slope of Blue Flat over bare rock we came to the summit of a precipitous wall bounding an anticlinal valley known as the Red Desert. This is an elliptical area bounded by a wall of reddish shale apparently only broken down at one point. The bottom of this valley is uneven and hummocky. The red beds are interspersed with whitish and bluish gray thin layers of shale entirely bare of vegetation and bedded nearly horizontally. On account of this coloring and the uneven weathering of the surface, the floor of the desert is striped and blotched and patched like a cross between a leopard and a zebra.

We climbed the wall to the south, first over the red rocks and then over a yellowish sandstone and conglomerate, followed a deep wash through the yellow sandstone southwesterly into the valley of the Dirty Devil, striking the road running parallel with the river about one mile above Caineville. Arrived 3:15 p.m. Very hot. We camped by the road at Curtis's Ranch, the first one we struck on reaching town, on the north bank of the river. We were very tired, hot and dirty, so at once made for the river to get a bath.

The Dirty Devil is full of silt, very shallow and very swift. George and I undressed on a mud-bank in full sight of the whole town, but there seemed to be no one there that we could disturb. We lay in the dirty water and rolled over on the pebbles, with each roll getting a little more of ourselves wet, and all the while fought mosquitoes that covered us like a blanket. If not cleansing, the bath was at least cooling, so that we were able to partially enjoy a belated lunch around 5:30.

After lunch or supper we walked "down town." The town consists of a few, perhaps 15, tumble-down shacks strung along the north bank of the Dirty Devil over a distance of a mile and a half. We asked a boy where the store was. He said Osterberg (a Swede or Dane) kept a little candy but there was no store. We found Osterberg's and were told that everything he had, which consisted solely of candy and tobacco, had been sold out on the 4th of July, except one box of chocolates which sold at $1.00 a pound and that apparently had been there for years. We induced Mrs. Osterberg, however, to let us have five pounds of sugar from her private stock.

When Rust was a boy his father had a ranch here and their cattle were grazed in the neighboring deserts. In those days the town is said to have been quite flourishing, but a great flood raised the Dirty Devil over the entire valley bottom and washed out practically all the farms. Everybody with any go moved from Caineville after that flood. Rust's father was glad to get $300 for about 1,000 acres of valley bottom land after the flood.

After leaving Osterberg's Rust took us to call on John Curfew, who had lived in Caineville when Rust was a boy there. We found Curfew sitting outside his house on a tumble-down bed covered with filthy, ragged quilts, among which it took no artist's imagination to see signs of life.

Curfew is about 60 years of age, has only one leg—the other was amputated after having been injured by a kick from a horse—thin, wiry, with a straggly gray beard. Curfew was formerly a mail carrier—one of his boys is driving the wagon now—and held various county offices. It was a surprise and shock to find him engaged in reading the *Literary Digest*, eager for news, capable of conversing grammatically and with a wide interest in affairs, all so much at variance with his appearance and surroundings.

Going along the street we met a young woman carrying a number of eggs. She was so agitated by our greeting her by doffing our hats that she dropped most of the eggs and then stooped to pick them up.

We sat with Curfew until dark. While there Osterberg joined the party and sat on the edge of the bed while Curfew made me read to the several parties a humorous editorial from the *New York Sun*.

In this country everybody uses a horse practically all the time and for every purpose. We encountered a little girl barely six riding bare-back a great work horse, and also a young man and his wife, a little slip of a girl carrying a young baby, the three riding bare-back on a single horse.

We started to make camp in the grass near an irrigation ditch, but Rust conceived the idea there were fewer mosquitoes by an alfalfa stack in Curtis's yard, so we moved over there. It was intensely hot and we had to keep our faces covered with handkerchiefs to escape the annoyance of the mosquitoes and the horses, who were in the corral near the stack, and kept nosing about it, so the night was not very restful. Bed 10 p.m.

Thursday, July 8–Friday, July 9. With their destination the Henry Mountains, the men headed south of town and climbed east over the saddle between South Caineville Mesa and Thompson Mesa, crossing the desolate Mancos Shale badlands. Pausing for lunch at what they called Lewis (Sweetwater) Creek, they sought relief from a hot southwest wind which "felt much like the draught out of a furnace." Farther south, Rust found a

Approaching the summit of Mount Ellen, Henry Mountains,
July 10, 1915. Photograph by George C. Fraser.

small spring in a tributary canyon, where they camped. On Friday they
began the long climb up the west flank of Mount Ellen, finding the going
tough and at one point nearly losing a packhorse when it caught its legs in
some boulders. Camp was made in a cirque 500 feet below the summit,
where a nearby snow patch gave water.

Saturday, July 10, 1915

Up 6:45 a.m. Strong wind from the southwest. Bright and clear. While
eating breakfast we saw a lone horseman approaching from the north
climbing the mountain. He turned out to be George Coleman, a cattleman from Teasdale, and a former acquaintance of Rust's. He took a
little food and explained that he was taking charge of a herd of "bucks"
(rams), belonging to a number of sheep men, which are herded together
at this season. He concluded he would accompany us over the mountain
for the day. So after taking some photographs, at 10:15 a.m. we left
camp and proceeded northerly to a saddle between the north and highest peak of Mt. Ellen and the central high point. Here we found a
Mexican sheep herder at his tent under some spruce trees and also a
man named McDougal and two small boys who had just ridden in from
Hanksville. McDougal has some sheep on the mountain. The Mexican
could not speak English. We tried to get some mutton from him but he
either did not or would not understand.

We left our outfit here with Coleman and climbed on foot up the north peak, where we arrived at 11:00 a.m. A strong southwest wind was blowing. The sky was clear save for light clouds on the horizon. This point is up 525 feet from camp, about 125 feet higher than the central point.

This was a geological survey topographic point, evidently the site of a permanent camp, for the rocks had been thrown out of a big hollow in which the men probably slept and a fairly good trail had been constructed up to the summit, so that pack horses could carry the necessary implements and supplies.

The view was magnificent. Away across the Colorado we saw plainly the La Sal and Abajo Mountains and in between them, far in the distance, snow mountains, presumably in Colorado. To the southeast with the glass we could make out the peculiar forms of Monument Valley. To the northeast the Book Cliffs stood out plainly. Marvine, Hilgard and Terrill were easily recognized in the northwest. The southwest horizon was formed by the long tongue-like Kaiparowits Plateau (50-Mile Mountain) ending at Glen Canyon opposite Navajo Mountain, and through a depression in this mountain we could make out the Kaibab.

From here we could see the marvelous structure of the San Rafael Swell better even than from Thousand Lake Mountain. We could not spare much more than an hour for this view, and at 12:20 started down, got our horses in the saddle and proceeded with them southerly along the arete forming the summit of the mountain.

At the Mexican sheep camp we encountered another sheep herder, a young fellow with red hair, who claimed to be looking for pasture and told distressing stories of how bad the feed was for his herd on the east side of the mountain where he had it now. Rust arranged with this youth to get a leg of mutton, figuring that we might camp near his tent this evening.

All along the summit we enjoyed practically the same view as from the high point, except only that the north was cut off.

I talked much with Coleman and was astonished to hear him make familiar references to Hawaii, Samoa, Australia and New Zealand. Not long ago he spent three years traveling through these countries as a missionary. He made this trip later than is usual, for he is now 49 years old.

Probably we covered between three and four miles before we descended from the arete on the east side of the mountain into a deep cut or draw in the upper reaches of which lay a large snow bank. The run-off of this produced a good sized brook, and here in a grove of quaking aspen and spruce, which extended well into a pass between two of the summit peaks, we made our lunch camp.

In the shade it was delightfully cool. The southwest wind was drawn down through the pass into the gorge where we were camped and made a sweater comfortable. I sought the shelter of the trees to write up my notes while Rust walked over a mile to a sheep camp in an effort to procure some meat.

5:15 p.m. Left lunch place. Climbed to Saddle, followed summit a little way and then descended on the east side into a great amphitheater sparsely wooded with fine grass. The slope of this amphitheater was exceedingly steep. We had to walk and found difficulty in leading our animals. I took a clinometer measurement of this slope and found it 35°.

It is in this amphitheater that most of the mining operations in the Henry Mountains have heretofore been conducted. It is full of prospect holes. An old road runs into it from up the east slope of the mountain and near the bottom by a running stream is a deserted mill. Here we found some specimens of copper ore. In his youth Rust worked in this mine for two summers.[6]

Rust's directions from the sheep herder were to keep down the amphitheater in which we were. As it grew dark we became doubtful of our direction, but the boys had anticipated an error and soon signaled us with a bright fire.

Arrived camp 12 8:15 p.m., altitude about 8,500'.

The sheep herders had pitched their tent near a small sheep corral and beside a running stream. We camped in the corral, but were not allowed to use any of our provisions. The boys had arranged to entertain us. They were Leland Busenbark, who lives at Notom, Utah, and Buchanan, whose home is in Caineville, both of them about 18 years of age.

Busenbark is a sheep herder and Buchanan is cook and camp mover. They have been friends from boyhood. Busenbark is the son of a Dane. His parents were separated when he was a small child, and at 10 years he went to work for his present employers, Bowns Bros. Of Provo. He was paid $5 a month and his keep to start, but in two months was so good that he was raised to $15. Soon he got $35 and now is getting and for a good while has gotten $50 a month, food, tent and boots. He has to supply himself with a horse and clothes and he is not very particular about the latter. He is in charge of 3,000 sheep and he takes his responsibilities heavily. He it was that we met near the north summit of the mountain. We were astonished to find that his sheep here enjoy the most beautiful pasture, with grass as tall as they are, plenty of water and conditions generally ideal. We asked him how he reconciled this with his depressing remarks to the other herders. He explained that he did not want anybody coming over to see how well off he was and that sheep herding required diplomacy as well as care.

Busenbark was reserved, courteous and very correct in his speech. Buchanan, on the other hand, was rough, profane and entirely uneducated in his method of speech. He showed and expressed unbounded admiration for his companion, who he told us had taken a winter off a few years ago and attended school at Richfield and held a certificate that he was qualified to enter the 8th grade of the Public School.

These boys had been out there for six months and had just pledged themselves to spend another year until July, 1916. Since April 1st they had not seen any one but sheep herders, except that Buchanan rode into Caineville on the 4th of July, spent the evening calling on his girl, and rode back again over the desert all night. It had taken us three days (of course with many meanderings and much time out for enjoyment of views) to make this journey one way.

Busenbark has an attractive personality and a strong character.[7] After dinner he produced a violin, with many apologies because it only had three strings. Nevertheless he played on it some familiar airs that did not sound cheering. I never realized how important a string could be.

The boys' tent was of heavy duck, A-shaped swung over a ridge pole. At the far end they had a mattress covered with blankets and near the door a light serviceable stove. They had a great quantity of canned goods of good quality and of course mutton. Cool as it was outside, the stove overheated the tent and put Rust to sleep. The boys sang us a few songs and begged us to reciprocate. As we were unable to do so George told them stories he had recently read, among them Arthur Train's tale about McAllister and his valet and Christmas in the Tombs.

Bed 10:45 p.m. Very cold and a tremendous strong southwest wind drawn down from the mountain top along the valley in which we camped.

Sunday, July 11, 1915

Up 6 a.m. The gale blowing. Clear. Fairly warm in the sun. The boys invited us to breakfast and we were glad of the shelter and warmth of the tent. While we were eating breakfast, the wind grew stronger and every now and again a hard gust would hit the tent as though to blow it over. Pretty soon a gust harder than the rest broke the ridge pole, but we managed to catch the two parts, propped it up with a forked pole and continued our breakfast. After we had finished, while George, Buchanan and I were seated on a bed, a still harder gust struck the tent, snapped the ridge pole, and blew down the back upright pole directly on my head, cutting a gash in the scalp about 1½ inches long. At the same time it hit Buchanan's funny bone so hard he thought his arm was broken. Beyond bleeding all over my cap and having a slight headache the rest of the day, the cut did no harm. On parting the boys gave us a leg of mutton. We tried to pay for that and our entertainment, but they refused to accept anything. Immediately after breakfast Busenbark went off with his dog, full of business, to look after the sheep which were huddled together half a mile up the draw. He moved them a little bit into some good grass and before we were packed up rejoined us.

We had had some trouble all day yesterday with old Yellow Neck, but under all the circumstances he came through pretty well. Buchanan had an old yellow horse that he evidently did not think much of, and Rust, after much talking, negotiated an even trade, so we went off with old Baldy Face, leaving poor Buchanan the miserable old Yellow Neck. It seemed to me like stealing.

We ascended the draw to the Saddle on the summit of the ridge, followed along the ridge for a distance, and then descended steeply into Penellen Saddle between Mts. Pennell and Ellen. From the Saddle we descended into a sandstone gorge draining westerly but dry. There was no water in it until the sandstone was cut through. There by a small brook at 12:45 we took lunch.

Left lunch camp 2:30 p.m. Rode and walked through a dense growth of scrubby pines, buckbrush, cedar and live oak. Exceedingly hot in the sun when out of the strong wind. On emerging from the canyon, running westerly from Penellen Saddle, we crossed a valley running substantially north and south and bounded on the west by hills of shale capped by sandstone dipping westerly away from the Henry Mountain mass. Through a pass in this mountain we entered another valley, followed that northerly and northwesterly for a mile or two, and left it through a pass similar to the one by which we had entered.

The westerly bounding walls of both these valleys presented striking illustrations of the sapping of cliffs. Near the point where we left the second valley there was an incipient landslide. The sandstone cap, cracked along lines of joint, was breaking off and ready to slide over the underlying shales into the valley below.

On emerging from the pass beyond the second valley we entered on a sandy and dusty plain with poor grass and followed this several miles, heading for a break in the flat top hills to the west. A short U-shaped narrow canyon led us into a great oval valley bounded, as it seemed, on all sides by sheer cliffs, where we were greeted by the welcome sight of bright green spelling cultivated land under irrigation, which we knew to be Coleman's Ranch.[8] The ride from our lunch camp here had been very dry, for we left the brook a short distance from camp and had been all afternoon in the burning sun without water.

Coleman's Ranch is fenced and as we missed the gate on its east side, we had to ride around the best part of 800 acres, a weary proceeding for man and horse thirsty, as we all were. Arrived Coleman's 7 p.m.

Coleman had left us yesterday when we turned down the east side of Mt. Ellen after lunch. Whether to see us and insure our appropriate entertainment, or because he wanted some supplies, or merely because he was tired of the bucks, was not clear; at any rate early this morning he had left camp and come into the ranch. We arrived at the psychological moment, for one of the ranch hands had just come in from Notom with a wagon load of supplies, among them a fresh cake.

The party at the ranch house consisted of Coleman, a young relative of his aged about 20, an American farm hand and a Hollander called Pat Brown. The names of the relative and farm hand were Reynolds and Lyman respectively.

The ranch house originally had one room, but a small kitchen had been built on the south. This was too small to hold all of us, so supper was served on a quilt laid on the floor of the bed-room. We had a wonderful spread—fresh cheese, which George and I agreed was the best we ever ate, honey, bread baked by some lady of Notom, the cake, mutton, preserves, potatoes, raw onions and some canned vegetables. In the midst of the meal the American farm hand sitting on George's right called the attention of Pat Brown, who was sitting on George's left, to a bed bug crawling over the quilt table-cloth, with a request that he kill it. We enjoyed our supper. Afterward we lay about on the floor or sat on boxes, bags of flour and the like and listened to Coleman tell tales, mostly about hard experiences in catching cattle.

Coleman and a partner of his, who lives in Teasdale or Thurber, about three years ago made a desert entry of this land, that is, each took up 320 acres. Actually they have more land than this under cultivation. They have ditched water on to the land out of a small stream in the oval valley and are growing principally alfalfa, but also some grain and vegetables. In the valley outside of the irrigated area is pretty good grass, which they will reserve for winter, supplementing it with hay raised on the ranch. For summer they have the whole wide country, especially the table-land or butte summits bounding their valley.

The sunset was magnificent behind the broken sky line of the valley's bounding mesas. The structure is similar to what we had seen at Bluegate, a substantially horizontal bed of hard sandstone underlain by soft shales. In places the sandstone cap has been broken away leaving pillars and castles and at one point toward the west the sandstone has been weathered along the joints so as to leave a round window through which the sun shone a moment as it set.

We slept on the grass beside the irrigation ditch near the ranch house. The night was comfortably warm and clear with a strong southwest wind. The altitude here is approximately 5,700'.

Monday, July 12, 1915
Up 5 a.m. Clear. Warm with a pleasant southwest breeze.

Coleman and Pat Brown especially, the others also, had a wonderful time using our binoculars. Pat Brown, while not gifted with a large English vocabulary, possessed a most uncommonly strong one. His cursing and blaspheming in his surprise at what he could see with the glasses way up on the Henry Mountains was an education. Coleman located his sheep camp, spotted the boy he left in charge, and even made out the color of the horse he was riding.

The horses had fine pasture and were in good shape. We all enjoyed the spot and had a most liberal and satisfactory breakfast. Coleman refused to accept any pay for his hospitality.

Left 9 a.m. Crossed Coleman's fields and proceeded westerly following for five miles the south branch of Lewis [Sweetwater] Creek on which Coleman's ranch is located. Our course lay northwesterly. We cut through a pass in the hills bounding Coleman's valley. Here we found some lignite outcrops lying in beds not over a foot wide under brown sandstone, fine rock carving into temples, buttes and needles. Leaving Lewis Creek we cut through hills formed by flexed beds dipping east by south and valleys caused by soft beds.

12:30 p.m. After about 11 miles of travel we reached Bowns's ranch.[9] A mile below we had struck Tantalus Creek,[10] here carrying very little water. In the canyon of Tantalus Creek were many black lava boulders.

We found these from here all the way along our route up on to Boulder Mountain.

Fraser found the reception at Bowns's ranch less than cordial, with one of the owners suspicious that Fraser was employed by the Forest Service: "I gathered from Bowns's attitude that he was not at all anxious to have his place inspected or advertised." Fraser explained that they were "just prospecting around," since they had learned that no one would believe that they were seeing the country for pleasure.

From Bowns's ranch the party headed up Tantalus (Oak) Creek, crossing the spectacular Waterpocket Fold in what is now Capitol Reef National Park. Finding a sandstone pour-off with an inviting waterfall, the men welcomed the chance to bathe and wash their clothes, and they enjoyed what Fraser called "the most beautiful camp site we have had."

Tuesday, July 13, 1915
Up 5:30 a.m. Clear. Beautiful warm night. Gray-back did not get on very well with the other horses. This morning he wandered off toward the ranch down stream. While George caught the other horses, Rust for an hour and a quarter chased this one.

Left camp 8:30. Followed up stream in the canyon, which now cut through the Vermilion Cliffs[11] and was no longer boxed. Leaving Vermilion Cliff we came into the permian where the canyon widened still further and should better be described as a valley. Large and small fragments of silicified wood were frequent. Accumulations of river gravel had been washed by rain, leaving pillars like those at Bozen.[12]

Above the permian we bore up the north wall of the valley, leaving the creek, and struck a deep canyon with dense growth of underbrush, oak, elder, etc., and here at 12:30 we lunched. Hot and flies troublesome. The growth was so dense that it was quite a labor to get to water.

All the way up we had been on the lookout for Bowns's reservoir, about the location of which we disagreed. As usual Rust had sensed it correctly and bearing northerly from the lunch place, we reached it in half an hour. The reservoir is formed by building two dams in a small valley, out of which into another valley the water is ditched. Leaving the reservoir we followed what is locally appropriately called Oak [Pleasant] Creek through a valley growing broader as we ascended. We found grass, yellow pine and spruce. On reaching the upper waters the character of the country we were entering was disclosed.

The Aquarius Plateau (Boulder Mountain) is a great table-top like

Thousand Lake Mountain and Fish Lake Plateau, but much larger. The easterly side of this table has been eroded into a segment of a circle from which rise various streams, including Tantalus Creek, which cuts through the water pocket fold. This amphitheater is heavily wooded and affords fine grazing.

About 5:30 we met a man and a boy on horseback and were surprised to receive a friendly greeting from the former. It turned out to be Curtis, of Caineville, by whose ranch we had camped. He has cattle on the mountain and a small hut and corral. We declined an invitation to stop with him, preferring to reach the Ranger Station, where Rust expected to find an old friend he has not seen in upwards of 20 years.

6:30. Arrived at Wildcat Ranger Station, where Rust was warmly welcomed by Ranger Hanks in charge. We camped a couple of hundred yards outside of the fence enclosing the Ranger Station yard beside a ditch carrying water from one of the streams that takes its rise from the melting snows of the mountain, under immense trees and on the best of grass.[13]

Walter E. Hanks lives at Grover, about 20 miles from here, where he has a farm. He is about 50 years of age and spends from May to October in each year at the Ranger Station. This year Mrs. Hanks, two small children, and a hired girl are with him. The Hanks have eight children. Mrs. Hanks and the girl run a dairy. Hanks has a number of milch cows out in pasture. The boys drive these in and the ladies make butter and cheese.

The forest service telephone keeps the Hanks family in touch with the outside world. Mrs. Hanks is a motherly person of very agreeable appearance and exceedingly hospitable. She is the least reserved of all the ladies we have met.

For supper Mrs. Hanks sent us fresh milk and butter, corn pone, raw onions and bread. We talked with Hanks till 9:45 and then went to bed. Strong wind blowing and quite cold.

Wednesday, July 14, 1915
Up 5:15 a.m. Clear night. Strong wind and some clouds.

Hanks undertook to guide us up the northeast point of Boulder Mountain—Tantalus [Chokecherry] Point. So after he had done some chores, milked the cows and looked after his 15 calves, which he showed us with pride, at 7:45 we left the Ranger Station in Hanks' company (pack horses and outfit left at Ranger Station) and at 9 a.m. reached Tantalus Point. The trail was faint, but easy, because Hanks had worked

Prof. A. H. Thompson's survey station, Tantalus
(Chokecherry) Point, Aquarius Plateau, July 14,
1915. *Left to right:* Walter Hanks, George Fraser,
and Dave Rust. Photograph by George Fraser Jr.

over the roughest places. To insure our safe return Hanks carefully
broke branches of the trees to mark the trail. Climbing was pretty steep
and we had to walk some. All the way pines, spruce, some quaking aspen
and fine grass.

Concealed in the stone monument at the summit of the point was a
can containing names of and some remarks by parties who had been on
the point, among them a memorandum of Thompson's party on its first
visit in 1872. Hanks set great store by this, so I suggested it would be
better to have it framed and hung in the Ranger Station than to be left

exposed to the elements and ravages of sheep herders. I accordingly brought this with me under promise to have it framed and returned.

Hanks is reserved and correct in his demeanor and speech and very resentful of the profane and obscene literature which sheep herders seem prone to produce. On every trip he expurgates the contents of the tin can. From the point we looked down on Hanks' farm and with the glass Hanks was able to make out his boys working in the field, told us the names of the horses on the hay wagon and various other details.

Hanks' personality is extremely attractive. He impresses one as possessed of great force and being thoroughly honest. His father was a noted scout and I think one of the pioneers.[14]

The view from the point matches that from the southerly tip of Thousand Lake Mountain. From here, however, the water pocket fold and its relations are better defined. We had an exceptionally clear morning, which perhaps aided our vision, but I think we appreciated this view better because we knew more of the country which we overlooked. For all the world the low-land is like a relief map colored geologically. The most striking features of the landscape are the temples in and west of the water pocket fold.

An hour and a half was too short a time to enjoy this view, but we had a long way to make this afternoon, so at 10:30 we started down on foot. Hanks left us a little before 11, and we proceeded rapidly to the Ranger Station. Arrived at 11:45. When we had the fire lit, the Hanks children brought us five trout, which they had got that morning, beside more milk and butter.

On leaving Mrs. Hanks invited us to return with our entire family and to spend the best part of any summer. I think she meant it. She gave Rust a large pot of wild elderberry jam made by herself, which we hugely enjoyed.

Thursday, July 15–Friday, July 16. Continuing their journey across the Aquarius Plateau, the party took a steep trail up the lava cliffs below Bowns Point, from which they enjoyed views out across the Circle Cliffs and the Escalante river basin—"the most confused, rough, cut-up country I have ever seen," according to Fraser—and then headed west to camp by some small, flower-strewn lakes.

Over the next two days the party wandered across the Aquarius, bothered by mosquitoes, losing the trail in places, and slowed by George Jr.'s lame horse. Descending Boulder Top, they reached Roundy Reservoir and

Spectacle Lake on the Aquarius Plateau, 1922. Its flower-strewn meadows brought respite from the desert heat.

followed telegraph poles to Jubilee Ranger Station, now a historical site. The station was unoccupied, and, not knowing where they were, Rust called the forest supervisor to ascertain their location. Continuing west, they reached Cyclone Valley, apparently a meteorological hot spot, for they witnessed several large dust devils close at hand. George Jr. let himself be caught in one, "from which he emerged covered with dust and filthy."

By Friday night the party had reached the western flank of the plateau, making a poor camp by a scum-coated pool somewhere in the seemingly endless, somber reaches of the Aquarius's spruce forests. Here they were ready to turn south toward their next scenic destination, Powell Point on the Table Cliff Plateau.

Saturday, July 17, 1915
Up 6 a.m. Cloudless and a white frost. A few flies after sunrise, but no mosquitoes. I got bitten in the hand by an ant and was pretty well swollen up and uncomfortable in consequence. Our provisions were low and we looked hopefully forward to finding a sheep herder or getting to a ranch.

Left 9 a.m. For about three-quarters of a mile we had easy going over a sheep trail, descending about 200 feet to a park marking the head water of Coyote Creek, which drains northwesterly. Here we met four sheep herders. One of these herders was an old timer with a wonderfully trained sheep dog that seemed to take great fondness to me. He lay close up against my back and as I would move from him, would immediately edge up to the same relative position. I discovered after a while that it was only my shade he was looking for. His master would not stand for such close proximity.

Of the other herders one was about George's age named Porter, a brother of the Ranger's, of which there are three on this forest. He is attending school and making money for his support by tending sheep. The other youngster had a good looking mule which Rust coveted. The boy rounded up the mule, brought him over and Rust tried every which way to negotiate a trade for our lame horse Indian. The negotiation was initiated by Rust with a seductive statement that the very best horse in our outfit had temporarily gone lame, and in view of the fact that we were in a hurry, he would be willing to trade him, although at a great disadvantage. The negotiation lasted for about an hour. The boy was half inclined to make the trade, but finally edged off with the remark that he guessed he was married to the mule.

In this valley was a fine meadow with a good growth of clover. The sheep were in good shape. From the herders we got directions how to reach the main road over the divide between the Aquarius and Table Cliff. On leaving them we followed the trail up an easy draw through a large park to a fine spring, from which a sizable brook drained to the south. Here we lunched at 12M.

In the parks on our journey this morning we found sweet william, wild strawberry blossoms, gooseberry and raspberry.

3 p.m. left lunch camp, followed through more parks over undulating country with occasional narrow bands of forest intervening till we picked up what we were told to look for—"a ranger trail." This trail looked to me like any cattle trail, but after careful inspection Rust diagnosed it correctly. He explained that he could see it was made by a single horse ridden at a good gait pointing in both directions.

Traveling down the break of the mountain was very bad—steep, strewn with boulders and impeded by close growth. After some time of such traveling we struck the road leading from Winder to Escalante at the summit of the divide between Table Cliff and the Aquarius. Here we turned west and followed down the road half an hour, say about two miles, to Sweet Water Ranger Station in a grove of quaking aspen in the valley bottom beside a fine stream. This is the summer abode of Ranger Joe Porter, his wife, and children. They live in Escalante in the winters.

Porter was not home when we arrived, but Mrs. Porter allowed us to camp inside the Ranger Station fence beside the brook and to put our horses in the pasture. Arrived 6:30 p.m.

Mrs. Porter gave us some bread and some plum jam and lent us Salt Lake papers. George was not feeling fit and went to bed without supper. He said it was due to the water out of the stagnant pond at Camp 18, but I diagnosed his trouble as too much bacon grease. After supper Porter joined us and talked until bed time. Rust induced him to accompany us to-morrow to the south point of Table Cliff. Rust and I figured that it was easy to make this trip in the morning, but Porter, who went there once about seven years ago, ridiculed that idea. We found out why.

Sunday, July 18, 1915

Up 5:30 a.m. Cloudless. George, not feeling fit, decided to remain at the Ranger Station.

At 7:50 Porter, Rust and I started. Porter was mounted on a large horse of the type locally called "blue," which I suppose we would designate as sorrel. Beside bearing a brand on his shoulder, this horse was branded with an "S" on each side of his neck. Porter explained that this indicated it was a stray. It appears that when a stray horse does one any damage, the horse is impounded, and if not claimed after advertisement, is sold, the proceeds going to indemnify the parties injured. Before a stray is sold, in order to avoid a controversy with his owner, he is branded on the neck. This horse sold for $1.50. Porter has had him 18 years and claims to have refused $200 for him. It gave our horses all they wanted to do to follow him.

We followed the road one and one-quarter miles and then turned southerly up a canyon in the northerly wall of Table Cliff. We ascended rapidly. The canyon petered out and we continued to climb up the slope of the mountain wall, where, having ascended 1,700 feet, we reached the foot of a clink stone lava slide. To this point we had climbed over sedimentaries—evidently the tertiary—first white, then pink, then white with gravel weathering out of some conglomerate similar to that found at the top of Terrill. Climbing over the lava slide was rough work and might have been appalling but for our experience on Mt. Ellen. Above this is a thin level cap of lava, the summit of which we reached at 9:30 a.m. We traversed the level surface of this cap southerly through dense growth with wild flowers in grassy open spots, then descended the canyon of Clay Creek, cutting into the westerly flank of Table Cliff. We were obliged to go down this canyon 1,400 feet and then climb 800 feet up another canyon, near the head of which we found a spring, clear and cold, where we stopped half an hour and ate most of the very little food we had brought with us.

At the head of the first canyon near the summit we found a herd of sheep and a small boy in charge. Porter was irritated at these sheep being within a reservation he had made for some other party. The owner of the herd was absent looking for strays and remonstrance with the boy amounted to nothing.

Leaving the spring, we climbed about 400 feet more to the summit of Table Cliff. This summit is an almost level table similar to the lava cap, but at about 200 feet lower altitude. There is no lava on its surface, which is of white sandy limestone. We proceeded rapidly over this surface keeping close to the easterly rim, through fallen timber, close growing spruce, fox-tail pine and quaking aspen. Skeletons of a few dead cattle indicated the depth of snow that lies here in the winters. We saw deer and bear tracks and on two large quaking aspen trees Porter showed me the marks of bears' claws, indicating where grizzlies had climbed.

We arrived at the southernmost tip of the plateau, a butte in process of being cut off from the main cliff, wholly of white limestone with little vegetation. This ended in a sheer drop, as steep a precipice as any point on the rim of the Grand Canyon. Beneath us the bare rock was exposed and the glare was terrific. Both Rust and Porter, accustomed as they were to the sun, found the glare so blinding they had to close their eyes for a long time and by degrees accustom themselves to it. My colored glasses left me free to enjoy the view.

Beneath us and to the east and west were fine examples of the Pink Cliff overlain by the white sandy limestone as mentioned. These cliffs are jointed vertically, and being of material yielding to the attack of the elements, are eroded out on the joint planes into a regular pattern of round uncompleted columns, eminently described by the name that has been applied to them of Pipe Organ Cliffs.

The absence of a foreground always adds to the impressiveness of a distant view. With nothing visible for 3,000 feet below, one's eye instinctively seeks the distance. Away to the south by west I recognized Cape Final and Vishnu Temple in the Grand Canyon. Rust ridiculed the idea that it could be seen from here, but when he got his eye sight recognized the shapes and relative positions of these two points just as I did. Further to the southwest we could plainly see Mts. Emma, Logan and Trumbull. The entire series of cliffs, except the Chocolate, were plainly to be made out. To the east we got a better view than we have had yet of Mts. Hillers and Holmes, and between them in the remote distance could make out the Blue [Abajo] Mountains. Again we could see the weird features of Monument Valley. The cut of Glen Canyon was plainly marked, and to the north and east of that we got another view of the Circle Cliffs and the Escalante Basin with Kaiparowits Peak at one end and Navajo Peak at the other end of 50 Mile Mountain.

This is a point where a night should be spent. We should have seen the view at sunset and sunrise. In the intense brilliancy of the midday sun the atmosphere has a smoky effect and individual features of the landscape are blurred and flattened. We took numerous photographs with hopes, but no expectations, and they were all bad.

Porter said that Powell spent the best part of a summer on this point. The remains of Powell's triangle made of logs still lay upon the point.

At 3 p.m. we left the south point. Returning we followed the same route, reaching the spring where we lunched at 4:30. Here we rested 'til 5 and then hastened on down one canyon and up the other. Darkness overtook us shortly after we descended from the lava cap and we had to walk, leading our horses through the forest, down the entire north slope of Table Cliff to the road in the valley below the divide. We arrived at the Ranger Station 8:30 p.m. after 10 hours in the saddle and having covered about 25 miles of very rough country. Porter, who is rather stout and about 45 years of age, complained of being tired. I was as fit as at the close of any day yet.

As we started to cook dinner, the Porter children appeared with surprises for us. Two of them bore a great iron pot containing a stew of mutton with noodles and rice, another carried a sponge cake and a third brought us bread and butter. We had a wonderful feast.

We found George thoroughly resuscitated and very well pleased with his day. He had braced up after we left and made friends with the small Porter boys, the oldest aged 12. There are seven children, running down to a baby 10 months old. George had cooked himself breakfast, then saddled his horse and taking one of the Porter boys behind, had ridden to Winder, about five miles off. At the store there he had bought some candy and raisins, which he shared with the Porter children.

The afternoon was spent shooting the .22 rifle, chipmunks, rabbits etc. The small boys located a chipmunk in a hollow log, and while one of the boys looked through a knot-hole at the chipmunk, another boy shot the gun into the hollow part of the tree and blew the chipmunk all to pieces into the face and eyes of the observer.

Bed at 10:30 p.m.

Monday, July 19–Tuesday, July 20. The Frasers and Rust rode west down Pine Canyon to the now-deserted town of Winder in Johns Valley. Heading south in this valley, Fraser was "surprised to find the tents and in a few places shacks of a number of homesteaders." Rather than take the dusty wagon road to Panguitch through Red Canyon, where Highway 12 now carries tourists to Bryce Canyon National Park, they elected to follow a shorter horse trail through Casto Canyon. Curiously, Fraser decided not to check out the Paunsaugunt Plateau, since the view from Table Cliff "convinced me that little of new interest would be seen" there. Thus, he and Rust missed seeing the colorfully carved amphitheaters of Bryce Canyon as well as the outstanding viewpoint at the southern tip of the Paunsaugunt. Still, their ride the next day through Casto Canyon's pinnacled bluffs held considerable interest: "The combination of color and sculpture in this canyon surpasses in beauty and interest any other we have seen. . . . It seemed curious that Porter never mentioned this canyon as of scenic interest."

They reached the Sevier River valley and the main road from Kanab about four miles south of Panguitch. Fraser's journal resumes:

Here we became conscious we were approaching a metropolis, for old Jake, the pack horse, whose existence heretofore had been peaceful, was nearly run over by a demonstration motor car containing the local doctor.

Arrived Panguitch 12:30 after a 15 mile ride. We made straight for the post office, where I expected to get letters, but met with disappointment. The town was filled with loafers in unusual number even for this country. Many of them were congregated about the post office. While I was making inquiries within, some of these remarked apropos our outfit that a wild west show had come to town. Rust bluffed them out with an offer to sell them reserved seats.

Riding down the main street of the town toward the hotel, we saw a familiar figure and were cordially greeted by our old friend, Isaac Duffin, of Toquerville.[15] Mr. Duffin turned out to be on a cruise with a prairie schooner full of Dixie fruit. He seemed to be overjoyed to meet us and gladly sold us a box of peaches for $1.00. He had run up from Toquer with this wagon load of fruit, retailing it at various points, and was now about sold out. He planned to restock with trout and lumber for the home market. I ordered from him as many 2 lb. boxes of dried figs as he could furnish and ship for $5.00 (paid in advance) to be received by Christmas.

We put up at Mr. Church's hotel, a large frame house with a corral and sheds in the back. On the ground floor was a sort of parlor or office, out of which opened a bed room that seemed to be occupied by various members of Mr. Church's family, male and female, and open to the use of guests. This in turn opened into the kitchen. Another door in the office led into the dining room. I changed my clothes in this public bed room, standing part of the time with my back to the door to the kitchen and the rest of the time with my back to the door to the parlor, taking a chance on who might come in the other, and entirely oblivious to the fact that a third door led to a porch, where most of the family were sitting.

We had a very good lunch with some fresh fruit the house had bought from Mr. Duffin. The only other guests were two drummers, one selling shoes. These men were evidently interested in politics, especially the prohibition question, and while I wrote home, debated this problem with Rust.

We found Salt Lake papers of yesterday, Monday and Sunday, which I read through. I was confident that there must be letters for us, so made a second trip to the post office. The Postmaster said he was sure nothing had come for me, because he always carefully noted mail for strangers, but he said that as there were a great many Mexicans there, he was apt to put mail for unknown people in the "M" box. So we looked over every-thing in that box, and finding nothing, the Postmaster ransacked the whole office. A large part of the population of the town came into the post office while I was there. Over the window was a post-card which had been mailed without any address. Every person who approached the window read this post-card through.

While I was thus engaged Rust was trying to trade Indian for a live horse. It seemed as though every man in Panguitch had a horse he wanted to trade. The street in front of the hotel was full of horses and at the post office I was approached by a man who said he had heard that a stranger in town wanted to trade a horse. On the street I was stopped by another man inquiring where was the horse that was open to a trade. Rust turned down all the bad ones and the owners of the good ones turned down Indian, so nothing was accomplished but talk.

As usual our intentions to start early were not carried out, so we stayed for supper at the hotel, and at 7:30 started out. We only got a block, however, when George and Rust insisted on getting ice cream and soda at the drug store.

The mule was opposed to leaving town and constantly veered off the road in an effort to get back to the corral and the feed there. As I had not partaken of the refreshments at the drug store, it fell to my lot to chase the mule, which involved a good deal of rough riding over the rear ends of lots fronting the street we were trying to go down. As I rode over one fellow's back-yard, the man stopped me and asked me whether I was the man that wanted to trade a horse. I pointed out Rust, so this fellow threw a bridle on a pony he had, got on his bare-back and started after us. Rust carried on negotiations with this man as we rode away from town for quite three-quarters of an hour. They split on the question of $5.00 which the man insisted Rust should give with Indian, so we left town with the same outfit.

We followed a good road toward Panguitch Lake for 10 miles under a moon shining rather dimly through light clouds. It was comfortably cool, but not cold. At 11 p.m. Rust's imagination told him that we had reached Seavey's Ranch, which was our objective, so we turned into a meadow through a gate and made camp beside a murmuring stream in deep grass without flies or mosquitoes, and at once went to bed at 11 p.m.

Wednesday, July 21 – Friday, July 23. The party continued up the dusty road along Panguitch Creek to Panguitch Lake. They visited with Mr. Seavey, the owner of the ranch where they had camped, who was trying to raise trout in Panguitch Lake for the Salt Lake City market, thus far unsuccessfully. They camped a little past Blue (now Taylor) Spring. On Thursday they continued on to the Forest Service ranger station on Lowder Creek, located in a mountain meadow and surrounded by a forest of quaking aspen and "glorious silver spruce."

From the ranger station they rode west onto Brian Head, the high promontory to the west. Fraser reveled in the view:

Here again we were in great luck. The sky was heavily clouded and sheets of rain were visible to the west. There was no rain on the mountains and the sun occasionally broke through the clouds and added to the beauty of the view. While the result of these weather conditions was to obscure the distance, the nearer effects were bettered. We saw again the series of cliffs: vermilion, white, gray and pink. There was a fine view into and over Parowan Valley and across the Escalante Desert to the Nevada mountains. The whole ridge of the Pine Valley Mountains stood up and charmed me more than ever, and Rust agreed we must see the view from the summit. The most marked feature of the landscape to the east and southeast was a great black lava flow bearing very few trees and looking as though it might have been laid down only a few years ago.

After returning to the ranger station and visiting with the wife of the ranger, they proceeded south to Duck Lake, through "shallow valley bottoms with rich grass and abundant wild flowers. . . . The parks are quite equal in beauty to those of the Kaibab, but bear much better grass, and in every valley bottom there is running water and we constantly encounter springs. This, the summit of the Markagunt Plateau, is by far the friendliest and in the way of vegetation the most attractive country we have been through."

On Friday, July 23, they reached Duck Lake, which Fraser also found charming, remarking that the pink-tinged beach gravels contrasting with the blue water "makes a very beautiful picture." Ever the observant traveler, Fraser examined a spring by the west end of the lake and "counted 17 points at which it bubbled up."

That evening, riding in a hard rain (Fraser had lost his mackintosh a few days before), they were happy to come across a sheep camp and to make acquaintance with another of the residents of the plateau country:

At 6 p.m. at the edge of an open valley with good grass we found a sheep wagon. Its occupant was absent, so we took possession, made camp nearby, spreading out our tent as an awning to keep our packs dry, lit a fire in the stove in the wagon and made ourselves at home. Pretty soon the owner turned up and philosophically welcomed us.

At 7:30 rain stopped and we enjoyed a charming sunset. The night was clear with a fine moon.

The occupant of the sheep wagon was named Lister, of Cedar City. He was temporarily herding sheep for the Cedar Mercantile & Live Stock Co., the regular herder being absent on account of illness in his family.

Lister is about 33 years of age, reserved, dignified and very correct in speech and manner. The wagon was as clean as if a dozen house-maids had scoured it every morning. It is built on the principle of a doctor's cabin on a ship. At the front end across the wagon is a bunk. Behind this on either side are chests serving as benches. On the right hand side of the door at the rear is a stove. At various points on the wall are lockers and drawers.

We had supper in the wagon, eating mostly Lister's food, although we supplied a little something.

Lister gave us a good deal of instruction and some figures about sheep. There are about 75,000 sheep herded hereabouts belonging to people in Cedar City. The magnitude of the industry in this Southern Utah country is indicated by the fact that this spring 135,000 sheep were sheared at Gould's, back of Hurricane. The shearing at Lund was even greater.

After supper Lister washed the dishes and the knives and forks, wiping them carefully on a dish towel. He presented me with a clean polishing towel and had me polish every article after he had finished with it, then he put everything in its proper place, closed up the drawers and cup-boards, swept out the floor and only then composed himself to listen. He was not a conversationalist. He only answered questions.

Saturday, July 24. The Frasers and Rust rode southwest, bypassing the upper reaches of the North Fork of the Virgin River, through much rougher country than before. After encountering several cliffs, they found a way down to the bottom of Deep Creek, where they camped. This being Pioneer Day, the anniversary of Mormon immigrants reaching the Great Salt Lake Valley, Rust entertained the Frasers that evening with pioneer stories.

A meeting along the trail that day illustrates the proprieties of travel in the backcountry:

Being short of shirts, I was traveling to-day in a long-sleeved undershirt. While we were lunching George told me that a lady was approaching on horseback. I thought this was a jest, but to my chagrin discovered a man and woman riding up to us, and the lady in ordinary attire astride a horse on a cow-puncher's saddle. I stepped to one side of the tent to put on a sweater to hide my undershirt, and when I came out in front was surprised to find the lady had gone behind the tent and swung her leg over the pommel of the saddle, so as to appear to be riding side-saddle.

Sunday, July 25. The party climbed out of Deep Creek and continued west, gaining views down into Zion Canyon and, later in the day, into Kolob Canyon. Rust was not familiar with the Kolob Terrace, which they were traversing, and led the Frasers south on a wagon track that ended above the confluence of Deep Creek and Kolob Creek:

It appeared as though we would get the chance we were so anxious for of looking into a deep canyon like that of Orderville Gulch which we traversed last year. So we left the outfit on the summit of the point and clambered down 400 feet to the rim of the canyon. The first 200 feet of descent was very steep over thin bedded sandstone containing a few fossils to a bench bearing some large pines. From the summit of the point it appeared as though this bench was at the rim of the canyon, but on attaining it, we discovered another bench below involving a still steeper descent of 200 feet more. Here the red jura shale gave way to the white cross-bedded sandstone, and we stood on the brink of a sheer precipice, which appeared to be 1,000 feet high, and looked into the canyon diagonally across from the point where Kolob Creek and Crystal Creek joined.[16] In the canyon bottom at this junction rose a great pillar of sandstone surmounted by a few trees. On every ledge, at every summit and wherever the canyon widened out at all spruce trees and occasionally pines had taken root. Utilizing these as stadia and judging their respective heights by our observation of similarly formed trees near by, we estimated the depth of the canyon as approximately 1,000 feet and its width at the bottom, which was filled by a muddy stream, as probably not over 10 feet.

The canyon is wholly cut in the white cross-bedded sandstone. The cross-bedding is a conspicuous and beautiful feature. The whole mass appears to be one bed. There is no sign of stratification. The rock is symmetrically and deeply jointed, one set of joints running parallel with the stream and the other at right angles. On the canyon walls in many places are masses of rock precariously poised, ready to break off in sheets along the surfaces of cross-bedding or the planes of joint. Although it was perfectly still and there was a considerable flow of water evident at the bottom of the canyon, the sound of running water could not be heard.

We spent an hour and a quarter on the rim of the canyon taking photographs and rolling stones and shouting to hear the echo.

We wanted to reach the summit of the slope above the west wall of this canyon. If we could have bridged the short distance from rim to rim we would have attained our objective in an hour or so. As it was, we made a long journey to the north until either at the foot of the slope marking the northerly boundary of the Zion drainage area or some distance up that slope, we headed this deep canyon. I was very confident that we would not have to go far and showed Rust a point where I thought we could cross. He was courteous and tolerant but modestly expressed the opinion that we would have to pass close to some rocks standing like statues on the north slope. The event proved Rust quite right. Although he had never been in this section before, instinct and experience together seemed to show him the way.

At 6 o'clock we left the canyon rim and in 25 minutes climbed the 400 feet up to where the horses were. This was no joke. For a little distance we followed our trail toward the lunch camp and then bore north and westerly along the slope surmounting the easterly wall of the canyon towards the breaks of the amphitheater. The slopes on which we rode were very heavily overgrown with oak. We were scratched and pinched against the trees and in many places had to dismount and crawl through the brush pulling the horses after us. There was no sign of a trail, but now and then we followed in the wake of some stray cow who had broken down the underbrush a little. By 7:30 it had grown quite dark and the sky was overcast, and it looked very much as though we would have to make a dry camp, which would have been hard on horse and man. Just as we were about to resign ourselves to such a night, at 7:50, by virtue of the good luck that never failed us, we ran across a clear small brook tributary to Crystal [Oak] Creek, and on its bank made a most comfortable camp.

The topography of this country was gradually becoming clearer. The cretaceous cliffs facing to the southward at the head of the Zion drainage are eroded in form like a number of horseshoes laid side by side with their closed ends to the north. The points dividing the several shoes are attenuated, forming long tongues of gradually decreasing altitude pointing south. Along the slopes of these closed areas, which I have chosen to call amphitheaters, are springs or seeps, the waters which, together with the precipitation, flow intermittently along established drainage courses toward a central depression, where they join to form the larger streams that had cut the deep canyons we have crossed and observed.

I was told by Rust and others that the tendency of streamlets to follow definite lines of drainage in the upper reaches of these slopes has been greatly aided by the pasturage of sheep there. Before sheep were introduced the grass protected the slopes from wash and in time of flood the water ran down in sheets quite evenly distributed, and in drier times sank in and as ground water found its way to the lower levels, where it seeped out into or not far from the main stream. The sheep, however, under grazing conditions which formerly were universal and still prevail to some extent, were allowed to eat out all the grass wherever they were placed before they were moved on. They were further allowed to string out as the expression is, i.e. to graze in lines, a number of sheep following close on the heels of another. Such grazing resulted in denuding the surface of the grass, loosening the earth into fine dust, and beating out trails like paths that men will soon wear over a meadow or lawn if they traverse it frequently on the same line. The rain water falling on such a surface picks up and carries in suspension the fine dust and selects for its run-off the sheep trails. A heavy storm may result in wearing down one of these sheep trails to a considerable depth and forming a dry wash with steep mud sides.

When a heavy rain occurs at the head of the drainage basin, the upper forks of Little Zion are at once filled with raging torrents of water charged with mud to the limit of its carrying power. These unite into Little Zion, which in turn is swollen way beyond its normal flood flow and debouches from its deep canyon onto the irrigable area of the Virgin Valley in such force and volume as to overflow its banks and wash out the farms. I began to appreciate the truth of what was told me by the men we talked with last year at Grafton.

Gradually the moon broke through the clouds. The rain we feared did not materialize. It was warm. There was a heavy dew. Bed 9:30 p.m.

Monday, July 26, 1915

Up 6:30 a.m. For the second time on the trip Rust was ahead of me with breakfast nearly ready. Soon after sunrise the clouds broke away and the sun shone through fleecy clouds. George got the horses except his own, which it took Rust to find.

Left 10 o'clock. Clear and strong hot sun and a southerly breeze. We proceeded northerly on the westerly sloping flank of the amphitheater, climbed a little, then descended into a dry wash and so on up and down all the time through very dense oak brush.

On mounting the first of these rises I could see that the point where I expected that we could cross the drainage of Crystal Creek was wholly impracticable. We had to go way up the side of the amphitheater and head the creek, as Rust stated.

Crystal Creek here is a mere brook of very muddy water flowing at a steep angle with many small water falls. It has cut numerous pot-holes into the shale. I measured one 3½ feet deep. It is here a miniature counterpart of the deep canyon below.

We guessed correctly that our way was now clear on to Upper Kolob, which lay at the summit of the west slope of Crystal Creek. We ascended gradually now along the westerly slope of the amphitheater, changing our course, which had lain northwest and north, to southwest.

There were not so many oaks and they did not grow so closely together. We encountered small swampy meadows of tall grass with wild flowers—a blue flower shaped like a daisy, and yellow daisies with long leaves. On the edges of these meadows were black birch, the long-leaved (mountain) cotton-wood, willows and a few maples. On reaching the summit of the plateau we found quaking aspen.

I inferred that the swampy condition of spots in the hillside were due to seeps of water from porous beds interbedded with impervious strata. On the slope under but near the summit, I observed incipient land slides where the saturated swampy soil of some meadow had broken away from the drier soil above, leaving an intervening crack and scarp from 3 inches to 18 inches high.

At 12:15 we attained the summit of the ridge, affording a fine view to the south over Kolob, with a few of the characteristic beehive peaks visible in the distance and also a view down Zion canyon. The atmosphere was misty, prohibiting photography, but affording cloud effects, which added to the beauty of the landscape.

We found the land to the west of the summit fell off gently into a broad dish-shaped valley flanked east and west by low hills, those to the east sedimentary and those to the west volcanic. We descended into this valley westerly, met a road and followed that southerly to Isom's Ranch, a surprisingly civilized looking place in such a location. Finding a way through the wire fence, we crossed a swampy meadow with a pool of water in the bottom, passed the ranch house, which we found empty, and threw down our packs in the corral. Arrived 1:30. The sun was shining strong and very hot, but under the shelter of an awning constructed out of a horse blanket the strong south wind made it cool enough to wear a sweater.

Our food was pretty low, consisting mostly of beans, dried beef and coffee and soup capsules. Rust and George went to the ranch and returned in a few minutes with bread, cheese, apples, cake, candy and honey. They reported finding a lady's night-gown. We enjoyed a very good lunch and Rust explained that he intended to leave a card bearing his name and address with the request that he be advised by mail of the amount of the damage, which he intended to remit.

The ranch was producing good hay. There were some potatoes planted and a few other vegetables that did not look promising. Some nice horses were in the pasture. There was a wagon and a reaper left out to withstand the weather.

After lunch while George and Rust packed up I rode east across the valley to the summit of the divide above Crystal Creek in the hope that weather conditions would permit of photographing the amphitheater

Zion National Park, view from rim, 1921.
Photograph by George C. Fraser.

at the head of the Zion drainage. It had cleared and the view was magnificent. To the north forming the westerly side of the amphitheater of what Rust called Crystal Creek, but some here call Oak Creek, is Thorley or Berry Point, with two great sandstone monuments on its flank and a heavy cap of basalt at its summit. In the foreground are the deep canyons of Crystal or Oak Creek and Kolob Creek, the latter heading near by and to the south of me.

On returning to the ranch I found Rust and George in conversation with a young man of about 25, who was seated on the fence, and looking not entirely comfortable. Pretty soon a man and a girl rode by and the former joined us. In a little while a third man and a second girl rode by and went to the ranch house. It turned out that Isom and his grandfather, both of Hurricane, owned this ranch, and that Isom and the two young men we had seen together with three girls, all from Hurricane, were here on a picnic, spending the usual Mormon vacation over Independence and Pioneer days (July 4–24). For some days ending yesterday a party of 25 young people from Toquerville had been with them. The food Rust and George had abstracted belonged to the girls. The situation was somewhat embarrassing. Rust offered to and insisted upon paying for what we had taken and finally put it up to Isom as the judge to impose the fine. He named $1.50, which seemed reasonable enough for pasturing six horses and eating up things irrespective of their value that could not be replaced. We parted on friendly terms.

Left Isom's 5 p.m. We crossed Isom's field in the bottom of the shallow open valley over good grass with sage brush through woods of small quaking aspen and a few large yellow pines, passed Imlay's cabin (empty) and gradually descended southerly and easterly over a basalt flow.

About 7 p.m. we climbed to the summit of the ridge whence we could look southwest and west down the North Creek drainage over Lower

Kolob. The foreground was sculptured in weird shapes, pure white bee-hive shaped peaks predominating.

The road ended at a cabin, near which many seeps of water gathered into a brook that 200 yards below the cabin broke over a cliff in a series of water falls on its way to the bottom of Little Zion Canyon. This cabin belongs to Eiseman of Hurricane, who had recently purchased a considerable acreage of state land, and is used as headquarters for his herders when the sheep are feeding on this range, locally known as "Horse Pasture." In the moist bottom by the creek some potatoes and other vegetables are making a poor effort to grow. Part of a deer's leg near the cabin indicates that some lawless hunter has lately been here.

Although it had threatened rain all the afternoon, we were not tempted to sleep indoors. There were too many signs of rats. George and I stretched our tarpaulin over some ropes and made a slanting roof, under which lay our bedding. At 10:30, just as we were ready to go to bed, a severe thunder storm broke. Rust declined the hospitality of our shelter and came through quite dry by wrapping himself, head and all his bedding, in his tarpaulin. The storm lasted about an hour with brilliant effects of lightning and loud peals of thunder.

Tuesday, July 27, 1915

Up 4:40 a.m. A full moon. Sun rose behind pink clouds; otherwise the sky was clear. We anticipated looking into Zion Canyon to-day and so made an early start. We made our way generally toward the southwest, at first by sheep trail. From a divide to the southwest over the broken, wooded, uneven plateau, we got a view of the Western Temple.

The going was bad. The heavy rain of last night made the grass slippery and left a layer of mud over sand quite dry because the water did not reach it. In this canyon bottom were some large yellow pines, some 10 to 12 inches in diameter and 25 feet high. We encountered maple, choke cherry, cedar, piñon, cactus—Spanish bayonets with withered flowers and prickly pears with red and yellow blossoms like roses—buck brush, mountain mahogany, and at two points where there were springs we found ferns and water cress.

A climb of 400 feet up the steep wall of a canyon brought us to a divide. The view from here was beyond description. We rode along the summit of the divide climbing higher till at 8 a.m. we attained a vantage point affording the widest range of vision.

To the south and west of us the land fell off abruptly, not precipitously, but in graceful curves of bare white sandstone forming a sort of saucer or basin out of which rose buttes and beehive peaks. To the south extended the rough plateau on which we were with the Western Temple rising above and appearing to be its terminus. A little to the west was a flat topped butte supporting luxuriant trees and grass, but effectually cut off from all the rest of the world by inaccessible bare slopes. Amongst the trees on its summit rose needles and monuments of red, remnants of the jura shales which cap the Western Temple. The angle at which the sun's rays struck the rock in this basin brought out sharply the cross-bedding of the sandstone, in appearance like an etcher's lines. It was brilliantly clear. Far to the west we plainly saw St. George and read the giant letter D (symbol of the Dixie High School) in cement on the hillside above it. In the distant background, we could descry the Hurricane ledge with a volcano on its summit, the Virgin, Beaver Dam and Pine Valley mountains.

After studying this view some time we proceeded southerly along the ridge here fairly level and open and found ourselves to be on a point of land, as it were jutting over the white bare sandstone sea. The end of this point fell off sheer. We descended on foot its easterly slope 300 feet and stood on the red shale on the brink of a precipice falling almost sheer 1,000 feet or more to a bare sandstone valley and jutting northerly and easterly into the plateau which we have traversed. There was a tremendous echo here, so distinct as to be uncanny. A word shouted into the depths is not reverberated, but about two seconds after its utterance is repeated plainly, and so with pistol shots.

After ascending the ridge to where we left the horses, we proceeded northerly along the easterly side of the ridge to the head of this canyon, which if possible here broke off more abruptly than at our last stopping point. It was a precarious descent over loose and slipping shales to the hard rock at the brink. Seated at the edge of the precipice taking pictures, I nearly knocked over the camera and just missed slipping down myself into depths from which there could be no recall. Rust stayed 100 feet higher up the slope. From both points of view we saw the bottom of Little Zion Valley at a point between Crawfords and the cable-way, and for the first time had a view of the superb Eastern Temple to the southeast of us with the U-shaped hanging valley at its flank. The Eastern Temple is concealed by surrounding peaks from the observer in Zion Valley. It is only on approaching the valley from the south of Rockville (as Dutton and Holmes did) that it can be seen by those not enterprising enough to scale the plateau where we were.

We enjoyed this view as we skirted the rim for a quarter of a mile northeasterly, which brought us into sight of one of those sheer precipices so characteristic of Zion Valley, but most often described in connection with the Yosemite.

The sun was out full. It was very hot and dry, for our single water-bag was quite empty. From the vantage point of the ridge we descended northerly down a steep wooded slope into a deep side canyon opening into the Little Zion drainage area. In the bottom of this canyon we found a little running water and a rich meadow carpeted with grass, blue daisies, ferns, yarrow, wild roses, pink flowers (whose name I did not know) and the brilliant red and yellow cactus flowers. Here we lunched. Poor feed for us, honey and mildewed bread stolen from Isom's party. We started with a can of dried beef but lost it.

We climbed out of the canyon up its north slope over red jura shales and slaty limestone to the most easterly point of the ridge. It was high noon with a dazzling sun intensified by the bare white rock exposed on every hand.

To the north, northeast and east we had spread before us the entire Little Zion drainage area, the great amphitheater through which we had traveled for three days, and the upper portions of the wall of the deep canyon in which we waded last summer. The white, cretaceous and pink cliffs stood out in their true relations. The ridge on which we stood fell off sheer for hundreds of feet toward the west and then sloped steeply to a bare saucer shaped bottom of white sandstone practically barren. We wished we might be witnesses of the effect of a heavy rain on this land sculpture.

We descended from the divide, arriving at the cabin at 2:30. It was too dark last night and we departed in too much haste this morning to permit of much prospecting around the cabin, so now to see where we were and search for a bathing place I walked to the rim of the cliff where the brook fell over. The brook canyoned in the sandstone immediately, flowing over a 60° slope about 20 feet into a pot-hole or grotto and beneath that in a series of bounds lost itself quickly in great depths. With care I was able to climb into the first pot-hole and there got a cold shower.

At 5:45 p.m. we left Eiseman's cabin and retraced our steps of yesterday, keeping to the road all of the time. At 8:15, it being then quite dusk, we arrived at Imlay's cabin, which we had passed on the way down. Here we found a man, very grouchy and apparently suspicious. We asked the privilege of putting our horses in the pasture and were refused. We asked where we could find water and he pointed to a dirty brook of meager flow. He allowed that we might hobble our horses and let them get what pickings they could outside the pasture, but did not encourage us even to do that. So in the darkness, about 100 yards from the cabin, we threw down the packs, lit a fire and began to cook. By this time another man came up and joined the first one. Rust got in conversation with these two. Pretty soon the second one left and then the first one edged over. By degrees we got him in conversation and learned that his name was Grant, of New Harmony, in the valley just below Cedar City, and that he had supervision over three sheep herds owned by Imlay of Hurricane. When he thoroughly thawed out, he gave us a great deal of information about the country we had been through. It was not until 11:30 that he left us.

A fine moon rose at 9 o'clock. Bed 11:30.

Wednesday, July 28, 1915
Up 6 a.m. Cloudless. The moon was still up. Fine view of the Virgin Temples to the south by east. On arising we found Grant very busy cooking. On starting to get our own breakfast ready he insisted we should eat with him. He apologized in a way for his cool reception of us, explaining that he had frequently been imposed upon of late by people riding up from the dry farms on Lower Kolob, turning their horses into his pasture and eating his food. By way of making good he gave us a sumptuous breakfast, including several kinds of canned fruit put up by the South Utah Canning Co. of Leeds, Dixie honey and native molasses.

Left 10 a.m. We kept to some wagon tracks called a road up the shallow valley past Isom's Ranch and swung northwest over a divide through a park containing two deserted cabins. We skirted westerly under Kanarra Peak. As we proceeded we found the road more and more used. We continued to skirt the side of the amphitheater for about two miles and then cut west into the horn of a saddle, this being the watershed between the La Verkin Creek and Cedar or Kanarra Valley. Directly beneath and on the easterly side of this saddle was a freak of erosion that might be called a rock-garden, innumerable monuments of weird shapes weathered out of the cretaceous sandstone or limestone and rising to all heights up to 40, perhaps 50 feet.

Descending from the saddle we skirted in a northerly direction the westerly side of the mountain. Here we found sheep grazing, got a good drink at a spring and crossed a small creek. A sheep herder appeared as soon as we threw down the packs. We asked if it was his tent we had passed a quarter of a mile above. He said it was and asked why we had not gone in and helped ourselves to some mutton he had hanging there.

Left lunch camp 3:45 p.m. Climbed a divide between the Kanarra Creek drainage and that of the creek to the north. From here down the road was quite good, although, of course, exceedingly steep in places. The road wound because the canyon made too steep a grade for wagon traffic. Beyond a gateway of hard limestone, the plain of Cedar or Kanarra Valley opened out, dry and dusty but bearing evidence of quite recent heavy rains and flood wash. Here the scarp of the Hurricane Cliff strikes north and south and dips with the limestone about 80° west. We kept along the base of the cliffs for 2½ miles to Kanarra.

About a mile above the town we came into the main highway from Lund to Hurricane via Cedar City, the "Grand Canyon Auto Road." Here for two miles we followed our route of last year.

6:45 p.m. arrived Kanarra. Put up at hotel kept by Williams. We found two tents pitched in the front yard and on the common across the way a good sized service tent and were advised that some Presbyterians were conducting a mission for the benefit of the Mormons. We found the mission headed by Dr. Paden, formerly of Salt Lake, and a Princeton graduate of the Class of '80. Dr. Paden was very friendly and started to tell Rust and myself a story about the Mormons. Before getting well under way he stopped and explained that he did not intend to hurt our feelings or say anything about our beliefs and practices that might give us offense.

It seems characteristic of the hotels in this country that the man of the family should sit about in a helpless sort of way and his wife run the hotel. So it was here. I found Williams sitting on a sofa in the parlor and quite uncertain as to whether we could get anything to eat or not, explaining that his wife had gone across the street to see a friend. His son came in and sat on a chair in an equally helpless attitude. Rust and George made the horses at home in the yard while I instilled into Williams' son the notion of the possibility of inducing his mother to come home and get us some food. Before he had quite compassed this idea, Mrs. Williams returned. In short order we had a fine supper, including new potatoes, eggs and cake.

After supper we heard strains of music emanating from the school house near by. Here we found a children's dance in progress to the music of an orchestra composed of two boys and three girls playing cello, violin and various kinds of horns. The dance broke up at 8 o'clock and the revival meeting immediately started. All of the children came from the dance, many mothers and babies attended, and also a number of men, so that the tent was entirely filled and a goodly number stood around its entrance. Rust and George sat outside in an irrigation ditch, where Rust fell asleep and snored so as to somewhat disturb the proceedings.

After the meeting Dr. Paden invited me into the tent and gave me a cigar. After weeks of Bull Durham, its strength took the roof off my head. The Doctor told me of his work and the courtesy of the Mormon Bishop, to whose good offices he was indebted for all the chairs in the tent, and other assistance. We talked until 10:30 and then as we were about to leave, the Doctor inquired of George where he intended to go to college, and on George saying to Princeton, the same place where I had been, the Doctor fell on my neck and confessed himself a Princetonian and talked for three-quarters of an hour more.

At 11:45 p.m. we left Kanarra. The strong wind that blew all day went down with the sun. It was pleasantly cool. We had a good road and no dust, and although there was no moon, the stars gave plenty of light, so we had no difficulty in making our way southwest by west across the valley to New Harmony.

Rust had telephoned in advance to a man named Davis and obtained permission for us to sleep in his back yard. Having no definite description of Davis's place, we were doubtful of being able to pick it out, but Rust's unerring instinct guided him correctly, and at 1:15 a.m., after 34 miles' ride, we camped all right in Davis's yard. George slept in the hay in the barn, having first aroused 14 young piglets asleep under the hay loft. Rust and I laid our beds in a sheltered spot and on awakening found the shelter was afforded by a pig sty.

Thursday, July 29. Another long ride took the party from New Harmony around the north end of the Pine Valley Mountains to the village of Pine Valley. The road was rough, their horses "stiff and tired." They arrived after dark, just as the moon rose, to find a dance taking place at the schoolhouse. The local bishop invited them to camp in his pasture, where Fraser and Rust "enjoyed a gorgeous moon-light view of the valley."

Friday, July 30, 1915
Up 8 a.m. Cloudless, a light breeze until 9 and then the usual strong southerly wind.

On awakening my eye caught the Newcastle water project irrigation ditch along the hillside to the northeast looking like a railroad cut. For some time I could not place myself and imagined this was one of the parallel roads of Glen Roy described by Tyndal.

We got good water out of a pipe in the yard back of the Bishop's house and Rust managed to procure some eggs, cheese and fresh bread for breakfast.

After breakfast we called at the Ranger Station and made the acquaintance of Martin McAllister, Ranger, who is first cousin of the McAllister of Kanab. McAllister had been about the mountain a good deal but never on the high point which we wished to reach. He thought he was pretty busy, but we managed to persuade him he owed it to himself to accompany us, which he ultimately decided to do; so we fooled about all the rest of the morning.

Pine Valley town is an old settlement. In the early days there were saw mills hereabouts and yellow pines were abundant. They have long since been cut out to furnish lumber to Dixie.

The town has the reputation of being slow and the people are talking about moving down to Dixie. It consists of good substantial houses and has fine large trees planted along the street.

The dance last night was incident to the breaking up of a picnic party of about 50 young people from all over the neighborhood. We saw a number of them riding about the streets in pairs, the girls nice looking in neat riding costumes.

Lunch at 12 M. in meadow where we camped. Then we stored our stuff in the Bishop's barn and at 1:15 started with our regular mounts and Jake and the mule, McAllister on his horse.

Leaving the town we rode southerly up a gentle slope to the north of the second canyon to the east of the village—Pole Canyon. The going was rough and we had to follow the creek bottom most of the way, but there were vestiges of a trail. Near the head of the canyon a trail came in from the next canyon to the west—Forsyth Canyon. This turned out to be a lumber road used about 25 years ago, still good in places, but frequently entirely washed out. All along were stumps of large pines and the stones paving the road showed marks of heavy wagon wheels. The destruction wrought to the road by the floods is a splendid lesson in the rapidity and effectiveness of erosion. In places the canyon was V-shaped between steep cliffs with only a few places where trees could grow and the sculpture was fine. At such points we were relegated to the stream bottom, difficult for the horses to get through and compelling us to walk.

Near the head of the canyon we passed the site of an old mill with piles of slabs much decayed. From there an easy ride over a gentle slope brought us to a pass marking the divide between the waters that flowed to Pine Valley and those that flowed into Santa Clara Valley. Here was a corral, some cattle grazing and a spring in a deep cut in the soil. The bottom of the saddle was covered with rich grass. We rose a little distance after crossing the divide down the other side and got a fine view of Santa Clara Flat.

After watering the horses at the spring and eating a little, left 5:30 p.m. and climbed easterly up a steep slope through a dense forest of small quaking aspen, none over 20 feet high, growing so closely together that it was difficult to thread a way. The going was complicated by dead timber. Above the quaking aspen we struck a region of burned out spruce.

At 6:30 p.m. we arrived at the summit, but on careful survey found a peak a mile or two to the southeast was higher. It was too late to get up that peak before sundown, so we decided to camp where we were.

Rust and I climbed a ridge or needle of volcanic rock (andesite) cleaved into enormous slabs dipping about 80° southwest, while George and McAllister climbed a similar small ridge.

It was cloudless but smoky and the light was unfavorable to photography. The view was very fine, especially to the south and southeast, where the light of the setting sun fell on the permian cliffs and brought out their color bands, so that they could be read like a book. We overlooked Hurricane bench and ledge and the entire Trumbull platform where we could make out the three big mountains and quantities of smaller peaks. St. George lay below us with the big "D" on the hill behind conspicuous, every detail brought out in profile by the shadows. Purgatory Flat showed up in its true colors as a red sandy desert with drifting dunes like a lake of fire in the dull valley bottom. To the west the horizon was formed by the Nevada mountains, behind which was a magnificent after-glow at sundown, while along the eastern horizon there was a golden band.

I watched the sunset and darkness fall from the summit of the rock, and on climbing down encountered a crack about 2½ feet wide, 20 feet long and 20 feet deep with a considerable depth of snow at the bottom. We melted snow for drinking and cooking and had a good supper, especially appreciating fresh bread baked by McAllister's little girl.

Bed at 11:15, as the moon was rising.

Saturday, July 31, 1915

George and I got up at 5 a.m. Cloudless, cool, but not cold. Rust and McAllister a bit late. There was no water to wash with, so we at once cooked breakfast, and then started for the high point. We followed the ridge about a mile, probably more, to the east and up a gradual slope covered with spruce trees to the high point. Altitude by forest map 10,400 feet. A monument there.

The view from this point in grandeur and beauty equals any we have seen. It is not as extended as those from the Aquarius, the Henry Mountains and Thousand Lake Mountain, but more varied and possibly more interesting. In view of its accessibility and proximity to the settlements, it is a wonder this point is not more frequently visited.

11 a.m. Left high point and slowly walked back to camp, keeping as close to the precipitous cliff over Diamond Valley as possible. Arrived at camp 12 M. A quick lunch mostly of canned horse, and then we packed and started at 1 p.m. McAllister filled a gunny bag with snow, which we loaded on Jake to be used in making ice cream. We walked, riding very little, down the steep slope to the meadow in the saddle at the foot of the peak, and continued the same road as we had followed going up. Arrived Pine Valley 4 p.m. We found all our stuff safe in Bishop Snow's stable and proceeded in the street to unpack, sort and repack everything ready for shipping. We washed in the yard under the eyes of five boys, who were supposed to be putting in alfalfa and seemed much impressed by the process.

McAllister came over about 5 o'clock and formally invited us to dine. George and I, beside washing, wore our coats at dinner and each of us put on a clean shirt. We had supper at 6. It was cooked by McAllister's daughter, aged 15, and his niece, aged 14, who were temporarily stopping with them. Their bread was fine. The meal consisted of fried canned oysters, fried onions and potatoes, raw onions and radishes, mildewed cheese, apple sauce and a blue grouse which Rust had shot on the way down when McAllister was not looking and out of respect for McAllister's official position was referred to as a "chipmunk."

Rust left soon after dinner to get the horses ready, while George and I continued with McAllister.

McAllister is about 40 years of age. He was formerly a motorman in Salt Lake City and told us he was the first man to run an electric car there. He is reserved, almost reticent, and it took him a good while to size us up. He told us of the very crabbed postmaster at Modena, who, he said, probably would not give us our mail. I suggested he give us a letter of introduction and say "I thought what you will when you get this, but they are not tramps." He said he thought he had better not give us any letter.

The horses are pretty well played out and we knew it to be impossible to make the long ride to Modena in any kind of time with them, so we decided to take a wagon. Rust found he could not get a team of horses in town, but on telephoning to Central, nine miles away, on McAllister's introduction to a farmer there, he got a tentative promise of a team, so Rust borrowed a wagon from one man and various pieces of harness from several other men, hitched up old Gray-back and his own riding horse Bird, and at 9:10 p.m. we started.

The road was very rough and it was pitch black dark, the moon not rising until very late, so we made slow progress, watching for boulders and keeping down hill all the time. At 12 midnight we arrived in Central. As usual Rust managed to find the right house. We woke up the owner, who led us into the corral, where we put up the horses. We laid our beds on an alfalfa stack, and in the morning found we were close up next to the pig-sty. The temperature was comfortable, but cool enough for a sweater.

Sunday, August 1, 1915

Up 6 a.m. Cloudless, cool. Cooked breakfast in the yard and had some poor bread from the house. While we were eating an elderly man in a panama hat came over. He was a Mormon refugee from Mexico. He had been Superintendent of the Madero Company in Sonora, where he had lived for 20 years. He told how his house had been destroyed, $200 worth of books and music had been torn up, his organ broken with an axe, and altogether his savings of about $10,000 were gone. He was trying to make a new start here at the age of about 65.[17]

Rust got a team—one white and one bay mare—of heavy farm horses from the farmer in whose yard we slept and we started at 8 a.m. The road was much better than last night. We traversed undulating country of barren, rounded sage-covered hills. At 9:15 we encountered the ranch at Mountain Meadows. This is a barren spot. Formerly the Meadows are said to have borne good grass, but careless sheep grazing in the early days ruined that, and now there is nothing but sage brush. The massacre occurred (1857) one mile to the south.

Here we encountered the road from St. George and turning north by west, crossed a divide and descended gradually, passing a small ranch through what used to be the town of Hamblin. It is marked by two deserted frame houses and a stone house, all of them built subsequent to Jacob Hamblin's time.

Arrived Enterprise 12 M., a village of perhaps 100 houses right in the desert with dusty streets and hardly any vegetation. As we drove up the street, the entire population came out of the meeting house from Sunday school. There had been a restaurant in the place as appeared from a sign, but it went out of business a year or more ago. So we put up at a place displaying the sign of a boarding stable, a filthy stable yard in the back of a dilapidated house. The sun was blinding and exceedingly hot. We cooked coffee in the street and ate our lunch in the wagon.

Leaving the town we turned west over some outlying hills and for about eight miles kept in the bottom of a valley between low rounded hills until we reached the desert again. The desert floor is of very fine silt and the road dusty. I was unable to see any traces of Lake Bonneville's terraces. There were some basalt flows obvious on the hills. In spite of the hot sun, it was comfortably cool under the shade of the wagon top while driving. About six miles east of Modena the team showed strong signs of being pretty tired.

A mile and a half out of Modena, having plenty of time before the train was due, we stopped, discarded our traveling clothes and put on our city suits. We strung what was left of our trousers on a telegraph pole and used them as a target.

Arrived Modena 5:30. At the Post Office got mail, the first letters we have had since we went into the country. At the express office we found our luggage forwarded by Doolittle from Lund. We packed up such of our traveling stuff as we wanted to keep and shipped the bags home. Then we settled with Rust.

Our train was due at 6:13, but an hour late. Left at 7:20. Dined on train—all very good, except the soup, but we ate too much, including beer, which was served after crossing the Nevada line.

So, on a note suggesting their tiredness, the Fraser's monthlong journey through the High Plateaus country came to an end. They continued west by rail to visit friends and business associates in Los Angeles, San Diego, and San Francisco. In San Francisco they spent several days attending the Panama-Pacific Exposition, held on the four hundredth anniversary of Balboa's reaching the Pacific Ocean. They returned home via Texas, where Fraser inspected his ranchland holdings north of Del Rio. There they experienced various adventures common to motor travel in those days, including a broken crankshaft, which a rescuer repaired onsite, and a mud hole, from which they were extricated by a cowboy on a horse. They returned home on August 19. The journal concludes with a detailed expense summary, showing that the entire journey, including train fares and hotels, totaled $1,274.85. Their horseback excursion with Rust cost $495.00.

Chapter 3

Lees Ferry and the Navajo Country, 1916

I had not thought much of the bridge as a spectacle, really considering it merely
an objective—a sort of excuse for taking a long journey into a desolate region
to see the beauties and abnormalities of a wild country; but in grace and
beauty of both structure and color it is all that has been said of it and more.
—George Fraser's journal, July 20, 1916, at Rainbow Bridge

George Fraser and his son returned to the Southwest in the summer of
1916, making a monthlong horseback journey across northern Arizona
and southernmost Utah from the Grand Canyon to Bluff, Utah. Once
again, Dave Rust guided them most of the way, although he was on
unfamiliar ground while crossing the Navajo Indian reservation and relied
on Navajo and Paiute guides for part of the journey.

A highlight of their trip was a visit to Rainbow Bridge near Navajo
Mountain, one of the most isolated of America's national monuments at
the time. This soaring rock span had been made known to the world in
1909, when Professor Byron Cummings, of the University of Utah, and
William Douglass, a General Land Office surveyor, engaged John Wetherill to guide them to the bridge.[1] President Taft proclaimed a quarter
section of land centering on the bridge as a National Monument in 1910.
Where today as many as three hundred thousand people see the bridge
each year via Lake Powell, early visitors had to make a difficult overland
trek from distant trading posts on the Navajo reservation. Among these
were author Zane Grey and former President Theodore Roosevelt, both of
whom traveled to the bridge in 1913. These men, as well as most other
early-day visitors, also employed John Wetherill, a well-known explorer
and Indian trader who operated out of his trading posts at Oljeto and
later at Kayenta, Arizona. The Paiute Nasja Begay, who had helped guide
the Cummings-Douglass party in 1909, also assisted with the Grey and
Roosevelt parties.

Roosevelt wrote about his adventure in an article for *The Outlook* magazine,[2] describing in his ebullient prose the joys of rugged travel in this

remote region. His account, along with that of Cummings, helped popularize Rainbow Bridge, and it is likely that his readers included George Fraser. Up until this time there had been no detailed geological surveys of this part of northern Arizona. Herbert E. Gregory's pioneering works on the geology and water resources of the Navajo country were published in 1916 and 1917, too late for Fraser's use. Nor did Fraser have the stimulating writings of a Clarence Dutton to follow as he had in 1914 and 1915.

Fraser's route, like Roosevelt's, began at the South Rim of the Grand Canyon, crossed the chasm and climbed out to the North Rim and the Kaibab Plateau via Dave Rust's trail, then headed north and east, down off the plateau, to a second crossing of the Colorado River at Lees Ferry. (Fraser uses "Lee's" Ferry, the older form.) Located at the onetime hideout of Mormon pioneer John D. Lee, the ferry was until 1928 the only practicable crossing of the Colorado from Moab, Utah, to below the Grand Canyon. Here the river emerged from Glen Canyon, where Dave Rust had placer mined for gold almost twenty years earlier. Borrowing a leaky boat left near the ferry by his friend Nathaniel Galloway, Rust rowed the Frasers a few miles upriver into the lower end of Glen Canyon. Rust had wanted to take the Frasers down the length of Glen that summer and was no doubt thinking about the tourist possibilities of this stretch of river—a business he ultimately started in 1923.

From Lees Ferry the most difficult part of the journey was to begin—the crossing of the Navajo reservation. This immense expanse was chopped and broken with steep-walled canyons and bewildering sandstone breaks; water was scarce and often depended on recent rainfall. Maps of the region gave extremely limited information. Fraser and Rust relied on General Land Office and U.S. Geological Survey maps, which displayed only sketchy topography and showed few of the extant Indian trails. Moreover, neither Fraser nor Rust knew the languages of the resident Navajo and Paiute Indians. All this made for serious route-finding problems.

Rust had heard from his father-in-law, E. D. Woolley, that there was an Indian trail leading from Lees Ferry up over the Echo Cliffs to the east.[3] Still, he felt compelled to hire a Navajo guide to head the cliffs and cross the expanse of the Kaibito Plateau to Richardson's trading post at Kaibito Spring. This was a fortunate decision, as their guide, "Old Dan," knew how to find the only reliable water source on their route between Lees Ferry and Kaibito. (John Wesley Powell had written of an area of water pockets called the Thousand Wells on the back side of the Echo Cliffs, but even in the relatively wet summer of 1916 these were not in evidence.)[4]

Leaving Kaibito and their guide, the Frasers and Rust made their way east and north through the sandstone breaks of upper Navajo Creek, heading for Navajo Mountain. Here they fortuitously engaged a young Paiute man named John to guide them to Rainbow Bridge. (The historian Stephen C. Jett identified John as Nasja Begay, of the Cummings-Douglass expedition, but Fraser makes no mention of this.)[5] John knew of the trail John Wetherill used for his tourist business, which crossed the maze of canyons draining north off of Navajo Mountain—a trail not shown on any map.

As the party continued east from Navajo Mountain, John also departed. Unsure of the route, Rust turned to the southeast up Piute Creek, wandering well to the south of the usual trail to Bluff, which looped far to the north through the old mine workings near the mouth of Nokai Creek. They were compensated, however, with unexpectedly finding enchanting canyons and, ultimately, riding into Monument Valley, only then becoming known as a noteworthy scenic destination. At times the party simply became lost in this maze of canyons, which, given Rust's usual route-finding skill, indicates the wildness of the country. Even Fraser's usually precise notes become vague and hard to correlate to map features; from his description it appears that the party skirted the head of Nokai Canyon or possibly Copper Canyon, both of which they successively mistook for "Moonlight" (Oljeto) Creek. Later, as they headed northeast from Monument Valley in search of a way to Bluff, Utah, they descended Comb Ridge into the badlands of "Chin Lee" (Chinle) Creek; here, incredibly, they figured they had reached the San Juan River, and were put straight only after talking with a local Navajo man. Rust clearly did not have the local topography down in the way that John Wetherill or Zeke Johnson, the Anglo guides who normally operated in this region, did. Still, Fraser cheerfully accepted these wanderings as a way to encounter stunning new sights.

At several points in the journey they appeared to have passed within a few miles of the ancient Puebloan ruins included within Navajo National Monument. They likely came close to both Inscription House in the upper reaches of Navajo Creek and Keet Seel in the Tsegi canyon system. Although the monument was established in 1909, Fraser and Rust either did not know of these ruins or chose to bypass them. By 1912 the ruins appeared on the General Land Office map of Arizona, but they may have carried an earlier version of the map.

They had many brief encounters with the Navajo herders who inhabited these far-off canyons. Due to language barriers, cultural differences, and perhaps prejudice, Fraser seemed unable to achieve the kind of rapport with them that he had enjoyed with so many of the Anglo inhabitants elsewhere in the region. Finally reaching the San Juan River and the end of the Navajo reservation, he describes Spencer's trading post at Mexican Hat (Goodridge), Utah, and provides an entertaining account of motoring from Bluff to Thompson, Utah, over the primitive roads of the day.

The first part of the journal is omitted, covering the Frasers' trip west from New Jersey by train, with side trips to Acoma and Laguna Pueblos in New Mexico and Meteor Crater in Arizona. The elder Fraser's curiosity for all things geological induced him to hike around the rim of Meteor Crater and climb down to its bottom, in spite of "almost unbearably hot" conditions.

Dave Rust met the Frasers at Flagstaff on June 28, whereupon they retired to the Commercial Hotel for "milk, sandwiches, grape juice and pop"—Arizona having gone dry the year before. From Flagstaff they climbed Agassiz Peak in the San Francisco Mountains, the prominent volcanic peaks northwest of town that Fraser had wanted to climb at the conclusion of his 1914 journey. From the top of Agassiz they were treated to views stretching 150 miles or more in all directions. Back in Flagstaff, the party engaged Lee Simmons, a local man, to drive them to the South Rim of the Grand Canyon and the start of their horseback journey.

George Fraser's Journal

Friday, June 30, 1916

Simmons is the man we met in Kanab two years ago, who had undertaken to drive a couple of Agricultural Department men over the Painted Desert, via Lee's Ferry, and had a breakdown in the desert, 65 miles from anywhere. I remembered him as using the most offensively profane, blasphemous and obscene language. This year in speech and action, and even in dress, he is particular to a nicety. For that reason I did not recognize him as our previous acquaintance until shortly before we parted. In the interval Arizona has gone dry, and he has gotten married. The moral is obvious.

Before leaving we checked our suit cases with our decent clothes to G. P. A. Peck, of the San Pedro at Los Angeles, who undertook to forward them to me at Thompsons, so we had nothing but our duffle bags, one tied on each running board, and another in the tonneau.

Dr. Duncan [a professor accompanying them] was no professional entertainer. Each of us separately, and all of us collectively, tried him on every subject of which we had ever heard, without eliciting a sign of interest or a spark of enthusiasm. Rust said the girls at Wellesley will be perfectly safe.

We passed Sunset Crater shortly before noon and had an excellent opportunity to observe the phenomenon of the Sunset effect. It looked exactly as though the last rays of the setting sun, obscured by a shadow below, were falling full on its top. Obviously the iron-charged lava slide on the mountain's summit, in weathering has oxidized, the rust color resulting giving the glow of sunset.

The party made a short detour to observe Sunset Crater, then undertook the dusty road north and west to the Grand Canyon, stopping briefly at Grandview Point. Arriving at El Tovar Hotel that evening, Fraser "asked at the desk for a water bag and canteen which I had left there exactly one year and eleven months ago. The clerk leaned under the desk, and produced them." That evening they enjoyed a lecture and movie given by Emery Kolb—an old friend of Dave Rust—and afterward stayed up chatting with Kolb and his wife.

Saturday, July 1, 1916

Up 6:30, clear. We had a double room with Rust next door and bath between. Rust disappeared before I got up and breakfasted with Emery Kolb and got from him a sketch map and detailed description of the Rainbow Arch trip. Breakfast was good, except some pigs' feet, which were spoiled and caused regret. Packed some plates and films and changed verascope plates. During all the time we were getting ready disagreeable subordinate employees of the hotel kept urging us to hurry our start. It seemed to be the policy of these employees, from my experience during this and two previous visits, to speed the parting guest without consideration for his convenience or comfort. There was no occasion for haste, because a start at one o'clock would have allowed time to get us to the river and have the guide bring the animals back before dark.

We got $10 in silver from the cashier as a reserve for use among the Indians. When I paid the bill of $46, he told me he did not think we would have to worry about our money, because there was no danger of our being robbed on the other side of the canyon.

About 10:30 we started under the guidance of a supercilious cowpuncher, each of us on a mule, with our stuff packed on another mule. We rode steadily and fast, breaking the rules and not dismounting even at Jacob's Ladder, and in one hour and 5 minutes (12:05 p.m.) reached

Indian Gardens, having almost overtaken the trail party which started one and a half hours ahead of us. It was warm on the rim and grew steadily hotter as we descended. There had been no rain for a long time and the trail was inches deep in dust, making riding behind the guide and pack, as we had to do, exceedingly disagreeable and especially trying on the eyes. The trail has been relocated in parts since my trip over it in 1911 and much improved. It is like a boulevard compared to the trails we have been accustomed to in the last two years.

Stopped for lunch at Indian Gardens one hour, the guide in conversation with another one, who had been detailed to work on the trail, complaining all the while about his job and disagreeable experience with tourists. This morning he resigned.

Leaving Indian Gardens 1:05 p.m., sun still brilliant and very hot, we followed the regular trail over the plateau approximately a mile to near where the regular trail drops into the head of a canyon in the granite. There we turned easterly, keeping on the plateau and heading two side canyons in the granite. The trail ran over the Tonto shales and was very dusty.

About 2 p.m., at the head of Pipe Creek Canyon, we stopped a moment for a drink at Burro Spring, and then keeping under the base of O'Neill Butte, still on the Tonto shales, went northerly and easterly to the head of a side gorge in the granite, down which we dropped very steeply to the river, arriving at the crossing 3:05 p.m.

On the way down this gorge I noticed faults in the algonkian on the west side of Bright Angel Creek. Beneath the Tonto sandstone are magenta beds of algonkian overlying the black schist (known as the granite) which is cleaved nearly vertically. In the canyon we descended there is apparently a fault, thanks to which it was possible for Rust to construct a trail along its southeasterly side. A breccia, the composition of which I could not make out, occurs in this canyon, possibly along the line of fault.

From the rim of the inner gorge, a mile or so from where we started its descent, we could see Rust's camp in Bright Angel Creek near its mouth, and with a glass made out Rust's man, Reese B. Griffiths, of Fredonia, Arizona, who had been left in charge of the animals. Three shots from the revolver and loud shouting aroused him, as we knew he would meet us at the crossing.

The mules went very well. I was surprised though to have mine buck at a steep place on the trail when one of the others butted into him behind.

The sun was blinding and at the river it was intensely hot. My minimum thermometer registered 112 deg. in a semi-shady spot.

The cage and two painters' swings attached to pulleys were on the south bank of the river. The cage is worked by a windlass on the north bank. Rust prepared to cross on a pulley to help Griffiths work the cage, but George was before him, jumped in a swing and started across pulling himself hand before hand without investigating whether his pulley was in good shape. The wire rope from which the cage is suspended by pulley wheels sags so that gravity carried the pulley to the middle. When George tried to pull up to the north bank he found his pulley wheel stuck for lack of grease and made poor progress. Rust overtook him, but was unable to help. George had failed to put on any gloves in his haste and thoughtlessness. The rope was frayed and of course burning hot. It took all of his strength and most of the skin off his hands to bring him to the north bank, and when he got there, he was entirely played out and unable to help with the windlass.

Rust and Griffiths set to work with the windlass and pulled the luggage and me across to the north side in short order.

I photographed the crossing with George and Rust suspended from the wire, but my efforts at autochrome[6] and with the kodak resulted poorly because of the intense brilliancy and lack of shadows.

The cable landing is in the steep granite cliffs, so we had to carry our luggage about 300 yards to where Griffiths had left a pack[7] and three saddle horses. George and I mounted horses and rode half a mile to Bright Angel Creek and a little above its mouth, threw off our clothes and got a good bath in the cold water. This resuscitated George so that he felt no ill effects from his experience in crossing the river beyond the soreness of his hands, which bothered him for two or three days.

About a mile above the mouth of Bright Angel Creek where the canyon widens, Rust formerly had his regular camp, and here some cots, blankets, cooking utensils, etc. are cached. The canyon walls rise high, probably a thousand feet, almost sheer, shutting out any breeze there might be, so it was intensely hot all evening. I washed three flannel shirts and two merino drawers before supper and in one and one half hours, although the sun had gone down, they were dry. Temp. 8:15 p.m. 88°.

Sunday, July 2, 1916

Up 5:15 a.m. Bathed in Bright Angel Creek, cold. Minimum air temperature 6 p.m. to 6 a.m. 72°.

At our camp there are good cotton-wood trees and the canyon

bottom supports a fair amount of grass. It would be an easy matter to irrigate the river silt bottom at this point and raise fruit, vegetables and alfalfa.

Left at 8:30 a.m. with four riding horses and two packs. Our equipment, beds, supplies etc. for the trip Rust left at Camp Woolley, so aside from our personal luggage our packs were light.

The trail runs up Bright Angel Canyon, which boxes in the granite about a half a mile above camp. For hours we rode in the canyon bottom, sometimes in the stream and fording it according to my count 83 times, this without figuring the number of occasions when we entered the stream and left it by the same side.

By 10:30 a.m. at ford no. 70 we emerged from the box canyon at the summit of the granite and thence followed in the algonkian, with occasional granite outcrops, to Ribbon Falls. George and I bathed under the falls. The water was very cold, but the force of its descent, probably aided by small pebbles and sand, beat on the skin so hard that it warmed one up.

The sun shining in a cloudless sky made intense heat, but in the shade of a rock shelter it was comfortably cool. Between the base of the falls and Bright Angel Creek, about 200 yards, the creek flows through a narrow cut in the rock with many pot-holes. In these George and Rust bathed after lunch.

Vegetation is sparse—I noted cotton-wood, willows, prickly pear, wild rice, yuccas up to 12 feet high, cat-tails, and cat's-claw. The only animal life observed were toads, lizards and tad-poles, the latter in semi-stagnant pools.

In the face of the northerly (left) wall of the side canyon, into which drops Ribbon Falls, is a rock shelter with stalagmites and stalactites in a deep friable calcareous deposit at the base. This looked like a promising point for excavation.

Left lunch camp at Ribbon Falls 2:30 p.m. and continued up Bright Angel Canyon, relatively open, in comparison with what we have been through. Boulders and brush made riding more trying, but we only forded the stream six times after lunch.

The trail, evidently originally well constructed, has not been worked for some time. While it is in generally good condition, at one point it traverses a steep slope in the algonkian and has become washed out. Here we had to unload one of our packs and carry the stuff across the slide. My horse was not in very good condition; he probably ate some poisonous weed during his stay in the bottom of the canyon, and while stopping on this slide he broke into a sweat, trembled and wobbled so that it looked as though he would roll over the precipice. Rust was quick to loosen his cinches and so I succeeded in getting him over.

About three miles above Ribbon Falls we passed on the west side of Bright Angel Creek the mouth of a side canyon coming in from the easterly base of Bright Angel Point and fed by Roaring Spring which takes its rise in the tonto shales.

From the summit of the cross-bedded sandstone at 7 p.m. we enjoyed a wonderful view with the colors and contour accentuated by shadows and lights cast by a fast setting clear sun.

Rust stayed with me while George and Griffiths proceeded to camp. Over the summit Kaibab limestone the trail is good, though zigzagging steeply. From the rim to Camp Woolley—about three miles—we ran our horses through the forest and caught up with the rest of the outfit just as they arrived at 8 p.m.

George and I slept under a yellow pine above the cabin, avoiding our previous sleeping place and escaping ants.

Monday, July 3, 1916

Last night Rust had extended the courtesies of a spring cot, said to be built for two. It was constructed on the principle of rising in the middle and falling on the sides, so that there was a constant effort during the night to keep from rolling out; beside it was too short and the night was cold. On awakening we found ice in the canteen. Temp. 7 a.m. 36°, minimum during night 22°. In the camp enclosure we found columbine in bloom.

Griffiths cooked the breakfast and fed us fine hot biscuits with Dixie sorghum and long legged "mutton."[8]

10:30 a.m. we all started in search of Uncle Jim Owens in the hope that he would take us on a lion hunt the next morning. Between Camp Woolley and the Ranger Station we encountered young Hirschi, son of the Bishop of Rockville, driving a sad looking horse with an open light wagon, and followed by a simple looking dude on horse-back, dressed in shiny tan puttees and otherwise looking miserable. They wanted to hire an outfit to go down Rust's trail. The Easterner wanted to walk up to the south rim and spend a day at El Tovar and return. Griffiths stayed behind to fix up this fellow's wants.

We found the Ranger Station deserted, but there were signs that some one had been there in the morning, so we proceeded to Bright Angel Point over the automobile road, now in excellent condition, and found Scott Dunham in charge of building a trail for the Forest Service out to Bright Angel Point. They were making a good job and in a few days would have finished as good a trail as exists on the south rim. From Dunham we ascertained that Uncle Jim had gone to the westward to meet some tourists and would not be back for several days. He said Blondy Jansen, son of our old friend, the inn keeper at Fredonia, was at Bright Angel Ranger Station and had two hounds. Jansen was temporarily employed by the Forest Service as a fire guard, but nobody thought that would interfere with his taking us out if he wanted to.

I had been distinctly disappointed with the view from Grand View and the little we saw of the canyon from El Tovar. The view from Bright Angel, though, proved fully up to recollection and expectation as affording an intimate panorama of the buttes, temples and towers in the most crowded and characteristic part of the Kaibab division of the canyon.

We returned to camp for lunch and Rust began storing his stuff preparatory to packing. He and George spent the afternoon riding after horses and succeeded in gathering in a few of those we would take on the trip.

Griffiths and I mounted horses at 3:50 and rode partly on the wagon trail, but principally straight away through the forest to Skidoo Point [Point Imperial] at the northeast end of Greenland. Arrived 5:10 p.m., having covered nine miles in one hour and twenty minutes, mostly at a gallop.

This is said to be the highest point on the canyon rim. It affords the most comprehensive and magnificent view of the amphitheaters and canyons at the head of the Grand Canyon and a bird's-eye view of the entire Painted Desert or Marble Canyon Platform with the Vermilion Cliffs, the Echo Cliffs and Navajo Mountain as a background. For a goodly distance one looks up the trench of the Marble Canyon. From this or some near-by point Holmes made his sketch (Plate 19 of Dutton's Atlas).

As I tried to photograph the immensities of the view, I knew my efforts were doomed to failure and thought of Alter's title to one of his pictures: "Trying to coax chaos into my camera."

I was for staying until the sun went down, but Griffiths' caution prevailed, and at 6:45 we left and riding hard made the nine miles back to Camp Woolley by 8:05.

The forest had suffered severely this year from heavy wind occurring after the thaw when the ground was soft. The result was the uprooting of quantities of trees, large and small. It was a constant matter of surprise to see yellow pines, close to 100 feet tall, down with their roots torn loose, making big holes in the plateau surface. Other trees of considerable size had been broken off three to six feet from the ground.

We found George and Rust had located Jansen and arranged for a hunt in the morning, so all hands went to bed early.

Tuesday, July 4. The Frasers and Rust spent the morning on an unsuccessful hunt for mountain lions, guided by Aldus "Blondie" Jensen (Fraser spelled his name Jansen). He describes Jensen as "a fine physical specimen, age about 22, 6 feet 4 inches tall and well proportioned, weighing under 200 lbs. He has been successful enough in a business way to accumulate a good bunch of horses, a few cattle and an Oakland machine, which he has at the Ranger Station. He seems to be the pet of the girls in Fredonia and Kanab and is otherwise pretty well spoiled. We were conscious of condescension mingled with courteously concealed contempt in his intercourse with us." Jensen had begun guiding horseback parties out of the Woolley cabin the year before.[9] The dry weather made it impossible to track the lions, and the party returned to the Woolley cabin and prepared for their journey into the desert beyond the Kaibab Plateau.

Wednesday, July 5, 1916
Up 7:45 a.m. Light fleecy clouds. We finished up the last of the "mutton."

Packing was a laborious and difficult operation. It involved sorting more than three weeks' supplies, besides blacksmith's outfit, beds and personal belongings, and kept Rust hard at work until lunch time. 1:30 p.m. we left Camp Woolley and Griffiths, the latter evidently regretful that he could not go with us instead of ministering to the wants of parties of tourists from Kanab and Salt Lake who promised to come soon.

Our outfit consisted of three riding horses, three pack horses and a pack mule. Rust rode his old horse Bird. George had a white horse which Rust had intended I should ride if Jane and Myra [two of Fraser's daughters] had come. I rode a light chestnut with a flaxen mane called Flaxey, a thoroughly well broken cow and trail pony, with good speed, and some reputation as a race horse. It belongs to a man in Hurricane from whom Rust hired it for Jane's use. As packs we had for the third year Jake and the mule Jerry, and for the second year the old gray-back we had acquired from the sheep herder on the Henry Mtns. last summer when our Yellow Neck horse broke down. The fourth pack was a little mare not well broken and who never had carried a pack until she went

Pleasant Valley, north of DeMotte Park on the Kaibab Plateau, 1913.
Photograph by J. Cecil Alter.

down to the river to meet us. Except that she would not keep in line and
was in constant disagreement with Jake and the mule, she proved a
satisfactory pack animal.

From Camp Woolley to V.T. (i.e. De Motte or Big Park) Ranger Station, where we arrived at 6 p.m., we followed the automobile highway, a
really excellent road nearly all the way, entirely worked over by the Forest Service since we were last here and comparing favorably with any
other road in the country we had been over. It was comfortably cool
riding for the sun was obscured by clouds most of the time. Barring
dust from the much traveled road the ride was enjoyable.

The beauty of the parks grows on one. The different shades of green
in the trees at the fringe of the meadow—yellow pines, spruce, firs and
quaking aspen—and the graceful curves of the wooded hills and the
grassy slopes of the park combine in rare beauty.

We made our camp at the drift fence across the park 300 yards south
of the Grand Canyon Cattle Company's ranch house, which is on the
east side of the park near the middle and three-quarters of a mile from
the Ranger Station, which is built on the westerly fringe of forest. Between the station and the ranch house in the valley bottom is a spring or
shallow well lined with stone. After supper Beauchamp (pronounced
Beecham), the Georgia boy, nephew of Stephenson, General Manager of
the Cattle Co., came over to renew our acquaintance of two years ago.
Ranger Haycock also called and with dignity laid down the rules govern-

ing a tourist's use of federal forests, which he expressed himself as doubtful about Rust and ourselves knowing.

Just before dark a fine buck came within 100 yards of camp and inspected us leisurely.

Thursday, July 6, 1916
Up 6:30 a.m. George had a chase of a mile and a half after his horse. As we had no option but to stop at Kane Spring to-night, we took our time about starting. Left 10:30. For five miles we followed the road northerly through V.T. Park and beyond its northerly end and then turned east by north, keeping on the high portion of the plateau and avoiding its canyons. As we progressed easterly we found the hitherto horizontal limestone dipping toward the east and commenced our descent along the slopes of the East Kaibab monocline.

From 12:30 to 1:15, we rested without unpacking and ate some cheese and bread. Soon we left the region of the quaking aspen, spruce and yellow pines for a region of cedar and piñon, with little grass.

In the descent from the plateau we followed the trail used in driving cattle from the desert winter range to the Kaibab summer range and vice versa. After descending 1,400 feet from the summit of the plateau, the limestone approaches the horizontal, making a bench or shelf a mile or perhaps more wide. We had descended the most westerly of the two East Kaibab monoclines. This cedar and piñon covered bench is known as Little Mountain in contrast to the Kaibab or Big Mountain.

Up to the time we broke camp, it was hot, the sun shining unobscured, though light clouds gradually growing heavier had begun to gather. By noon it became overcast and we saw heavy rains and lightning to the north and northwest but few drops fell on us.

Leaving the relatively level summit of Little Mountain, we followed the surface dip of the second East Kaibab monocline over thin soil and much bare rock. The canyon to the north of us, deeply cut and draining east, disclosed in section the monocline with Kaibab limestone, crossbedded sandstone and the red supai shales in series from top to bottom. Here the trail was very rough. The limestone beds dip easterly to the margin of the desert, whose flat surface slopes gently also easterly.

At 4 p.m., after 15 miles' ride, we arrived at Kane Spring, down 3,050 feet from V.T. A strong southwest wind was blowing and rain threatened, so we laid our beds on the porch of the ranch house. This is the winter headquarters of the Cattle Co. Water is piped in from a spring up the canyon above referred to.

The change from the bracing coolness of the Kaibab to the oppressive heat of this place was trying. We were all tired, and in spite of ants and flies, glad to lie on the dirty porch floor.

From the ranch house we got a view that began to make us familiar with the Marble Canyon Platform. The canyon appears as a trench sunk in an apparently perfectly level plain. The platform is bounded as if by walls by the Vermilion Cliffs marking the southerly end of the Paria Plateau, higher and more majestic than they appear in the vicinity of Pipe Springs and Kanab, and the Echo Cliffs in the far distance. Behind the break between the two rises 50-Mile Mtn. and Navajo Mtn. In the center east of the canyon is a conspicuous butte (mapped as Shinumo Altar) rising solitary, the only eminence on the desert.

Friday, July 7, 1916

We planned to start early—in fact that was our expectation every morning. We had begun to learn though that packing was a laborious and lengthy operation. We had already found that Rust could not get much help from us. George managed to get the horses sometimes, where no special difficulty was involved. Where there was trouble or a long walk involved, Rust wrangled them.[10] Of course each man saddled his own horse, and George took charge of packing Jake, who carried our personal stuff. That left Rust with three horses to pack, which meant under the best conditions a full hour's work. So it became 8:30 before we left.

Our route lay across the desert substantially east by north, making an almost direct line for the south point of the Paria Plateau, where the Vermilion Cliffs appeared to be highest. Within a mile of Kane's were a few cattle which escaped the round-up when the herd was taken to the Kaibab. From that point until two miles west of Lower Pools we encountered no animal life, except for a few jack rabbits, some chipmunks and some lizards, yellowish with black spots, up to eight inches long. Heavy clouds were on the northerly horizon. The sun shone full and it was very hot in spite of a strong southwest wind.

At 11 a.m. we arrived at Lower Pools, an empty log cabin two miles south of Vermilion Cliffs, with water piped into cattle troughs, corrals, etc.

I stopped on the rise above the cabin to take a photograph. When I caught up with George and Rust I was surprised by the apparition of a man from behind the cabin. He was the picture of "Weary Willie" in the comic supplements. He had on a dirty cotton shirt, leaned on a long stick, and his face, overgrown with a two weeks' coarse black beard, was rugged and sunburnt. His left arm was gone at the shoulder.

My attention was distracted from this apparition by a herd of buffalo watering at the troughs. On the approach of our horses they started to leave the corral. I ran after them and snapped three chance shots as they made off southeasterly in leisurely fashion. A large bull stood facing me with head lowered, covering their retreat.

Rust rode out after the herd and counted 41 head, including calves. These are the buffalo brought out originally by Buffalo Jones on joint account with E. D. Woolley and the Grand Canyon Cattle Co. The purpose was to breed the bulls with the better breed of range cows. Such hybrids are called cattalo and their hides are nearly as good as buffalo robes. After Buffalo Jones left the country, his associates lost interest in this enterprise, especially as the result of this breeding was only to breed cattalo cows, not a single bull having been born.

We had lunch in the cabin, which afforded the only shade and which was reasonably cool in contrast to the intense heat outside. Our "Weary Willie" friend ate with us and gradually unfolded his experiences.

He is J. R. Bevard, of Marysvale, Utah, where he owns a little place. He was born near Paris, Ky., I should think about 40 years ago. I don't think he is a Mormon. Last winter his health was bad and he sought relief by finding a new location, finally landing in Flagstaff a few weeks ago. There he consulted a doctor and was told he has tuberculosis. On learning this fact, his wife deserted him. He invested what funds he had in a broken down buggy and a horse and started to drive over the desert from Flagstaff to Kanab via Lee's Ferry. He got along all right as far as Willow Springs. Ten miles past there a wagon track he had followed failed him, and he began to realize he was pointed wrong, but his horse had been so long without water and his canteen was so nearly empty that he thought it would be best to go on to the Marble Canyon, where he supposed he would get relief. Somehow he made the rim of the canyon and of course saw the impossibility of getting to water there. He drove northerly, parallel with the canyon, until his horse was so far gone he knew that further progress was impossible. He let it loose and so was hopelessly stranded, alone, west or a little northwest of Shinumo Altar. Somehow in the cool of evening he started to walk northerly 45 miles to Lee's Ferry. He claimed to have been without water 72 hours. The ferryman brought him safely across, fed him up and cared for him. After two day's more recuperation he started in the early morning to walk to

Kanab, about 95 miles across the desert. He had come about 18 miles yesterday and 12 miles this morning, wearing a pair of woolen trousers and a coat to match. The sole on his right foot was almost torn off and his toe was sticking out. His left foot was but little better.

We unfortunately had no extra shoes in the party. We gave him three pairs of socks and such food as he could carry—beef cubes, veal loaf, etc. I imagined he was broke and tendered him a loan. He declined at first, but finally accepted $10, taking my address and promising to send it to me as soon as he had gotten a job and earned a bit.[11] At 2:30 Bevard hit out, hoping to make House Rock Spring soon after dark. Then he planned to walk to Jacob's Lake in the hope of getting a job herding sheep or finding a conveyance to Fredonia.

At 3 p.m. we started to pack. There were heavy rains on the Echo Cliffs, the Paria Plateau and the Kaibab. A half mile to the north of us a cyclone raised a cloud of sand about 50 feet. Just as we got packed up at 4 p.m., a heavy rain and wind storm hit us. We stayed in the cabin spinning yarns until 5:15, when it blew over. Cloudy with a breeze so cool that I wished my sweater had been left out. We headed straight for the south point of Paria Plateau along the base of the cliffs, rounded that point and turned slightly east by north.

There was no dust and with such good going, we made fast time. But we had started too late to make camp by the only water between Pools and Lee's Ferry—Soap Creek—so at 7:15, when we found ourselves in fair grass, we made a dry camp about four miles west of Soap Creek. We had no fuel but sage brush and no water, but the feed was fairly good. Bed 10 p.m. Clear.

Saturday, July 8, 1916

Up 5 a.m. Clouds on the horizon obscured the sunrise. The horses started back for Pools with the first light and Rust had a two mile chase on foot to head them off. The atmosphere was dead. A mist hung over the Kaibab and light clouds lay back of the Vermilion Cliffs. Without shade of any kind, we were at the mercy of the blazing sun, especially trying in the early morning when one feels entitled to protection and there is work to do. We made our fire with matchweed and sage brush, about all that grows here, except grass and brigham tea. The weed when boiled like tea makes a beverage Brigham Young commended to his followers. I wondered whether the Mormon prohibition of tea and coffee was not originally for economic reasons. I remembered Mr. George A. Low telling me that tea which he imported from China sold at Salt Lake City at

$10 a pound in the early days. I can imagine Brigham Young's injunction was to keep in the community the money that might thus be spent.

At 9 a.m. we left camp, very uncomfortable for lack of washing and with but little water left to drink. We continued along the base of the cliff northeasterly and at two miles crossed the mouth of a canyon in the cliff, a regular rock garden with boulders weathered into curious shapes by wind and rain, some supported on shale pillars four feet high and even taller.

10 a.m. arrived Soap Creek, an alkali seep. Here the horses drank, but we feared to take much of the water. A mile below Soap Creek, George and I left Rust with the packs to continue on the road while we went out about two miles to the rim of Marble Canyon at the mouth of Soap Creek. It was intensely hot on the canyon rim, but I tried a few photographs while George sought relief on the brink under a ledge that threw a little shadow.

We rode hard northwesterly, picking up Rust about two miles beyond where we had left him. Rust produced a can of tomatoes and some bread, which we ate, sitting under our horses Indian fashion availing of their shadows for shade. There was no other.

12:20 p.m. started again, continuing under the cliffs. In the distance it rained, but the sun poured on us as it had all day. Our water was all gone and we suffered from thirst, which was aggravated by the dust. I did not take the temperature, but found my maximum thermometer had registered 108° in its case wrapped up in my coat.

We proceeded fast at a jog trot, and by 1:30 reached the narrows where the Echo and Vermilion Cliffs approach the river. Here we climbed over the spur or shoulder of the Chocolate Cliffs and got our first view of Lee's Ferry. The sculpture of the Chocolate Cliffs here is fine—tall buttes, monuments and columns.

The road came down close to river level 100 yards from the bank. We resisted the temptation to stop out of pity for the horses and so pressed on. Arrived Lee's Ferry ranch 2:30 p.m.

To-day's ride was trying, both because of the heat and lack of water. The sun was never obscured a moment. The maximum thermometer got up to 108° in the shade of the trees, but I suppose the sun got on it through the leaves.

After eating something at 4 p.m., we walked up river one mile to a deserted mining camp, where the Johnson boys, custodians of the ranch and ferry, had a boat. While George and I bathed, the Johnsons took out the boat, set off four charges of dynamite in the river at its deepest

Approaching Lees Ferry across the forbidding House Rock Desert of northern Arizona, July 8, 1916. Photograph by George C. Fraser.

point, and with a gaff pulled in all the fish that came to the surface in consequence of the explosion. They got about 25 fish—bony-tails characteristic of the Colorado River, the largest about 15 inches long, one small cat-fish, a number of large fish with a sort of hook nose and mouth like a sucker, a flat belly and a white silvery scaly back.[12] These large fish were very good eating. The bony-tails too were good, except for innumerable large bones.

The river carries much silt. It flows so rapidly that swimming against the current was out of the question. We had to content ourselves with staying well within our depth on a sand bar, avoiding the regular down current and back eddies, which were equally strong. In color it was to-day light yellowish brown. The walk up and back was very hot, and after the trying ride, tuckered me out pretty well.

The ranch lies 300 yards west of the Colorado along the bank of Paria Creek, from which its 40 acres now under cultivation are irrigated.

The ferry proper is about a mile and a half upstream from the ranch. At the ranch we found growing alfalfa, of which five crops are produced annually, corn with stalks up to 11 feet tall, cotton-woods this year attacked by some pest that is rapidly destroying their leaves, willows, mulberries, wild plum trees with fruit ripe, early apples, also apricots, their season over, peaches not yet ripe, melons just beginning to turn, pears not yet ripe and locusts. The boys keep two cows, five hogs, a dog and lots of chickens. There are many wild doves.

The ranch house is a two-story frame affair, with glass windows screened. This stands in the place of John D. Lee's original house. Near by is a log cabin built by Johnson after Lee left. In addition to these are a shed and a blacksmith shop, both of logs.

Lee's Ferry is full of romance. After the Mountain Meadow Massacre, in 1857, John D. Lee, having first hidden himself in Shinumo Canyon, established himself here and resided in peace for nearly 20 years.

During Lee's time Mormon emigrants into the country east of the Colorado used Lee's Ferry frequently, so after Lee's death the church delegated Johnson, father of the Johnson boys now at the ranch, to take charge of the ferry. For 22 years Johnson lived there, and then in the later 90's old Jim Emett came in possession of the ranch.

The Grand Canyon Cattle Co., soon after coming into the country, had trouble with Emett and charged him with stealing cattle. Emett defended himself successfully, but stories of one kind and another derogatory to him were in circulation. After Emett's acquittal on the cattle stealing charge, E. D. Woolley negotiated a sale of the ranch by Emett to the Cattle Co., coupled with the tacit understanding that Emett should leave the country. He accordingly moved north of Kanab and later to Beaver, where he now resides.

The Cattle Co. sold or gave the ferry to Coconino County, which now operates it through Jerry Johnson, who with his half-brother Frank (they are sons of the same father by contemporaneous wives) has charge of the ranch and works jointly for the Cattle Co. and the County. The gross revenues of the ferry amount to about $200 per annum. Johnson has discretion to pass free anybody he is satisfied is broke.

Emett got about $10,000 for the ranch and certain water rights he had acquired adjacent to the Cattle Co.'s range.

The Johnson boys are from 30 to 35 years of age. Frank was born here, but Jerry was born up north of Kanab. Frank's family lives at Short Creek. He has lately bought some unimproved land in the outskirts of Hurricane, which seems to be the goal of all enterprising Dixie people, and expects to move there. Jerry Johnson's family is at Hurricane. He bought a place there on borrowed money, which his wife and children are farming. They boys get $100 a month for tending ranch and ferry. They have been there five years now, part of the time with their families.

The mining camp is a relic of a promotion by a man named Spencer, who is now operating in Flagstaff. Spencer organized the American Placer Co. to reclaim gold from the Colorado River sands, and enlisted the backing of some Chicago people. He must have raised a great deal of money, both according to report and from what is still left at the mining camp. Besides shacks for workmen, there is a well-equipped blacksmith shop and assay laboratory. Sunk in the river is a good sized steamboat and on the bank are two expensive gasoline launches. He hauled in two heavy boilers, which it took 30 days and 50 teams of oxen to haul from Marysvale via Paria.[13]

Jerry Johnson worked for this outfit a long while and ended by being stuck $800, which they owed him. He showed us a pay-roll sheet for a week shortly before the outfit broke up, which contained accounts with workmen, all overdue, some amounting to over $1,000. Not satisfied with the wrong done Jerry Johnson, Spencer, who was employed by the county to operate the ferry, sublet his job to Jerry Johnson. Spencer went to live in Salt Lake, drew the pay for running the ferry, blew it in and never paid Johnson anything. That was bad enough, but in addition he left Johnson all winter at the ranch without sending supplies, as he promised, and without any means of getting out of the country. In spite of all this Jerry seemed to have no special hard feelings against Spencer and spoke as though he expected ultimately to be paid if Spencer made good on the irrigation project he is now promoting that contemplates utilizing one of the craters near Flagstaff as a reservoir, from which to irrigate some virgin soil.

Neither of the Johnson boys smokes or drinks alcohol, tea or coffee. They are scrupulously correct in their conversation and talk grammatically in spite of what must have been the deficiencies in their earlier education, in view of their bringing up in this remote place.

We had a fine supper, mostly fish, but I enjoyed best bread and milk, of which there was an unlimited supply.

The dining table was round and had a movable center on a pivot. All the food was placed on this turn table, so that any one could help himself without bothering his neighbor. The equipment of the ranch belongs to Z-Bar. They were a little short of ordinary plates, because, when the plates ran out a while ago, Mansfield, on consulting the Sears-Roebuck catalog, took a fancy to some perforated plates there listed and ordered a couple of dozen. He thought they were decorated, but they turned out to be pie-plates with holes in them.

After supper the Johnsons told stories. That such a remote place as this should have so many visitors of various kinds is peculiar.

Some years ago, early one morning, the Johnsons saw a boat with one man in it go down the river. They called to the man to stop, but he shot past on the current. They had received word that a fugitive from justice was wanted for murder in Wyoming and was suspected of having taken to the river. Nearly two months afterward a man appeared at the ranch, stating he had been wrecked in Marble Canyon. His clothes barely hung together and were patched up with rabbit and other skins. They recognized him as the person they had talked to, but the man denied it. They subsequently ascertained that this man brought the murderer down the river and dropped him just above the ferry, whence he made his way to Tuba. Fearing to be held as an accessory, the man had gone into the canyon and lived as long as he could on a liberal stock of food he had brought with him, and when that was gone, climbed out thinking to escape detection.

Bed 9:30 p.m. very tired, under the cottonwoods.

Sunday, July 9, 1916

Up 6:30 a.m. Flies very bad in the early morning. Damp and hot and very perspiry. A bath in the river before breakfast was refreshing.

We had been doubtful how to get into the Navajo country and determined, if possible, to avoid the 75-mile hot ride over the desert at the foot of the Echo Cliffs to Tuba. We had hoped by chance an Indian might turn up who could guide us over the plateau above the cliffs.

The Johnsons receive mail once every five weeks, when an Indian they hire at $6 for the trip rides in from Tuba. That Indian is due on the 11th and we may have to wait for him. Sometimes the Navajo sends his boy, sometimes he is a day late and sometimes a week late. If he does not start on the day of the week when he is due to leave, he waits until the corresponding day the following week, so there is a delightful uncertainty as to whether or not he will come. Rust felt we might get through over the plateau, but first wanted to prospect the land, so at 9:30 he rode up to the ferry with the Johnsons and George to climb the Echo Cliffs and take a look at the plateau.

I was glad of the rest and lay around all day, writing up notes, letter home and the rest of the time talking with the Johnsons. At 4:30 George and I bathed and washed our clothes in the Colorado. The result of such washing was to make them light yellowish brown.

By 5 o'clock the rain, which had been threatening all day, fell heavily on the Paria Plateau and along the Vermilion Cliffs. It was a gorgeous sight to see the desolate dry precipice glistening with water and waterfalls breaking over the brink. A few drops of rain fell on us, but not enough to wet the rain-gauge. Jerry Johnson, among his other duties, reports to the Water Bureau the rain-fall at Lee's Ferry. He is not kept very busy, because there rarely is any rain-fall.

At 5:30 we heard three shots and George and I, who had not returned from our bath at the mining camp, saw Rust across the river. I hastened back for Frank Johnson while George went to the ferry. Frank took my horse and met Rust while I enjoyed a cool breeze and drop in temperature.

Rust reported a heavy sandy trail up to the Echo Peaks with marvelous views from the summit and a broken rock country to the north and east which we would have to traverse. Everything dry and no rain up there. The prospects of getting through with no water and without a guide were poor, and promised great discomfort. We determined to wait until the Navajo arrived or we were certain rain had fallen along our route.

Monday, July 10, 1916

Up 4:45 a.m. Last night's rain had swollen the Paria, which was now hardly a stream of water but rather of gray mud. I bathed in the Colorado before breakfast.

At 9 a.m. we arrived at the mining camp and took a boat left by the great hunter Galloway on his last trip.[14] The boat leaked like a sieve and there were only two oars, which meant hard work pulling upstream as we intended to do. Rust took the oars and pulled us across the river without losing much distance. He handled the boat very skillfully. By keeping close in shore we were able to utilize back eddies to help us up stream and occasionally where the scrubby growth on the river was not too thick, it was possible to tow the boat short distances against the rapid current.

We rowed about three miles above the ferry into the mouth of Glen Canyon. A sheer vermilion sandstone wall rises on the right bank of the river. The left bank is of sand with the cliffs rising further back. It was intensely hot and there was no shade. We bathed before lunch, being careful to stay well within our depth and out of the fast current.

On the left bank of the river is a dug-way run by the mining outfit for use in their operations. I walked up this a mile, perhaps more, beyond where we brought the boat, say three miles above the ferry, and from

George Fraser Sr. and Jr. cooling off in the Colorado River three miles above Lees Ferry, July 10, 1916. Photograph by Dave Rust.

there could see around the first curve in the river in Glen Canyon. The river doubles on itself in a great ox-bow or horse-shoe and above this point the walls close in rising sheer as in the Little Zion. At the first bend in the canyon the bounding cliff is cut more than half way down by a dry hanging valley.

The walk through deep sand in the sun was distressing. Perspiration poured off me like water and my glasses were constantly befogged.

It took us about two hours to pull up the river and less than 20 minutes to float down with the current. It was an almost irresistible temptation to go on by the ranch into Marble Canyon, but that meant infinite labor in getting back and perhaps the loss of the boat.

At 3:30 we arrived at the mining camp. Clouding over. We took refuge from a dust storm in the blacksmith shop, where we left the horses while we were on the river. Soon it rained and hailed hard for about 10 minutes. To our surprise we found not a drop had fallen on the ranch a mile away. After another bath we rode back to the ranch, gathering plums and apples along the way. I took advantage of the evening light to climb the hill on the southerly side of Paria Creek and take some photographs. Bed 9 p.m.

Tuesday, July 11, 1916

Up 6:45 a.m. When I got to the river for a bath, I was astonished to find its color changed from the grayish brown comparable to cocoa with milk of yesterday to a deep red, almost vermilion. Jerry Johnson explained this as due to rains in the Chin Lee Valley. The river had risen a little and was carrying more debris than any day so far. The Paria also was swollen and more muddy than yesterday. Its gray chalky colored waters mixed slowly with those of the Colorado. It was a wilting morning, cloudless and without breeze.

At lunch the Johnsons expressed confidence that old Dan, the Navajo, would arrive at 4 o'clock, so Rust began to pack and we sat about listening for the bell. Having heard nothing up to 5 o'clock, we rode up to the mining camp again and took a swim, on the return climbing the up-slope of the Shinarump ledge above the ranch to John D. Lee's lookout. After we had given up hope on Dan's coming at 7 o'clock the bell rang and by 8 Jerry had him at the ranch.

I was eager for a newspaper. The only one that came was the *Great Divide*, a Colorado weekly or bi-weekly publication, which scrupulously avoided anything in the way of news. It was made up of Sunday Supplement stuff and this issue gave most of its space to a discussion of the problem as to why dancers made better marriages than show girls.

The Johnsons speak a few words of Navajo. In spite of their years of residence here, they know nothing of the country across the river, except the main road to Tuba and Flagstaff. They interrogated Dan and explained to us that he could guide us over the plateau to a store about two days' journey. From the maps we assumed we wanted to go to Kai Peto Spring, but Dan did not recognize the name, so we entered into elaborate negotiations with Dan, who had every excuse for not taking us. It meant for him an extra two days' ride, probably 50 miles out of the way.

Dan brought with him some saddle blankets, which he wished to sell, and as part of the trade we bought for Rust a saddle blanket priced at $3.50 and retained Dan's services as guide for a total of $10. He demurred at closing though because he said we did not have the money, so I showed him a $10 gold certificate. He looked at both sides of it, held it up to the light and then said "check; no good." The Johnsons persuaded him, however, that it was all right and he agreed to take us. He compared the distance we had to go to the store, which he said was near Navajo Creek, to the distance we had come from Kane's Spring to Lee's Ferry.

Jerry Johnson seemed disturbed by the advent of the mail and retired soon after dinner to write. It developed he received a letter from the supervisors saying that Spencer had presented a bill for $200, claiming equipment of that value had been removed from the mining camp and utilized in the ferry, all without authority from him. This last annoyance seemed to irritate Jerry more than the loss of his $800 and the appropriation of his wages as ferry-man, and he sympathized with Dan, who had been done to the extent of $10 by Spencer, due for carrying mail. Dan's idea of a remedy was to tie a weight around Spencer's neck and drop him in the river. A man, who worked as superintendent for Spencer in his mining operations at $200 a month and was never paid, is now herding sheep on the Paria Plateau and carrying a gun in anticipation of meeting Spencer. I think Johnson would like to have that man as a guest in case Spencer shows up.

The Johnsons worked until 2 a.m. on their correspondence. We went to bed at 10:15, hot and bothered with mosquitoes.

Wednesday, July 12, 1916

Up 4:15 a.m. We intended to get started at 3:15, but the alarm in my watch did not wake me. In spite of working late, the Johnson boys were up and had breakfast ready, so we were able to leave at 6:30 and to quickly cross the ferry.

The ferry boat is a double-ended scow running on a pulley attached to a wire stretched across the river. By means of a slack wire below, the boat can be pulled where the current does not aid it.

We paid the Johnsons the prescribed ferry tolls and at the rate fixed by the Z-Bar people for the horses' feed, aggregating $16. They refused to let us pay for our entertainment, but Rust added $4 and made it an even $20. They entertained us hospitably and courteously. No one has done more for us.

At 7:45 we left the ferry and followed the old dug-way up stream one-quarter of a mile and then climbed a steep sand slope leading to the Echo Peaks. We had hoped to get away early enough to make this climb in the shade. The sand was fine and deep, making very hard pulling for the horses, and after we came into the sun at 8 o'clock it was a hot trying ride. By 8:45 we had reached the top of the sand beneath a saddle in the Echo Peaks. From here we had a magnificent view around the first bend and up the second stretch of Glen Canyon with Navajo Mtn. and 50 Mile Mtn. as a background. The bends of Glen Canyon follow generally the line of vertical joints.

George Fraser *(notebook in hand)* and Old Dan, his party's Navajo guide, in the Echo Peaks above Lees Ferry, July 12, 1916.

At the foot of a cliff before us on the way up I observed a conical hill of talus. I had seen the same on the Shinarump Bench under the Vermilion Cliffs. John D. Lee's look-out on the brink of the Shinarump shelf over Lee's Ferry ranch was such a hill, but it was a quarter of a mile or more from the foot of the Vermilion Cliffs. I was puzzled by these occurrences, but the hill before us made plain their origin. Above this hill a dry wash terminated at the brink of the cliff. When it rains, that wash carries boulders, pebbles and sand from the plateau above over the face of the cliff and so builds up the equivalent of a delta or river fan. The hill at Lee's look-out was formed in the same way before the cliffs had receded through sapping by erosion of the soft shales lying between the conglomerate ledge and the Vermilion Cliff.

Beyond the saddle we descended 200 feet, then up and down again over the bare sandstone, here dipping steeply as at Lee's Ferry. The cross-bedding as we ascended becomes more marked. We had fine views of a broken red sandstone country bounded northerly by 50 Mile Mtn. Trail rough and rocky. We descended into a sandstone canyon, the summits weathering into beehives and out of the canyon into a maze of sandstone domes and ridges forming the summit of the plateau.

At 10:45 Dan left the trail and crawled into a crack in the rock and called us. There we found a water-hole in a miniature Little Zion

George Fraser Jr. *(above pool)*, Old Dan *(leaning against rock)*, and Dave Rust *(standing)* at a hidden waterhole on the Kaibito Plateau, en route to Richardson's trading post at "Kai Peto" (Kaibito) Spring, July 12, 1916. Photograph by George C. Fraser.

Canyon. Dan assured us we would find no more water until after one sleep, so we unpacked and got out lunch. A light breeze was blowing, the sun was somewhat obscured by clouds and we felt cool in comparison to Lee's Ferry. This water-hole was most extraordinary. It was in the bottom of a cave or tunnel in the cross-bedded sandstone open at each end and roofed over. The water accumulating in the pot-hole is protected from evaporation by the shade of the roof, and probably nearly all seasons water is to be had here. Without Dan we would have passed this place by and suffered great privation, unless, of course, we had been favored by rain.

After lunch we ascended the highest of the neighboring pinnacles and enjoyed an extended view including Navajo Mtn. and 50 Mile Mtn. We continued easterly over the plateau toward a low ridge of white cross-bedded sandstone, which we ascended. We ran parallel with the line of the White Cliffs northerly from us, making good time over fine light brownish sand. At 4 p.m. we encountered an exposure of bedrock with basins containing rain water, which we and the horses drank. By this time clouds had gathered and there were heavy storms to the east and south. For five minutes it rained sharply and grew so cold we were glad to put on our coats.

At 6:30 p.m. we made a dry camp under and south of the White Cliffs, here capped with red, perhaps marking the summit of the cross-bedded sandstone as it does in the Virgin temples. The details of weathering of this white ridge are similar to Dutton's illustration "Midsummer night dream of the Kolob."[15] At the camp we have cedars and tall sheep grass, the latter growing in circles from 1½ feet to 5 feet in diameter. Up 2,600 feet from Lee's Ferry. Night overcast and damp.

Thursday, July 13, 1916

Up 4:45 a.m. Clear, much dew and cold. Left 7:15. Light clouds. We continued easterly parallel with the white sandstone ridge. At 8 a.m. Dan stopped us at some water-holes or rock basins. One of them was four feet deep and two feet in diameter. Dan stopped me from drinking there, saying that it had been polluted by the coyotes, whose cries had bothered us in the morning. We got plenty of good water out of shallow basins.

Dan showed me what he claimed were antelope tracks. We saw cotton-tails, jack rabbits, lizards and hawks.

At 12 M. made lunch camp among white cross-bedded sandstone

beehives with a water-hole in a valley between two of them. Nowhere have I seen the cross-bedding so accentuated as here. The weathering of the rock brings the planes of cross-bedding in relief as much as 12 inches. From the summits of these beehives we got a fine view over a broken canyon country with red towers to the Henry, Navajo and 50-Mile Mtns.

Dan consented to be photographed at the water-hole, but demanded 50 cents for any further poses. He is not sufficiently picturesque for the price.

Near the lunch camp we encountered some cattle and two Navajo ponies. Dan tried to catch the latter, because his own was pretty well played out, but failed. Around 3 o'clock we passed a deserted Navajo hogan and sheep corral, the first sign of human habitation we had seen since Lee's Ferry.

At 4:30 a Navajo joined us. His apparition was sudden as though he had sprung out of the ground. He was equipped with a saddle of native workmanship, but wore no hat. Instead he had a handkerchief around his head and wore over-alls and a shirt with its tail out. We found he was rounding up some horses inside a drift fence made of twisted cedar limbs.

At 5 p.m. a mile north of us in the white cliff we saw a natural bridge. Leaving Dan, who resented the waste of time, we rode over there. The bridge occurs in a spur of the cliff jutting westward, at the point of contact of a hard band of red sandstone with the underlying soft or friable white cross-bedded sandstone. The spur forms a divide between two canyons. In the most southerly of those canyons are water pockets, and there we found two Navajo children, with two burros and water flasks getting drinking water, for near-by hogans.

Retaking the trail we continued easterly over reddish shale, here overlying the white cross-bedded sandstone, and over red sand to a ridge forming the margin of the plateau, from which we had a fine view of White Mesa with its outlier "Square Rock" due east of us. Dan assured us the store lay at the bottom of this valley. It was quite concealed, and we could see no sign of life. We rode directly east down a gentle slope of drifting dune sand with little vegetation at the bottom, and on crossing a bench, found Richardson's store in the valley bottom under a cliff of pinkish to white sandstone to the eastward.

Arrived 6:30 p.m., and ascertained we were at Kai Peto [Kaibito] Spring. We made camp under the west wall of the house and received a hearty welcome from Ray Talley, Richardson's clerk in charge of the store, and a boy Jim, about 16, Richardson's brother-in-law, who is spending the summer here and beginning to learn the business.

The store is constructed of rock quarried out of the adjacent cliff and consists of a store-room about 20 x 20 feet, with a storage shed about 30 x 35 feet off to one side, and in the back two sleeping-rooms, a dining room and a small kitchen. Close to the store is an empty building erected by the Agriculture Department. One of their men spent a little while here trying to teach the Indians to dry farm in the sand. He soon became discouraged and resigned and the place is now deserted.

Back of the store is a canyon draining westerly out of the cliff and about 400 yards up this canyon the water seeps out above the red shale, which overlies the cross-bedded sandstone. Richardson has boxed up the spring and fastened it securely with a large pad-lock. A small amount of water drains into the creek bottom and forms a very soft sand or quick-sand. Here I found a yearling steer embedded up to his neck and two Navajos trying to extricate him. One of them had a rope around the steer's neck and in trying to pull him out choked him. Each time the rope caught on the horn of the saddle and the horse pulled, the steer's head would be pulled under the mud and he would be nearly suffocated. I induced the other Navajo to rope the steer around the horns, then both pulled, but without effect, because the steer was anchored firm.

After trying to direct operations for a while, I went to the store and told Talley of the trouble. He said it was a nightly occurrence and started out with a rope to help. By the time we had got there the Navajo tried a new tack. One of them had taken off his trousers, rolled up his shirt and was out in the quick-sand treading it close to the steer, which loosened the mud so that the steer by frantic efforts was able to extricate himself. I was standing at the edge of the quick-sand and as soon as the steer got free, he made for me head down. I dodged and ran, but he followed me up, the Navajo hanging on to the rope and running behind. Finally the steer started up the trail, the Navajo after him, and when they reached a cedar tree, the Navajo deftly got a hitch around it and threw the steer and tied him.

This is the most remote trading post in the Navajo country. It is about 135 miles from the nearest railway at Winslow. Richardson established it about a year ago and lives here with his wife and daughter. He has a machine and makes the run from Winslow, via Blue Canyon and Red Lake, in one day. It was unfortunate that Richardson was away, because his boys could give us no information about the country and they could not talk with the Indians. An Indian boy, John, who looked after their stock, was able to interpret a little.

The boys entertained us sumptuously at supper and invited us to sleep in the house, but as it was pretty hot, we preferred to sleep out-doors.

After supper half a dozen Indians congregated in the store smoking Bull Durham, which is provided free. The store is arranged with an open square place in the center and high wide counters all around, except at one point, where there is a door with a spring lock, which cannot be reached outside.

We paid Dan as agreed with the $10 bill. He at once showed it to Talley and asked him whether it was good. When Talley offered him 10 silver dollars, he decided to keep the note, and pretty soon began to make purchases.

One Navajo, 40 or 50 years of age, indicated he might be induced to guide us to Navajo Mountain and the Arch. He was a hard looking surly Indian. We did not press the negotiation, but arranged to talk to him further to-morrow.

Bed 9:40 p.m. The horses had poor feed and did not like the water, and about 10 o'clock we heard them hitting out for the west. Rust got up and returned with them at 11 o'clock and tied them up for the night. At 3 a.m. it rained a little, but we kept dry under our tarpaulin.

Friday, July 14, 1916

Up 6:30 a.m. A gentle rain for about an hour. Breakfast in the store. Afterward our prospective Indian guide turned up with a cow for sale. He had a loan of $127 against the pawn of a neck-lace and applied the proceeds of the cow, less a little spent for flour, on account of the loan. He asked for $3 a day for his services or $10 for the trip to Navajo Mtn. and the Arch and back to the Mtn., which he said would consume six days. He did not speak a word of English, and was so surly, not to say villainous looking, that we determined to go on without him in the hope of picking up a Paiute along the trail, those Indians being more likely to speak English than the Navajo.

Dan bought some dress goods and a pair of child's over-alls. In the pocket of the latter he stuffed some tobacco. He encourages the use of Bull among his young progeny, but abstains himself.

Bought a Mexican silver, with opal, bracelet, $1.50, and Navajo silver turquoise ring, $3.50.

Richardson does considerable business in pawns, lending as high as

$125, perhaps a little more, on first class turquoise necklaces. He has between $1,500 and $2,000 loaned out in this way. The pawns are redeemable in six months without interest. Talley says they are very rarely unredeemed, except where articles of trivial value have been pledged. The profits on this business are indirect. A good part of the money borrowed is at once spent at the store, and when the pledge is redeemed, cattle, sheep, piñon nuts, blankets, pelts or the like are brought in for sale and the proceeds applied in payment. The Indian regulations prohibit trading with the Indians in kind. Everything must be done on a cash basis.

The Navajo (we found the same custom among the Paiutes) wear a leather wristlet with silver mounting called a kato on the left wrist. One of these priced at $4.50 was for sale in the store and in the design carried two arrows. George explained this as probably a survival of the days when bows and arrows were used, the kato serving as a protector against the bow-string. We ascertained this to be the fact later from Hyde, at Bluff. The only present use of the kato seems to be to scratch matches on.

The store was well stocked with blankets, which are bought at from 80 cents to $1.00 a pound, depending on quality.

Early in the morning a very old and decrepit man appeared. He spends every day at the store, never buying anything, but smoking the free Bull and sitting curled up in a heap under the counter or in the shade of the house. A hunch-backed Paiute on a donkey also came in, bought some tobacco and sold a goat skin. A young woman, about 16, bride of a week, came in for supplies, and later two older women, one of them with finely molded aristocratic features, came in for supplies.[16] They wore a cheap kind of imitation velvet waist of dark bluish or purple color. Some of the men wore home-made blouses or shirts of the same material. In every instance these appeared to be ripped beneath the arm-hole. Actually they are finished with an opening there for purposes of comfort and ventilation. The women wore skirts a little below the knee and had their legs swathed in heavy cotton material, giving the effect of clumsy trousers.

At 10 o'clock it was clear with light clouds and a cool breeze blowing from the southwest. By noon heavy black clouds had gathered in the distance and it thundered and lightened. A strong wind blew from the north. Between 12 and 1 we packed and then had lunch with the boys. At 2 o'clock the wind veered to the west, blowing hard, and at 2:10 it began to rain, not lightly, but in torrents. The cloud-burst lasted for 30 minutes. The dry sand wash close to the store became a raging torrent in a moment. We had seen no running water since leaving the Colorado River. Streams of mud poured from the rock ledge back of the store, rocks fell over the cliff and sand and gravel poured down like water-falls. The packs were out in the rain while we weathered the storm in-doors. The warehouse became flooded with 12 to 18 inches of water seeping in under the stone walls and over the door-sills. We helped the boys get the perishable stuff off the floor, but considerable sugar, flour etc. was damaged in spite of strenuous efforts. The rain stopped just as suddenly as it had begun. We found the main canyon at its intersection with the small wash running with mud three, perhaps four feet deep, absolutely impassable by horse or man. The flood subsided in less than 10 minutes to such proportions as would permit crossing but for the danger of quicksand, and then equally quickly rose higher than before, the storm in the meanwhile having circled about and expended its force on the White Mesa where the canyon heads. This storm was an enlightenment. The amount of detritus transported and the erosive effect on the cliff, canyon bottoms and slopes was astounding.

We bought $3 worth of provisions, but were not allowed to pay for our entertainment.

Talley had been a few miles north of the store, but could give us no advice about the trail, and we had been unable to glean anything definite from the Indians.

The trail ran at the base of the cliff to the east of the store, following some and crossing other washes. In view of the flood, we decided to avoid this, so leaving at 3:30 p.m., we scaled the cliff at the first available point and made northerly without a trail in the general direction of Navajo Mountain. The sky was overcast in the afternoon. Cool.

Two and a half miles from the store we encountered the main trail with wagon tracks, but we followed it only a little way, as it turned easterly, apparently around the northerly end of White Mesa. Here we encountered a strong horse trail running north. Between five and six miles from the store we encountered a 200-foot deep box canyon in the crossbedded white sandstone draining westerly. We were compelled to follow the rim about ¾ of a mile easterly before we could cross.

Our horse trail petered out, so we continued easterly without trail heading another canyon and getting fine views from every rise and divide, especially of White Mesa and Square Rock.

White Mesa has a red summit, the run from which has discolored the white precipitous cliffs below. Near the bottom are other red-beds. Its face is broken into pinnacles and towers exceedingly picturesque and similar to the structure at Acoma.

The further we got from the store, the drier it got. At seven miles we found little sign of recent rain. Scaling a rock ridge running approximately east-west, we had a fine view to the north and northeast, including Navajo Mtn. and the rough broken country in the breaks of Navajo Creek. Descending this into a valley, we struck what is evidently the main trail in this section deeply worn with an old wagon track. We followed this north across the westerly draining valley, and at 6:30 found a white cross-bedded sandstone outcrop with basins, in which we were disappointed to find no water. So we continued up the northerly gentle slope of the valley to the top of the divide. Arrived 7:30 at more white sandstone outcrops and here we found very little water in small pockets. Made dry camp here in the sand close to the rocks. The sky was overcast and a strong southwest wind was blowing.

Rust tied Bird to a sage-brush about 100 yards from camp, leaving him there while he unpacked. Darkness was rapidly falling, and as it looked so threatening, George and I hastened to make our bed and protect the stuff with covering. Then while Rust was taking the horses out to where there was fair feed, we built a fire and boiled some water. As darkness fell, the wind increased in intensity until we experienced a genuine sand-storm, blinding and cutting and filling everything with drifting sand. We made out for supper with beef cubes and crackers hard to eat on account of the sand.

While thus engaged Rust came up leading Bird and showed me two holes in Bird's upper lip beneath the left nostril. I supposed the horse had stuck his nose in a cactus, but Rust said it was a rattle-snake bite. We immediately proceeded to treat it with the Forester rattle-snake antidote. Rust made a tourniquet out of the flour sack which he wound as tight as possible around Bird's head between the nose and eyes. I then took the lancet in the kit and punctured each wound five times until it bled quite profusely. Then Rust took the permanganate of potash and after moistening it, rubbed it into the wounds with the palm of his hand. Bird looked pretty bad and his nose swelled rapidly. We tied him to a cedar tree close by and kept watching him.

While this operation was going on I heard a voice and soon there appeared a Navajo boy about 18 mounted on a brood mare with a young colt. He dismounted, inspected the horse and by graphic signs explained that he had been struck by a rattle-snake and would soon fall down and die. Rust's melancholy, sufficient before, became intense. He reminisced about the horse's good qualities, the fondness of every member of the family for it and had Bird dead and buried in imagination.

The wind-storm, which subsided about 9 o'clock, cleared the sky and so we were able to observe a partial eclipse of the moon, which began about the time the sand storm occurred. The Navajo was greatly interested in this phenomenon. At first the northwest corner of the moon was obscured, then the entire northern and part of its southern hemisphere, leaving only a brilliant crescent at the extreme south, and gradually the earth's shadow passed off at the northeast segment. The moon was full to-night.

Having little else to enjoy Rust and I made the best of a cigar apiece. I had brought 50 good cigars and we made it a point to smoke one each night after supper. The Navajo apparently had never seen a cigar before. He watched us smoke with intense interest. Of course we had given him a bag of Bull, with which he was making good progress. When Rust's cigar had been pretty well smoked down, the Navajo snatched it out of his hand and stuck it in his mouth. He smoked with expressions of delight, inhaling every puff, and stuck to the butt so long I feared he would swallow it. It could not have been a quarter of an inch long when he finally dropped it in the fire.

Not knowing but other Indians might be in the vicinity, who mischievously or with ill design would be tempted to drive off our horses, we promised the Navajo boy 50 cents if he would stay over night and wrangle the horses in the morning, which he accepted.

Bird's heart kept strong, but he looked very miserable and his nose was swollen tremendously. Bed 11:15 p.m.

Saturday, July 15, 1916

Up 6 a.m. We found ourselves due south of Navajo Mtn. We had to wake the Indian, who speedily brought in the horses. While at breakfast another Indian boy turned up. Both ate and smoked. The feed here has been poor and the horses look pretty tired. A light breeze was blowing. It was cool and there were fleecy clouds in a clear sky. Left 9 a.m.

In looking for water last night we had left the trail and now failed to find it, so we rode north by west over whitish sand, the weathering of the cross-bedded sandstone cliffs. At 9:45 we struck the main trail and soon encountered two Navajo, who indicated our route. They had a herd of sheep and goats, who had eaten down the grass.

At 10 we saw an occupied hogan. In it were two women, a papoose tied to a board hanging from the side of the hogan, five children, two kids, a cat and a dog. In front of the hogan was a weaving frame with a partially made blanket. On the floor were goat and sheep skins, blankets and a couple of large jars of wicker work apparently plastered over with gum from spruce trees. In these utensils the Navajo keep their water for drinking and culinary purposes. We gave each woman a quarter for the privilege of photographing her.

Two other children of these women were herding goats near by. The women showed us a water-hole in a shallow canyon, where we were able to water the horses, but the water was too bad to drink.

From here we proceeded westerly and a little north parallel with Navajo Creek. We had been descending gradually from the divide between Navajo Creek drainage and that next to the south. Soon we passed another hogan on a ridge half a mile from the trail. Two Navajo came out to shake hands and get some tobacco. We could get nothing intelligible out of them.

At noon we turned northerly to the rim of Navajo Canyon and got a magnificent view over a bare broken country toward the head of the Navajo Creek drainage. Below us from the rim to the west we saw the canyon bottom and on a sand bench a small corn patch. At 1:15 we reached the canyon bottom, which we followed down stream west a quarter of a mile to the farm. Here I climbed a 40-foot sand bank to the terrace we had seen from above and walked through the corn patch hardly over an acre in extent. There was alfalfa, also some peach trees and cotton-woods. We made lunch camp under the cotton-woods.

Navajo Creek is a surprisingly miserable little stream from 5 feet to 12 feet wide and nowhere over 6 inches deep, with a treacherous bottom. Drift-wood, and markings on the sand indicated a recent flood level of quite 6 feet above the present level of the stream.

It was terribly hot in the bottom of the canyon, for we were shut off from all breeze. There was no feed for the horses and flies and ants were troublesome, but the water was very good.

While we were eating two boys, aged 12 and 8, appeared. They approached silently so we were not conscious of their presence until they stood about 10 feet away from us. The smaller boy was beautiful, perfectly formed and with finely molded features and delicate skin. The small boy wore a shirt with broad pink and lilac stripes running ver-

George Fraser changing camera plates at lunch camp in
Navajo Canyon, July 15, 1916.

tically and a sort of pajama effect by way of trousers split up the side to the knee. Neither boy had on shoes. They were timid and kept out of reach. On inquiry by signs about feed for the horses, they both ran away and soon returned with armfuls of alfalfa. We made them repeat their mission and gave them five cents apiece for their work.

At 4:30 p.m. we left the lunch place and continued down the creek bottom a little over a mile. We turned right (northerly) up a side canyon. Here we found another spring of good water. We followed this canyon generally northerly, but twisting a good deal, riding in the bottom over sand and bare brown cross-bedded sandstone rock.

At 7 Rust found some promise of some feed on a bench to the east of the canyon. Having watered the horses at pot-holes below, we made dry camp in the canyon bottom beneath a picturesque dome to the south of us. We found some drift wood and cedars, from which to make a fire on the rocks and sleep comfortably in the sand of the canyon bottom.

Clouds obscured the moon, but during the short intervals when it was unobscured the dome above us was beautifully illuminated.

Sunday, July 16, 1916
Up 6 a.m. No breeze. Some of the horses wandered a mile and a half up the canyon and others went down, making trouble to catch them. We found a little water in a pocket and got a kind of a wash.

Left 9 a.m. For nearly three hours we continued up the same canyon, mostly in its bottom, but occasionally climbing a bench on one side or the other to avoid falls.[17]

The rock scenery became more picturesque as we progressed toward the canyon head. We climbed a bench or mesa and here got an open view, finding ourselves directly between Navajo Mtn. on the north and White Mesa on the south. The trail traversed this bench, ascending gently until we turned right and ascended a very steep trail over bare rock with steps cut in places leading to the plateau at the base of Navajo Mtn. From 12 to 12:45 we climbed very steeply, walking most of the time.

12:45 arrived at the summit of the plateau leading by a gentle slope to the base of Navajo Mtn. Very hot, good grass, sage, cedar and piñon. About half way between us and the base of the mountain I saw a column of smoke rising straight in the still atmosphere between two bare sandstone hills about a mile apart. We followed the trail north over the plateau, making straight for the smoke. A quarter of a mile from the house we encountered a woman with a 12-year-old boy. She was shy, but consented to sell us a canteen full of water out of a water jar. The water tasted of resin, with which the jar was lined. She showed us where a spring is, about three miles to the northwest at the base of the mountain.

After lunch we climbed the dome 90 feet high and took panoramas west, north and east, including Navajo Mtn. As there was good grass here, and we knew we could get water at the spring and the mountain held all sorts of uncertainties, we concluded to make camp here and defer our ascent of the mountain until to-morrow. So at 5 p.m., leaving our packs, we rode northwest over the plateau to the foot of the precipitous cliffs at the southwest base of Navajo Mtn. to the spring. The water-seep is at the contact of yellow sandstone overlying a red shaly sandstone. The flow is small, but the water fine.

The effect of the rattle-snake bite on Bird was to swell his nose and face so that he had the appearance of a rhinoceros. His upper lip projected so far beyond the lower that he could not get any suction to drink as a horse ordinarily does, and had to lap up what little water he could get with his tongue. The swelling was beginning to go down, and at the spring he got a fairly good drink, though it took him 15 minutes. Rust kept a very light pack on him since the bite and now that he was beginning to eat and drink a little, he looked better.

At the spring we filled our two kegs and three canteens and got a good wash. On the way to the spring I rode ahead alone and though I could not make out where the spring was, the calls of birds led me to it.

Arrived camp at dark. When unpacking the food for supper, Rust found a scorpion in the luggage. Bed 10 p.m.

Monday, July 17, 1916

Up 5 a.m. Cool and dry, no flies or mosquitoes, fleecy clouds and no wind.

Left camp 8:15 a.m. and went east on the plateau, rising gently. All is sand with a sparse growth of cedar and piñon, grass and sage. Near the southeasterly base of the mountain we struck a faint trail leading up a canyon coming down from the south face of the mountain. We followed the bottom of this canyon over boulders growing larger as we neared the mountain. We ascended rapidly. To the east of us the steeply tilted sandstone beds are broken into picturesque yellow-brown to reddish pinnacles. At 10:45 a.m. we reached a bench marking the summit of the steep cliffs at the south base of the mountain. The bench is narrow and soon again we ascended steeply. At 11:05 we reached a second bench of sandy soil supporting large yellow pines. At 11:30 we encountered two Paiutes, each riding a mare with colt. The formality of shaking hands and giving Bull having been observed, we entered into negotiations with the older of the two, called John, for guidance to the top of the mountain, to Rainbow Arch and back, and in an incredibly short time reached an agreement at $1 a day. The young boy wore a kato, which after some bargaining I purchased for $4.50.

John speedily got another horse, changed his saddle and then led us further up the mountain and in 40 minutes, at 12:30 p.m., brought us to a spring.[18] On the way, we ran into the quaking aspen and I observed sego lilies and balsam.

John's companion soon joined us. We all had lunch.

John is probably 22 and his companion about 18. John wore two cotton shirts and a pair of blue over-alls and over them a ragged pair of corduroy trousers, cut to fit a man six inches taller than he, so that they were wrinkled like an accordion around the ankles and the crotch came a little above the knee. He had to pull up his trousers every time he wanted to take a long step. He wore a felt hat with a horsehair braided band. Both he and his companion were Paiutes, much darker in color than the Navajo.

While we lunched, it rained a little. The spring is at the foot of a boulder slide in the black humus of a bench sparsely covered with quaking aspen. The water is cold and fine. Visitors have used the quaking aspen as a register. We found Kolb Bros.' autograph dated August, 1913 and troop H, 5th U.S. Cavalry, dated 1908, among others.

The trail up to the spring had been reasonably good.[19] Leaving our belongings and pack animals, we took the saddle horses and at 2:45 started for the top of the mountain. John led the way up a boulder slide east of the spring. This seemed too rough for the horses and we demanded that he find another way, so we rode back to camp, and at 3 o'clock started westerly, first climbing gently, then very steeply over boulders, down timber and through dense growth of quaking aspen and pines. At 3:30 p.m. we encountered a narrow bench. From here we climbed still more steeply to the top of a second bench. Still more steep climbing brought us to the summit, which is relatively level, and at 4:30 p.m. we reached the extreme northwest tip of the mountain.

The view to the north is grand and extended. To the north by west of us is the whole Henry Mtn. group visible in profile. Climbing about 500 yards over large angular boulders down from the northwest point, John showed us to the west by north the Rainbow Arch, which spans its canyon at right angles to our line of vision. The view directly west was obscured by the lowering sun.

At 5:45 we left the northwest point and rode over the summit half a mile to the north point of the mountain. From here we got a better view north and east. The foreground tributary to the Colorado River on both sides is chaos—a maze of red, brown, black and white cliffs and buttes cut by deep canyons. We saw the San Juan River in its narrow canyon, Escalante Canyon, the water pocket fold, the Aquarius, Table Cliff, Brian Head, the south end of the Paunsaugunt, Henry Mtns., the Orange Cliffs, Elk Ridge, the Blue Mtns., Monument Valley and the Carrizo Mountains. Shadows cast by the setting sun and light clouds shading portions of the landscape brought out the color and contour.

We were unusually fortunate in having such a clear atmosphere. Had we brought a blanket apiece and a little food, we would have spent the night there to witness the sunset and the sunrise. As it was we lingered too long. We left at 6:30 and rode over the plateau to the south break and down by another route leading us east of the spring. John selected a place where there was no trail and our way lay mostly over big boulders overgrown with brush and trees. Going was bad enough for a man—we all walked—but especially hard on the horses. Jake, whom Rust was riding, nearly broke a leg.

A curious feature on the descent was our observation of the shadow of the mountain ever lengthening as cast upon the plateau.

Arrived camp 8 p.m., down 1,125 feet from the summit. Altitude of camp, therefore about 9,300 (Navajo Mtn. is mapped at 10,416).

Tuesday, July 18, 1916

Up 4:45 a.m. Cold, wind, cloudless. A poor night on account of mosquitoes and flies. John's horse got away with the other horses he had been running with. Four of our horses got loose and caused Rust 1½ hours' chase.

Left 9:45, keeping on the trail we had taken yesterday. Near the mountain base we turned east on a mesa and at 11:30 we reached the sandy plateau. We then rounded the southeasterly corner of the mountain, and at 12 M. made lunch camp under cedars at the foot of a cliff. In the cliff is a shallow rock shelter 7 or 8 feet deep and 10 to 12 feet high, with picture writings made by daubing red sand on the white face of the rock.

There was no grass in the canyon bottom, so Rust turned out the horses on the plateau at the summit of the cliff. They got lost and so did John's horses. It was intensely hot and Rust had to walk two miles before he found the horses. John also was gone a long time and returned very sulky. John said he would go to Bluff and see lots of Paiutes and eat peaches and not accompany us to the Rainbow Arch. He had told us of a ruined house near the spring and with difficulty we persuaded him to take George and myself there while Rust recuperated in the shade from the hot walk for the horses and back.

This house stood on a ridge and shows evidence of the land about having been terraced. The house proper seemed to have been rectangular, 100 feet by 126 feet, but as the outer walls were all down, it was difficult to trace their lines. We saw one sculptured stone, the zigzagging lines, according to John, indicating snakes. John's story was that the Navajo attacking the Moqui, who lived here, put them to death and destroyed their belongings. I found four broken grain grinders, quantities of broken pottery and flint pebbles, but nothing complete. The sun was intensely hot.

Left 4:20, riding hard, arrived spring 4:40. Rust was nearly all packed, and we were ready to start. John reiterated his statement that he "go Bluff see Indians, eat peaches." We offered him $10 to take us to the bridge and to Bluff. He declined to contract that far ahead, but demanded $2 for the work so far and $5 to go to the bridge and back to this point. As this figured out practically $1 a day, our original contract, we were glad to accede, so we started, all in good humor, 5:30 p.m.

While at the spring we saw two hummingbirds. Only once before (last year) had I ever seen these in this country.

We made good time over the firm red sand desert, which may be described as level in comparison with what we have been accustomed to, although it undulated considerably and we repeatedly crossed shallow drainages, all dry, which carried the run-off from the mountain. There was a fair trail, which we followed while John took the .22 and rode close under the mountain looking for rabbits. He shot one, which we had for supper.

After about five miles of progress northerly, we veered northwesterly and then west, keeping at the north base of the mountain. The drainage on this side into the San Juan is cut more deeply than on the east side, and at one point on a divide between the two canyons, we enjoyed an unobstructed view to the north and northwest over the breaks of the San Juan. This was just before sunset, the light bringing out in richest hues the red sandstone sculpturing of the country and the beehive domes and other characteristics of Kolob weathering in the foreground. The trail had been worked with some care and on steep places into the canyon on the bare rock steps had been cut.

We passed a long flat-topped black spur extending northerly from the mountain, and in the dusk traversed a narrow trail on a ledge along a precipitous cliff, then descended a deep steep rock canyon wall, and 8:45 p.m., it being quite dark, made camp by a brook in a rocky box canyon cut in red shaly sandstone underlying the red brown cross-bedded sandstone.[20] It was warm. The water was clear and cold. There was good feed on a bench on the west side of the canyon and plenty of fire-wood. We made our bed on a rock shelf 18 inches from the brook and slept free from sand and ants better than for a long while past. It was a perfectly clear night and the sky showed more stars than I ever saw at one time before.

Wednesday, July 19, 1916
John went for the horses at 5, but I lay abed until 6 and then got a bath in a pot-hole in the brook, very cold (58°) and invigorating. The pot-hole was about 6 feet wide and 10 feet long and carried a depth of 4 feet of water clear as crystal and free of animals, except a hair snake 8 inches long. We should make Rainbow Arch to-night and return here by to-morrow night, so we determined to give all the packs but one a rest and divided our luggage, taking only what was necessary, not even beds.

Left 9 a.m. George and I rode our horses, Rust rode Bird and Jake carried the packs. We found the mule following after we had proceeded a little way, and rather than take a chance of his wandering off, brought him along, which proved fortunate.

After ascending to the westerly rim of the canyon, we continued westerly for an hour alternately descending into and climbing out of canyons draining northerly from the mountain. From Byron Cummings' description and Kolb's story and his movies, we were led to expect the trail would be dangerous. For a stretch of over a mile between 10:30 and 11 we traversed bare rock part of the time, very steep, with steps cut, and part of the time along narrow ledges on steep slopes. To this point our course had been generally west. Beyond here we worked more southerly, but the trail wound so much in, out of and through the canyons that it was practically impossible at the rate we were going to keep direction. At every turn something picturesque was in view—tall domes of reddish brown sandstone, columns, caves, arches in the cliffs due to the weathering out of sheets of sandstone along the crossbedding planes, box canyons and most of the time the ragged slopes of Navajo Mtn. rising majestically.

At 1:30 we found ourselves in an open canyon with a small flow of running water.[21] On the bank of this creek we made lunch camp under a cedar that furnished sparse shade. It was very hot and we eagerly sought relief by bathing in a small pool in the creek. The bottom of the pool was of soft mud and the water so shallow one could not get entirely wet, except by lying down in the mud. John was immensely amused at my lying face up in the mud and water, with my face shielded from the sun with a handkerchief, and kept calling "usque." I found out this meant "to sleep."

John had given us to understand that he had a horse in this region. He evidently located the horse's trail, because he rode off after we made camp and at 2:30 returned with a new mount.

Left lunch camp 4:30. As George's horse had not been acting very fresh, we left him with John's first mount and proceeded as before, except that George rode the mule.

At 5 p.m. on our left in the upper reaches of the canyon we encountered the Owl Natural Bridge, sculptured in a red sandstone spur dividing the main canyon from a side canyon. The span of the bridge and the height of its opening are somewhat larger than the bridge near Kai Peto Spring. Like that bridge though, the base of the opening is well above the canyon bottom.

We climbed steeply out of the canyon near its head and then westerly and southerly over a boulder slope under the northwest shoulder of Navajo Mtn. with a finely sculptured and gorgeously colored red topped butte to our right.[22]

The westerly slope of Navajo Mtn. is sculptured into pinnacles due to vertical jointing, and in one of these pinnacles is the Crag Natural Bridge, probably as large as the Owl Bridge, though appearing small at the distance, about a mile and a half, from which we viewed it.

We left the boulder slope abruptly and descended steeply into the head of a box canyon in the white sandstone, here dipping westerly, as it is still affected by the uplift of the Navajo Mtn. laccolite.

We were now in Bridge Canyon, the bottom of which we followed, except for occasional digressions on account of falls (the canyon here is dry). In the upper reaches we were in the fine white cross-bedded sandstone, but lower down ran into the red-brown cross-bedded sandstone. The walls rise sheer and in places, probably on account of the joints being slightly off the vertical, the walls overhang.

By 7:30 we got down to the base of the cross-bedded sandstone at its contact with a 2-foot layer of dark red shaly sandstone. This was worn away at the base of the cliffs, sometimes 2 feet or more, undermining the massive bed above, and beneath it was a ledge of hard dark red sandstone stratified 2 feet to 3 feet in layers making a fall. We climbed around this on the right side of the canyon on a ledge at the foot of the red-brown sandstone cliff to a spring at the contact. Arrived 7:45 and to the west by north of us down the canyon, which here takes a bend, we saw the Rainbow Arch. Good water. For half a mile we traversed the hard sandstone bench, and at 8 p.m. we made camp under the arch. It was intensely hot, not a breath of air stirred and the rocks radiated heat like the inside of a brick kiln. We took a very light supper and slept on horse blankets in deep sand. The moon rose late, but gave us a fine view of the bridge at night.

Thursday, July 20, 1916

Up 5 a.m. No sun in canyon until 6. Very hot. It was so dark on arrival we could not well orient ourselves last night.

The Bridge Canyon is cut in the red-brown cross-bedded sandstone rising precipitously from a bench of the dark red horizontally stratified sandstone, into which an inner canyon has been cut about 50 feet, perhaps 75 feet. In the bottom of this inner canyon there is a small flow of water. The walls of the outer canyon certainly rise 400 feet, perhaps in gradually receding steps 600 feet. The bridge spans the inner gorge. On the left (I refer to the direction of the flow of the stream) the arch is connected with the outer canyon wall. On the right it sweeps free in a graceful curve. In a sense, therefore, the arch is in the nature of a flying buttress supporting the left wall of the outer canyon.

Rainbow Bridge, July 20, 1916. Nearly three hundred thousand people
now visit the bridge each year by boating up Lake Powell.
Photograph by George C. Fraser.

I had not thought much of the bridge as a spectacle, really considering it merely an objective—a sort of excuse for taking a long journey
into a desolate region to see the beauties and abnormalities of a wild
country; but in grace and beauty of both structure and color it is all that
has been said of it and more. It is perfect in its proportions and entirely

symmetrical, and there is nothing of the colossal like the Egyptian or early Gothic about it. On the contrary its lines are so graceful and well proportioned that one is reminded rather of the best style of Renaissance architecture.

The arch is the remnant of a point in the canyon about which the creek made an ox-bow.[23] This is plainly evident on examining the space intervening its right base and the cliff bounding the outer canyon on the right.

It was too hot and involved too much labor to climb to the canyon bottom and back for a wash; beside I wished to avail of the early morning light for pictures, so I started at once to photograph, running off six from different points before breakfast.

Breakfast 7:15 to 7:45, and then climbed a low rise in the canyon north of the arch and took more pictures.

As the arch is only six miles from the Colorado River, we had anticipated going down to Glen Canyon, but as John assured us it was impossible to get horses through and a 12-mile walk in the intense heat did not appeal to us, we decided to make the best time possible back to our base camp and so at 8:30 a.m. started. After stopping at the spring for water and a wash and photographing a little, we proceeded in intense heat over the same trail as yesterday. The only exception was for about two miles, where we found John had taken us off the trail through a canyon where he thought he might find his horse.

The overhanging bluffs in the Bridge Canyon are due to long joints or cracks in the massive cross-bedded sandstone; the canyon generally follows the direction of these cracks, which run in two parallel series.

At 11:20 we emerged from the canyon and turned north on a boulder covered mesa. Before us a little to the left rose the magnificent Red Top Butte with the white wall below referred to in yesterday's notes, and to the west of us, turning back, we saw the abrupt face of the 50-Mile Mtn. At 12:30 we struck the head of a deep canyon, the one in which we lunched yesterday. Bathed as before and tried to get a little relief in the shade of a scrawny cedar. John got his horse and George's without much difficulty. We put the pack on the mule and I rode Jake in the afternoon, giving my horse a rest.

At 4:10 we descended into a red-brown sandstone canyon and found water in a pocket. Leaving this canyon we rejoined yesterday's trail and traversed the bad mile of rock trail. In crossing these rocks we ascended 400 feet, and I measured angles of bare rock slopes which we ascended at three points—24°, 27° and 30°.

It grew much cooler due to heavy rains on the Henry Mtns. and a little on Navajo Mtn. We benefited to the extent of a few drops. We continued up and down across shallow canyons, over sand and boulders, to and into the canyon where we had left our outfit. Arrived 7 p.m. Comfortably cool. We estimated the distance from here to Rainbow Arch at 20 miles. It took us eight hours to come back. An outfit, rough-shod, fresh and not heavily loaded, might make the trip in six hours.

Friday, July 21. Following their visit to Rainbow Bridge, the Frasers, Rust, and John, their guide, retraced their route back to the northeast side of Navajo Mountain and headed east toward Piute Canyon. John refused to continue on with them to Bluff and left, only to return a few hours later to warn them they were following a dead-end trail and direct them toward water. That night they camped near other encampments of Paiutes and Navajos and tried to get directions from them about the route to Bluff. They decided to head across Piute Canyon toward Oljeto and the store at Douglas, evidently not knowing of a route, used by miners some years before, that headed more northerly. They were not able to induce any of the Indians to guide them further.

Saturday, July 22, 1916
Up 5:15 a.m. at sunrise. Warm, clear, with a pleasant breeze and fleecy clouds. We set out to the southeast over the red sand, striking the trail that was to bring us into Piute Canyon. The trail into the canyon is very steep in places and not in good condition, so that we had to walk a good part of the way. At the base of the lower bed of red-brown sandstone was a drift fence, to which eight head of horses had retired as they heard us coming. Two of the horses jumped the fence and the rest got through when we made an opening for ourselves.

We turned left and went down the canyon easterly until 9:45 where it joined the main Piute Creek. The canyon we had descended was a side gorge, but not much smaller than the main one. Here we turned southerly, upstream, riding in deep sand and making much dust. There was a small flow of muddy water in the main canyon. From the easterly side a quarter of a mile above our point of entry a small clear cold creek flowed in through a meadow of rich grass. While drinking here we heard weird and piercing shouts which reverberated from wall to wall in the canyon depths. Rust's guilty conscience at having let the horses through the drift fence made him think their owners were after us. Soon there came from the canyon above the meadow the wildest Navajo we had seen yet riding a pony bare-back. His hair, tied with a string at the nape of the neck, hung to his waist. He wore brilliantly striped pajama trousers split at the knee, long stockings, and moccasins, a bright shirt open at the neck with its tail hung out, and had a handkerchief tied to his head. He would not approach us nearer than about 30 feet, although we offered him tobacco, and after looking at us suspiciously, he struck his horse and galloped off up the canyon.

At 10:20 we turned easterly up a side canyon in the bed of a pleasing brook. After 20 minutes' ride the trail petered out. Rust prospected for some means of egress, but there was no point at which the canyon walls could be scaled, so we returned to Piute Creek and followed it farther up. Here we encountered a few maples, cotton-wood, oak, wild rice, good grass and a very few wild flowers. At 12 M., finding good grass and shady cotton-woods, we made lunch camp. Rain threatened, clouds obscured the sun and it was comfortably cool. While we took it easy Rust prospected about on foot and finally located a trail leading out of the main canyon, but on the opposite side that we had intended to go.

At 5 p.m. we reached the rim to find the ridge from near which we had started in the morning hardly five miles to the northwest of us. We were apparently at the head of Piute Canyon instead of being well across it on its easterly side. Here we struck a wide cut trail running south by east with wagon tracks. This we followed, climbing gently over sand and cross-bedded brown rocks, and discovered we were on the divide between Navajo and Piute Canyons. We were fortunate enough to find water-holes in the bed rock, so we felt safe to go ahead and make a dry camp, if necessary.

We were entirely off our trail and had nothing but our knowledge of the direction in which Bluff lay to guide us. We sought consolation in the maps, but found them worse than useless. On the horizon to the southeast was a long dark mesa, which we imagined to be Skeleton Mesa. So reasoning we assumed the road we were on led to Kayenta and Red Lake. The Geological Survey map showed an Indian trail running northerly along the west base of Skeleton Mesa. The intervening country appeared to be a level plain without any deep canyons, so we decided to try to reach that trail by cutting straight across country.

We descended from the high point of the divide quite gently about two miles to the bottom of a canyon draining southerly to Navajo Creek and, finding water here in pockets and fine grass, made camp at 7 p.m. Thunder and rain in the distance. We prepared for a shower, but only got a few drops. It was still and murky but not uncomfortable.

Sunday, July 23, 1916

Up 4:30 a.m. Clouds. Damp. The water in the pockets was plentiful and good. We fortified ourselves for the day with a bean and mutton stew, the last including the bone of the leg we got from the Navajos. Our attention was attracted by a tremendous flock of cedar birds flying together as if in migration, and followed by a few big crows.

By 7:45 it had cleared and the sun shone strong. We ascended gently the slope of the canyon and kept a course east by north, without trail, over the plateau rising gradually to the eastward. We crossed a number of wide shallow canyons draining south (evidently near their heads) and some broad flats overgrown with stink-weed bearing blue flowers.

At 10:45 we struck a trail running east by north, evidently a very old one, for it was worn two feet deep and more in places. A wagon had been here since the winter. From a rise we saw Navajo Mountain nearly 20 miles west of us. On the divide between two canyons draining respectively north and south we encountered some yellow pines.

Up to 10 o'clock there was evidence of recent rains and we found some water in holes. From that time on it was dry. All morning we traveled either over red-brown sand or the red-brown sandstone rock. From the divide last mentioned, the trail descended into a canyon draining northerly and then climbed its easterly side, soon coming to the rim of a very deep box canyon with precipitous sides. Here we made our lunch camp 12 M. We imagined this must be Moonlight Canyon or a principal feeder to that canyon. How to proceed was the question. Rust figured there must be some way into the canyon, but I could not imagine any, its sides were so steep.

After lunch Rust and I walked along the trail to reconnoiter, and were surprised to find we were within 300 yards of the rim of a deep canyon. The canyon terminated within a mile of where we stood, bounded at its head by a sheer, semi-circular cliff. It was not far from 1200 feet deep, that being the depth measured barometrically of the adjacent canyon into which we subsequently descended. If one imagined the Niagara River dried up, and the depth of the Falls increased six or seven times, and the width of the gorge below widened about three times, the resultant picture would be comparable with what we saw. This is evidently a case of the principle of recession of cliffs, so familiar to travelers in the Utah-Dixie country. In places the canyon walls are literally precipitous for a greater distance than I have seen anywhere except in Little Zion. Near the mouth of the wash where we made lunch camp, I counted seven seconds before hearing the drop of a 10 lb. rock I threw over the rim.

The canyon bottom was green. I recognized yellow pines, quaking aspen and oak. The massive red brown sandstone was weathered into caves at many places due to water seeps at its contact with the horizontally stratified red sandstone below. In one of these caves, on the opposite side of the canyon, we saw a cliff dwelling, and beneath was fine growth of deciduous trees, ferns, etc.

We studied the maps and Rust decided we were at Moonlight Canyon, and must soon reach Oljato, that is, provided we could get to the canyon bottom. We were lost, and glad of it, for if we had stayed on the trail, we never would have come this way.

While I studied and photographed the canyon, Rust on foot followed the old trail which had led us to our lunch camp, and returned saying he had found a way into the next canyon on the east, so we returned to camp where George had stayed to sleep. He had been interrupted by a call from a Navajo, who had some sheep and a hogan nearby. The Navajo was very shy and could speak no English, so we were no better off for his acquaintance. This is the first person we have seen since yesterday morning, when we encountered the wild Navajo in the bottom of Piute Canyon.

At 3:40 we reached the adjoining canyon's rim, at the head of an Indian sheep and goat trail. Here we literally dropped down. The trail was incredibly steep. I do not think many men would care to risk their pack outfit on it. It had been carefully and liberally worked, and was evidently much used. Sheep and goat tracks were everywhere, and we frequently encountered wool caught on the brush. At the steep points steps had been cut in the sandstone for horses. Of course we walked and led our riding horses. The packs, as usual, found their own way.

We reached the bottom of the canyon, here dry. A little below, water seeped from the basal shales, and thence we followed a small creek. At the mouth of the canyon, the creek entered an open plain, and here, two miles north of the junction, we encountered a corn field, about two acres in extent, not irrigated. Close to the corn field were four hogans, one of them completely furnished with blankets, skins, simple cooking utensils, etc., but there was not a soul to be seen. The corn and a single peach tree were the only signs of civilization.

Rust was sure we were at Oljato, and that we had descended into and traversed Moonlight Canyon. The Piute John had stated Oljato was inhabited only by Indians, and that there was a white man's store not far east from it. We therefore determined to push on down the valley.

This settlement, whatever it is, is most picturesquely situated. Immediately to the south is the mouth of the canyon we had descended, with sheer walls receding westerly and northeasterly. From the east another canyon debouched from red cliffs capped by domes of the red-brown sandstone.

For a mile beyond the hogans we kept in the valley bottom close to the stream. The water was bitter, and tinged red. There were incrustations of salt along the margin of the creek which the horses licked. Here we watered the horses, filled our canteens and water barrels, and then crossed the stream to its right bank and traveled northeasterly over the mesa on the Shinarump, following a faint trail which soon dispersed in the manner characteristic of cattle tracks. A better marked trail ran northerly or northwesterly to the left of the stream. We chose the other route because it headed in what we conceived to be the direction of Bluff. After going two miles on the mesa, we made dry camp under some cedar trees on a flat overgrown with sage and good grass. While the light held, we studied the maps, but they helped us not at all.

By sunset, the sky had cleared, and as the moon rose late, the stars stood out in wonderful profusion.

Monday, July 24, 1916

Pioneer Day. Up 5 a.m. Clear. To the north by west of us over the plain we saw the Henry Mountains. Left 7:45 a.m. For something over a mile we continued northeasterly over the mesa on which we had camped. We dropped off a sheer cliff in the Shinarump about 30 feet high onto chocolate shales beneath. The detail was weird and picturesque. Blocks of sandstone, large and small, perched on shale columns, deep washes with strong water rills and on the canyon sides rocks of many shades, all barren and hopelessly dry. The trail, for we picked up one a little east of our camp, was very faint.

For over an hour we zig-zagged across the bottom of the wide amphitheater at the base of the cliffs, alternately threading dry washes and climbing and descending divides between, until at 9:30 a.m., we ascended very steeply the northerly margin of the amphitheater at the only point in sight where the sheer face of the summit bed could be scaled. Here the Shinarump was only 10 feet thick. Its unconformable deposition referred to by Dutton, Gilbert, etc. and observed on the Kanab Desert is apparent here.

We were again on the mesa. It had been very hot in the bad land bottom of the amphitheater, and the slick water gotten out of the creek last night did not satisfy our thirst. We rested ten minutes, and proceeded northeasterly, joining a well worn trail which we took to be the one we left last night. On the surface was much silicified wood in large blocks of fine texture and color, and numerous geodes. We descended steeply into a V-shaped canyon cut well into the underlying cross-bedded sandstone, weathering into beehives of the Kolob type and ripple marked. The trail direction was marked at several points by horse shoes and moccasin tracks sculptured into the sandstone.

We kept on the summit of the cross-bedded white sandstone and descended along the dip planes, with the main canyon on our right. The cliffs rose steeply on our left. Everything was bare, and we got the full force of a very hot sun. At first the view to the east was cut off by a projection of the chocolate shale cliffs. On rounding that projection, we were astounded to see before us a wide, practically level plain, extending many miles to the east, and probably six to ten miles wide north and south, studded with immense temples and monuments. We recognized this at once as Monument Valley, and knew we were 30 miles or more south of where we thought.

The view was magnificent, and under other circumstances we would have rejoiced at missing our way and landing here. As it was, our water was gone, it was intensely hot and humid, clouds hung over the valley, but none were friendly enough to get between us and the sun. The valley appeared absolutely dry, and its sandy character was attested by two whirlwinds which raised sand columns 50, perhaps 100 feet, and made a leisurely progress northeasterly across the valley. Except for a little stale water in a pocket, the horses had had nothing to drink since last night. They were feeling the strain.

To the southeast there rose from the valley floor a massive but grace-ful monument. We guessed this to be Crown Rock, indicated on the maps. Beyond this, still to the southeast, on a plain above the valley level, rose an impressive rock which we inferred to be Ragged Top. Due east, forming in appearance a sort of chain across the valley, rose the monuments we have seen pictured.

Though good, the trail was steep, very steep in spots, and we had to walk. As we progressed to a point where it was possible to see close under the base of the anticline, Rust descried a sheep and goat herd, which, of course, spelled water, so we hastened on and reached the valley bottom. We seemed to be in a desert, and to save the horses any unneces-sary exertion, Rust left us and rode a mile to the goat herd to find water.

In the course of the descent the clouds gathered and it rained heavily to the southwest of us. It was probably pouring on the route we traversed in the morning.

In half an hour Rust called us, and we proceeded southerly along the base of the anticline to the mouth of the canyon whose rim we followed down to the valley. Here we made lunch camp under a scrawny cedar. From basins in the white sandstone in the canyon bottom we watered the horses, and got some goat flavored water for ourselves. This was refreshing and palatable in contrast with the slick, salty water we had to depend on since last evening.

While traversing the Shinarump Mesa in the morning, Rust shot a rabbit, which we ate for lunch.

The herder in charge of the sheep and goats came over while we were cooking, and by appropriate signs indicated he would eat with us. He spoke no word of English. He was dressed in cotton trousers of pajama cut, split up to the knee on the outside of each leg, blue with white polka dots outside, and lined with red with black spots. He wore a brown dirt colored shirt with its tails out, a breechclout, and no hat. Of course he understood place names, and so comprehended my inquiries as to the route we should take to Mexican Hat and Bluff. He drew in the sand, marking various points appropriately with twigs and stones, an excellent, and as we afterward ascertained, accurate map of the trail. According to his advice, we would find water at the base of one of the monuments, which he indicated, and should there camp, proceeding thence northerly to the bridge across the San Juan River to Spencer's Store (called by all the Indians "Spence Sto"). He indicated we might make Bluff the second night.

I let the Navajo look through the field glasses. His astonishment and delight was interesting to witness. When he handed me the glasses, he extended his hands and drew them toward him to indicate the magnification of his vision.

The rabbit did not make four very large portions. With the courtesy practiced, if not enjoyed, by the civilized, the most dainty morsel was left to the last. While George and Rust were pressing it each on the other, the Navajo reached into the fry pan and took it. Rust never spoke a good word of any Navajo after that.

Although it rained close to us in the west, not a drop fell in the valley. We got some relief though from cloud shade and a slight drop in temperature. At 6 p.m. we set out due east toward the monuments. We encountered a young Navajo girl with a burro saddled with brilliantly colored blankets, carrying water jars. The girl was wild and hid behind the burro. Beyond the creek we continued in deep sand with very little vegetation, part of the time following some wagon tracks. The sand must drift constantly. We encountered a sheep corral of cedar roots and branches, almost buried in the drifted sand.

At 7:30, the plain stopped, and we stood at the summit of the white cross bedded sandstone, here forming a ridge or broken wall facing easterly. This rock, as where we first encountered it, is picturesquely sculptured into domes and beehives. To the east of the summit of this wall, we had an unbroken view of the series of monuments. Ten of them (not counting minor projections) were visible in profile. We intensely regretted not having started an hour sooner so that we might have enjoyed this view in the light of the setting sun and photographed it.

It grew dark early, for the entire sky was clouded. There was little feed and no water, so we jogged on, making the best time possible, in the hope that we might reach the water which the Indian had indicated. The most westerly of the monuments toward which our course lay, seemed never to get any nearer. On the contrary, it appeared as though the monument moved with us *pari passu*.

Finally, at 9 p.m., in the darkness, we did reach that monument, and threw down our packs a couple of hundred feet west of its base, having come as we estimated 12 miles from our lunch camp.

In the evening coolness there was a perceptible radiation of heat from the bare rock face of the monument.

We made a light and hasty supper, but before we were finished, it began to rain. We had laid the tarpaulin under and over the bed, and to save our stuff from getting wet, I crawled in with my boots on. In the darkness we had not been able to make up the bed properly, so it would be water-tight. Along in the middle of the night I woke up with a peculiar coldness. The water that had settled in the depressions of the tarpaulin, on one of us rolling over, had been dumped in to the bed and wet me from my knees to my chest, but no harm was done.

Tuesday, July 25. Continuing their journey to the east and northeast, Fraser noted a prominent ridge to the north near the San Juan River, likely the Raplee Anticline, which they would not reach for another two days' ride. They were fortunate to find water pockets, and later that day they reached Chinle Wash. At first they took this to be the San Juan River. Conferring with several Navajo men who lived there enlightened them somewhat as to their location, but they still could not determine which route they should follow. They camped under the shelter of a sandstone rim by the creek, "[a] very dreary place, no feed for the horses, and the water in the stream muddy. . . . Rust was very much discouraged."

Wednesday, July 26, 1916

We had chosen the wrong side of the creek for shade. The sun rose and continued to shine full upon us, and it was intensely hot and trying. While Rust was looking for the horses, George and I gathered drift wood from the creek and cooked breakfast. We found the creek swollen to a mighty torrent, not of water, but of mud, drift wood and brush. I filled the pail, and the weight of the muddy substance bent the handle. I poured the mud and water out and the pail was encrusted with reddish silt, as if it had been filled with badly mixed paint. When I put my arms and hands in the water to wash, they emerged caked with the same red mud. Later we learned from the Indians how to treat such water. Two of them waded the creek, and on emerging, rubbed themselves with dry white sand, which removed the mud.

At 7, after nearly two hours' chase, Rust returned with five horses. Jake and George's white horse were missing. He had had a long, hot walk, which did not stimulate his spirits. After a short breakfast, Rust left again, and at 9 returned with the white horse. In the meanwhile two Indians had waded across the creek, which had gone down about 18 inches since we first saw it this morning. I approached the Navajos with all the courtesy and tact I could summon, and we all smoked Bull together in the shade of a cotton wood tree some distance up the valley from camp. Neither of these Navajos spoke any English, but one of them was exceedingly intelligent, and with the sign language we made out very well. He drew a map in the sand and made me understand that getting to Bluff was out of the question because we would have to ford the San Juan up to our arm pits and swim the horses. I delicately broached the suggestion that he guide us to Spencer's Store, and after prolonged conference, I gathered that he would do so for $4, but I was not very sure because he indicated that he had no horse. However, his companion left us and climbed the cliff above our camp, while our prospective guide took off his trousers, rolled up his shirt, and again forded the stream. About 10 Rust returned, still without Jake. He was fearful that Jake might have crossed the creek before it rose, and to make sure took one of the horses bare-back through the torrent, returning without finding Jake's tracks. Presently some other Navajos came up, and then our prospective guide reappeared across the creek, carrying a saddle, some hides and something wrapped in burlap. His companion came down from the plateau with the horse. As the Navajo forded the stream with his burdens, the horse broke away and crossed to the other side. This did not seem to irritate the Navajo at all, who immediately re-forded the stream and in the course of time caught the horse and rode it back to us. I was relieved to find that he actually did intend to guide us.

By way of preparation for the journey our Navajo took off the hand-kerchief bound about his head which he wore when I first encountered him, and put on a beaver skin cap with a visor, although the thermome-ter in the sun was upwards of 120. Before we packed up, he handed us the burlap bag, evidently as a gift. In it was a leg of mutton. We enjoyed that for lunch, but had to throw the rest away the next morning.

We were then confronted with the question what to do about Jake. Rust decided it was most probable that Jake had gone back on our trail of yesterday, and determined to start in the hope of finding him. If we failed to pick him up Rust planned to come back and look for him after leaving us in Bluff.

While George and Rust packed, I sat under the cotton wood with the Indian. There was very little air stirring, and it was intensely hot. Within an hour, while I was sitting under the tree, the creek rose more than a foot above the high level of last night. At this level it carried large logs, and we saw go by a number of heavy hewn timbers such as might have been used in the construction of a bridge.

We left the creek, climbing its southwesterly wall over the trail we followed last night. Rust soon picked up Jake's tracks on the trail, and we found him grazing peacefully near the water holes where we had gotten our water the night before. The glare and reflection of the sun on the white sandstone was trying. We watered the horses, then washed our dishes and made lunch camp nearby under a scrawny cedar standing in the dune sand.

At 2:45 we left lunch camp. We turned to the right, westerly, leaving the trail we had followed yesterday, and keeping on the white sandstone plateau, reached the summit of the cliff bounding Monument Valley on the east, striking it probably five miles north of the saddle through which we passed yesterday afternoon.

The summit of the cliff here is surmounted by red sandstone pinna-cles and buttes, jointed vertically. At the base of one such butte, tower-ing over our trail, we found two very slight water seeps, the water no better than what we had gotten from the rock basins. Rust insisted this was Moses Rock, partly because there is such a rock marked on the maps, and partly because he remembers some of the Old Testament.

The plateau terminated abruptly in a palisade facing west, and it looked as if the trail would have to stop there. But somehow it extended down the cliff. We literally dropped off the cliff and slid down its face, a descent of 300 feet, to a sand dune slope. We made good time down this, crossed another trough in the chocolate cliff with very deep sand, and climbed to a white sandy plain sloping west. We could not make out from the Navajo how long the journey was to Spencer's Store. None of the Navajos we had encountered understand miles or hours. They designate distances, if long ones, by the number of sleeps required during the journey, and if short ones, by pointing the distance the sun will travel in the heavens. From our early morning conversation I had gathered if we started then, we would make Spencer's Store about sunset, so we pushed the horses very hard.

The anticlinal hill or ridge to the north across the San Juan had come into view at the top of the cliff under Moses Rock, and so continued from every rise. It looked as though the anticline we traversed at this point was a continuation, but with a lesser dip, of that conspicuous fold. Its face was dissected into V shaped canyons, leaving flat surface divides between, shaped like a series of shark's teeth—the same topography photographed in the easterly face of the Water Pocket Fold.

Beneath, to the north of us, lay a dreary, barren, desolate bad land country, deeply dissected by a canyon draining northwesterly to the San Juan. We continued down this canyon. There was a little water in the canyon, very red and salty, which seeped from the shales. We tried to drink at one of the larger seeps, but the water was too slick to tempt even the horses.

At 6:40 we left the canyon to our right, keeping northwesterly over an undulating, rough surface in the bare weather of the red shales, and passed through a highland to the west. From here we had an extended view over the bad lands and up and down the San Juan Valley. The brilliancy of the coloring was enhanced by the setting sun. The prevailing tint was maroon, soft and rich like velvet.

Before us lay a plain sloping to the San Juan, the waters of which were concealed in a deep canyon. On the other side we could see buildings and a road leading to them from the canyon. To the east of the buildings, on a shoulder of the anticlinal ridge, silhouetted against the sun, was a mushroom shaped rock, in outline similar to the peaked hats (sombreros) Mexicans wear. From this rock Goodridge derives its other name of Mexican Hat. The land office map of Arizona shows Mexican Hat as on the San Juan, and Goodridge as 20 miles to the north. It was only when we got to Spencer's Store that we discovered the identity of the two places. This error in the map caused us no end of trouble in our efforts to get directions from the Indians.

We hastened down the plain toward the river, and soon saw the bridge, where we arrived at 7:10.

The San Juan here is about 100 feet wide, of deep gray color, and runs in an inner gorge with sheer limestone walls about 50 feet deep. The bridge is made of wood, of the suspension type, anchored with cement in the limestone.

The road from Monument Valley, which we should have followed in the first instance, came into the southerly bridge head from the southwest.

Led by the Indian, Rust and I crossed the bridge, turned right, upstream on a dugway, and in less than half a mile arrived at Spencer's Store in Goodridge. George had considerable trouble getting the packs across the bridge and did not join us until half an hour later.

All day we had figured it would be possible to hire an automobile, or certainly a wagon, from Spencer to take us to Bluff, with the idea of making an early start in a motor and catching tomorrow night's train from Thompson. Spencer soon dispelled all such thoughts. There never had been an automobile at Goodridge, and he did not even have a horse. His brother had taken his team upwards of a month before for a trip to Chin Lee settlement. In the meantime he had no means of transportation. Before we had time to inquire about supplies, Spencer said he had nothing left but one can of tomatoes, and bacon, flour, coffee and sugar, which he needed for his family. So we resigned ourselves to delay.

Spencer is about 45 years of age, six feet tall, a little too large around the waist, but otherwise of good shape. His first greeting was rather formal and distant, but after he had sized us up in 10 minutes' conversation, he invited us to be presented to his wife, with whom, and his five-year-old daughter Helen, he lives here.

We found Mrs. Spencer seated under a sort of shed connecting the store and the kitchen quarters, and evidently used as their bed room, being airy and cool. She appeared embarrassed because we had caught her unprepared. She had on a calico dress, sneakers, and no stockings. She made us very welcome, however, and proved extremely interesting, intelligent and witty.

Spencer is a brother of the man who ran the mining operations at Lee's Ferry. He was attracted to this region by an oil boom, which raged eight or ten years ago. He showed me the prospectuses of the London and San Juan Oil Co., naming him as treasurer and general manager, also a town site map of Goodridge. From what was said, and in the appearance of things, I inferred he had sunk his all in the oil boom and was staying here in the hope of working out something, in the meanwhile operating a trading post with the Indians. He and Mrs. Spencer have lived here eight years. For three years past, Mrs. Spencer has not left the place. She has not seen a white woman since late last summer, and they have had very few white visitors, as was evident from the guest book they had us sign. The child knows nothing outside of this place. Living here, therefore, is not so bad for her.

Both Spencer and Mrs. Spencer have cheerful dispositions and evidently unbounded courage. They are busy all the time. Mrs. Spencer is largely occupied in making trousers for the Indians. We had an illustration of their shopping. Our guide selected two pieces of calico from which he wished a pair of pants made. He measured the size by the breadth of his hand, and using a piece of board as a ruler, marked out the pattern. Mrs. Spencer lent him a pair of scissors with which he laboriously cut out the calico, scrimping to the inch, and hardly leaving anything to turn over. She explained that the Indians were required to cut their own cloth because otherwise they were apt to make complaint that the trousers did not fit. After doing the work of his own cutter, the Indian handed the material to Mrs. Spencer, who in an incredibly short time, sewed the cloth up into a pair of pants, with a sewing machine. Our Indian seemed satisfied, wrapped up the pants, and went away.

The Spencer's stock was very small. They had a goodly accumulation of sheep and goat hides, and about a dozen good blankets. A good Navajo blanket here sells at from 80 cents to $1.30 a pound. We went over the stock, and with Mrs. Spencer's help selected what seemed to be the best of the not too gaudily colored ones, which weighed 14 lbs. 10 oz., and which they sold us for $15.

The only things that seem to thrive at Goodridge are chickens. Mrs. Spencer was so tired of eggs she did not think them worth mentioning, though to us they were a luxury. We enjoyed scrambled eggs and the lone can of tomatoes for supper, which Mrs. Spencer served us in front of the kitchen.

After sundown the sky became overcast. There was a heavy wind and quite a sand storm. Although there had been no rain in Goodridge for many months, it looked as if some might fall to-night, so we slept in a tent which Spencer's brother occupies when at home. A few drops of rain fell about 11:30, but not enough to dampen the dust.

Thursday, July 27, 1916

Cloudy and cool. We breakfasted with the Spencers and shaved and dressed to an audience composed of our guide and a high class Navajo who had ridden in early to do some trading. It was his sister who made the blankets we bought. Both the Spencers speak Navajo, and Mrs. Spencer is pretty well acquainted with all the Indians who trade regularly. She told us our companion is one of about ten sons of an important high class Navajo, whose wealth in sheep and goats is the envy of white people as well as Indians. Although about 40, our friend is classed as one of the boys, and subject to his father's control. He told Mrs. Spencer he would be in trouble because of leaving his hogan where there was work to be done. He was very curious to make out what we were doing. He intimated that he and his family thought we were somewhat crazy because we insisted on going to Bluff by the short trail from Chin Lee Creek, a route entirely impracticable at this time because of the high water in the San Juan.

The clouds which had made for a cool early morning dispersed about 8 o'clock, and it was intensely hot. Spencer's Store stands on a bare plain about 200 feet above the river at the summit of its inner gorge. The plain is almost all bare even of brush, sandy, with chips of stone. The horses had to be driven a mile or more up the valley's side before they found any feed. For fuel Spencer depends entirely on drift wood brought down by the river. It would be hard to find a more dreary, desolate and forbidding place to settle.

In the vicinity of the store, and for many miles to the eastward, along the road to Bluff, we encountered oil wells, a few with their derricks left, but mostly capped pipes projecting two feet or so from the ground. The oil is light and suitable for illuminating.

We left at 10:30, in very hot sun, going northeasterly over a wagon road away from the river. About three-fourths of a mile above Spencer's Store the river emerges from a deep canyon where it cuts through the anticlinal ridge on which our attention has been focused for two days past. In about a mile we encountered some deserted shacks and a group of oil wells. This is Mexican Hat proper, and was the center of the oil boom. Above it on a shoulder of the ridge is Mexican Hat Rock.

After traveling nine miles, we stopped for lunch, seeking such shade as a large sage brush afforded. Fortunately the sun kept pretty well hidden under the clouds.

Beside our saddle horses, we took Jerry the mule, carrying our personal luggage. The other horses we left near the deserted oil camp, and Rust left his stuff at Spencer's all to be picked up on his return from Bluff.

We continued on the sage plain, ascending gently, until we attained the summit of a ridge, the westerly boundary of a wide, barren valley, which we afterward learned to be Comb Wash, which drains southerly into the San Juan. Comb Wash is the prototype, and probably the northerly continuation of the fold we had crossed going to and returning from Chin Lee Creek. As viewed from the ridge on the west side of the canyon, and also as seen at a distance from the east on the road to Bluff, the ridge bounding Comb Wash on the east appeared like the teeth of a saw rather than like those of a comb, from which, by analogy, its name is probably derived.

About three miles west of Bluff we passed a camp of Utes. Eight men were playing cards, all of them dressed in brilliant colors and wearing their hair braided into pigtails instead of tied up as the Navajo and Piutes do. On the road to this camp we encountered Tis-ne-gat, the leader of the rebellion in the winter of 1914, which was quashed by General Scott. From the stories we heard it would appear that that Indian trouble was occasioned by lack of common sense and tact on the part of the U.S. Marshal.[24]

Rust had made the mistake of riding Bird, who though entirely recovered from the snake bite, had not regained his full strength. In the early afternoon Bird showed signs of giving out, so Rust had to walk a great deal. On the last stretch Bird was very groggy, so George and I went ahead in order to get located before dark. This may have humiliated Bird, for he pulled himself together and made haste so as to come in with the rest of us.

At 7 p.m. we arrived in Bluff, which is quite like the Dixie country villages. It is built along two main avenues with four or five intersecting streets, all lined with irrigation ditches and poplars. Many of the houses are built of logs, some enlarged by frame additions, and except for three or four modern houses, none of them painted. Each house stands in an enclosure of an acre or two, planted with garden truck. The alfalfa and grain fields, about all that is raised, except for individual consumption, are on the outskirts of the town. As we rode up the street we encountered a man letting the water into his field, and asked the way to the hotel and the post office. With characteristic courtesy he offered to hunt up the postmaster, whom he knew to be off duty.

We put up with Mrs. Pearson, a widow with a 16-year old daughter, an 18-year old boy and several small children. I tried to telephone Monticello for messages, but the wire would not work. The lady in charge was sympathetic and promised to spend the evening ringing Monticello, and to send for me if she got the connection.

Agreeable to custom, the post office was located in the most remote corner of town. I rode over there and found it locked up. While hunting for the postmaster, George was addressed by a man in an automobile, who said he understood we were looking for mail. He took George in the machine to the post office, and I got the first word from home, the latest letter dated July 18th. The postmaster asked George whether I was a Presbyterian missionary. He said at first he thought I must be because he could not otherwise account for our presence in the Navajo country, but said he was doubtful on the subject because he did not believe a missionary would ride around town smoking cigarettes.

In the meantime Rust reported having engaged a young fellow named Nielson, with a new Hupmobile that had only run 1800 miles, to take us to Thompson in a day for $40. Hardly had Rust delivered himself of this pleasing information when Nielson drove up and said he would have to raise the price $10. He had expected to have another passenger, who had given out. Of course we had to stand for the raise, and Nielson agreed to be on hand at 6:30 in the morning.

Rust and I settled accounts in the privacy of the sitting room while Mrs. Pearson lay in bed on the porch outside the window and listened.

Friday, July 28, 1916

We left Bluff 6:30 a.m. in Nielson's new Hupmobile, saying farewell to Rust, who up to the last minute was inclined to go with us. It seemed warm and murky, but riding without a coat in the open car was chilly. The road runs due north from the town up a narrow canyon cut in the sandstone bluff.

The climb up the canyon set the water in the radiator to steaming. We had to stop repeatedly while Nielson fussed vainly with the engine, and whenever we passed any water, which happened five or six times, he filled the radiator. I ascertained at Moab that the last time Nielson came through his car was giving trouble. Our prospects of getting through to Thompsons, as we hoped, looked bad.

8:40 a.m., 25 miles, arrived at Blanding, formerly Grayson, evidently a trifling village until quite recently. Numerous frame houses of the present day magazine design type are in process of erection. There seems to be quite a boom on.

Leaving Blanding 9 a.m., we turned easterly, in order to round the base of the Abajo (Blue) Mountains, running first through a canyon cut into the shales underlying the crossbedded sandstone and then on the southeasterly shoulder of the Blue Mountains. At this altitude we encountered a few yellow pines. Here the south bound mail Ford truck passed us, and 1½ miles beyond we were stopped by a ranger who had apparently overslept and thereby missed the mail. The road here was very rough, and riding most uncomfortable.

As we progressed northward, signs of recent heavy rains increased, until nearing Monticello, we encountered mud and puddles in the road.

11:45 a.m. arrived Monticello. Nielson made for the garage kept by a good natured, stout fellow named Adams, intending, as he said, to fix up the car while we had some lunch. Adams greeted us cheerfully with the statement that we might as well lay up for the night because the road to the north was washed out.

Unlike Blanding, Monticello is busy. There were four automobiles on the streets and a number of wagons, and we found two eating houses in prosperous operation. Adams directed us to Mrs. Hanson's, and told us we were sure of a good dinner, so at 12:30, we knocked on the door of an unpainted frame shack with a tent annex, all carefully screened against the flies. Nobody paid any attention to the knock, but on repeating it, we were told it was customary to walk in. We found about ten men, two of them plumbers installing the first bath tub in the town, the rest farm hands and wagon drivers, and were shown where we could get washed and provided with a clean towel. In a moment dinner was ready.

Dinner was served in the tent annex—fourteen men at a scrupulously clean table, with excellent food, all put on at once, Mrs. Hanson's daughter, a pretty girl of sixteen, serving the drinks consisting of green tea, coffee and milk. Regulation price for meals in this country is fifty cents, but a commutation ticket may be purchased entitling one to board at $7. a week. As our outfit finished, another crowd took possession of the table and was fed. Mrs. Hanson weighs about 250 pounds, has a bass voice and a blacksmith's arm, and looks capable of handling 100 men without exertion.

We got a room at Mrs. Jones', seventy-five cents for two of us in one bed, all that was available. The Jones' are branching out, and installing a bath tub with running water. In consequence of these plumbing operations water was only to be had from a pump in the yard, and we again had to defer an overdue bath.

Everyone we talked with (and that was pretty nearly the whole town) told us there was no hope of getting through for a couple of days. We found Nielson and another man at the garage blacker than coal-heavers and the insides of the car all over the place, but still without anybody having discovered the trouble.

Everybody who came up wanted to know what we were doing. To say we were looking at the country seemed to be regarded as equivalent to saying "None of your business," so I came down to our reply of last year, "Just prospecting around."

I went to bed at 9:30, leaving George to talk with two nice looking girls, 14 and 20, grandchildren of the Jones'.

Saturday, July 29, 1916

Up 6:45. Mrs. Hanson served us breakfast, but with a look of disapproval referring to our lateness. At 7:30 we found postmaster Walton. He had gotten telephone communication with some one up the road and learned that the motor stage was stuck in the mud about 18 miles to the north, where it had been all night. He said he would send out a wagon with the mail to meet the motor which would turn back and go to Moab. He was sure a wagon could get through the creek where the bridge was down, but was doubtful about a motor. We located Nielson who looked hopeless, and said there was no chance of getting through to Moab and anyhow the car was broken. Although we had come a little less than a third of the distance, he charged us $20 for the ride to Monticello.

We packed up hastily, and at 9:30 left in a covered buggy (two seated) and drawn by a pair of well fed heavy horses, and driven by a young man called Elmer. We had one fellow passenger, Dr. Christiansen, an itinerant dentist from Castledale, about 60 years of age. He travels around the country mostly off the railroads, stopping wherever there seems to be business.

The road was fair, but muddy and heavy in places. We made good progress, six miles in the first hour, over generally level country. Then we came to a narrow, shallow canyon. A heavy flood in the creek had undermined the road which had fallen away almost entirely in places and washed out the bridge and its abutments at the bottom. Men and teams were engaged here in repair work, but not in sufficient force to warrant expectations of the road being opened for some days. We took the old road veering to the left westerly, rough and steep, and forded the creek below the bridge.

Soon after attaining the northerly rim of Indian Creek, about a mile up a flat valley draining northerly, we saw the stalled motor truck. In front of us the road was under water, so we turned right through the fence and drove over the fields heavy with mud, until we reached the motor and a buggy that had been sent out yesterday. 11:45 reached the motor, which, for the time being, was stuck in a mud hole. It was a one-ton Buick motor-truck, with a driver's seat in front, and folding benches running longitudinally at the sides of the truck body. It had left Moab early yesterday morning in charge of Charlie Fisher, with mail, express and parcels post, and the following passengers—a woman with a five-weeks' old baby and a two-year old boy, a Scotchman and wife with a six-months' old baby and a three-year old girl. They had made reasonable progress to La Sal, where they lunched, and from there on had met with difficulty, finally getting stuck in a small flood at this point. The water soon rose to the level of the floor of the truck, wetting the passengers some and filling the carburetor and crank case with mud and water. The passengers had a small package of crackers which the children ate, and one of them fortunately had a little whiskey. The young baby and its mother were ill all night; they thought the former would die, but whiskey and water, heated at the camp fire, kept them going.

We helped transfer the passengers from the machine to the buggy, and they immediately set off toward Monticello with the team, now fresh, which had started last night. Elmer proceeded with our team a few miles to the north expecting to meet the southbound mail truck and drive in the day's mail.

Fisher was an inspiration and an education. He had had nothing to eat for 24 hours. All night he was soaked through and working hard on the car. The engine was running badly when we joined him, and required more work. In spite of all this, he kept at his job patiently, never complained or even swore, and assured us that the only regrets he had about the machine's misfortune were on account of the babies and ladies.

Fisher managed to get the truck running, and with the Frasers he turned back toward Moab. They became mired again at a wash where the truck had gotten stuck on the way down. Here they were met by another mail truck, proceeding south from the town of La Sal. This truck managed to pull out the first truck, and the Frasers continued on in the second truck to Moab, where they spent the night.

Sunday, July 30, 1916

Up 4:30. 5 a.m. breakfast at the short order place, presided over by a middle aged lady, who prattled all the town gossip while we ate. Excellent eggs, first class coffee and hot cakes. The postmaster showed up promptly at 6. His name is Bryan. The mail car was not ready to start until 6:30. It was a Ford truck, very dirty, ramshackle and noisy. The driver, a big fellow about 23, treated the machine like a horse, and tried to make it go by cursing.

We went 2½ miles down Moab Valley to the junction of Moab Creek with the Grand River, which we crossed on a substantial iron bridge. Here the engine of the Ford began to give trouble. After several ineffective efforts to keep it going, a new spark plug got all the cylinders in operation at once.

When 11 miles from Moab, while going at the rate of about 20 miles an hour, we brought up with a jolt. The driver cursed and put on the brake, and I saw our right hind wheel running ahead of us on the side of the road. It hit mile post 25 (from Thompson) and stopped. We had broken the rear axle. The driver produced a box from the back of the truck, carried it over to the telephone line about ¼ of a mile to the west, pulled up one of the poles and bent down the wires so he could reach them, and attached them to his box, tapping them so he could telephone to Moab for relief.

At 8:30 he returned saying he had a promise of a car coming pretty soon.

It was cloudless, and very hot, otherwise I would have been tempted to climb part way up the cliffs and see the view. To the east of us, against the sun so that no photograph could be taken, there ran a ridge of broken, jagged, red cliff, weathered into needles, and with two windows or bridges.[25]

10 a.m. a Hupmobile arrived with Newkirk, owner of the Ford car, and a mail contractor on this route, and a couple of men. Newkirk, one of his companions and our driver started to put a new axle in the Ford, and we proceeded slowly with the other man.

After going about seven miles, we came to a canyon with a small, poor spring. Here we met a number of freight outfits on the way from Thompson to Moab. This being midway between those points, the freighters have a camp here called "Courthouse." It takes two days to make the 36 miles from Thompson to Moab, and they ordinarily camp here for the night. Last night they were all out, stuck in the mud hole which we still had to cross. Freight outfit consists of two large prairie schooners, hitched together, drawn by four horses and loaded to the guards. Sometimes three and even more wagons are hitched together with three, four, and sometimes more teams.

11:30, arrived Valley City. This consists of a deserted house built years ago by a man who dammed up an adjacent canyon expecting to irrigate the place. A flood washed him out after a season or two, and the ranch was abandoned. The recent storms wrought havoc here. The canyon was flooded high, and the waters spread all over the plain at the canyon's mouth, settling into a mud hole or quicksand that hitherto had been impassable. By today, the place had dried up pretty well except for a width of about 10 feet. Just as we approached the mud hole, two cars bound east came along. They had crossed by means of planks, which I thought would answer our purpose. The driver, however, was timid, and insisted on waiting for a buggy which Newkirk had ordered to meet us. In a few moments the buggy appeared bringing the mail from Moab, and one passenger. Our driver transferred the mail for Thompson, and we were about to get in and drive the remaining distance, when a Ford car came along driven by the rival garage keeper at Moab. He had room, so we got in and without difficulty crossed the mud hole and sped over the desert, making the 12 miles to Thompson in ½ hour. Fare Moab to Thompson, $3 each, ⅔ of which we paid to Newkirk's man, and ⅓ to the last man.

Arrived Thompson 12:30. We put up at the Thompson Hotel, meal 50 cents, bath, very hard to get, 25 cents each. The floods have put the water system out of business. Drinking water had been brought in from a spring a few miles away in a barrel.

If the Ford had not broken down, and the mud hole had been passable, we might have got a morning train east. As it was, we had to wait until the train due at 10:50 p.m. arrived over an hour late. We spent the afternoon watching automobiles on the transcontinental road, and talking with some of the occupants. None of them displayed very much enthusiasm over their journey.

The lights in the hotel were put out about 9:30, and we found great difficulty in keeping awake until D. & R. G. #4 pulled in at midnight. The railroad men kept very busy all day. There were 21 trains through in the 24 hours preceding our departure.

The Frasers returned home without incident. After having ridden on horseback hundreds of miles through desert and canyon, the vagaries of automobile travel must have been frustrating. But they were witnessing a balance point in history, after which the automobile would quickly supplant horse travel, even in the backcountry of the Southwest. Within a year, the first tourists in automobiles would be visiting Monument Valley and other scenic destinations in the Navajo country. While long horseback journeys would still be possible in the deeper recesses of the canyon lands, the unlimited horizons Fraser and Rust faced were becoming circumscribed.

Dave Rust returned home to Kanab via Monument Valley and Kayenta, where he missed meeting John and Louisa Wetherill, who had established a trading post there in 1910. Traveling with the principal of the high school at Bluff, Rust made the return journey in ten days.

Epilogue

For as long as he was able, George Fraser continued to make adventurous summertime excursions to the Southwest, never exhausting the region's possibilities for geological and cultural study. One or more of his family would come along, and the automobile played an increasing role in his later trips. Following their Navajo trip in 1916, Fraser took a short hiatus due to the war. He wrote to Dave Rust in May 1917:

> I have no right to go far from my base, even without disappearing in the wilderness as I would like, and have liked to do. . . . When, with the end of the war, normal conditions are again in sight, you may look for a communication—probably by wire—inviting you to hitch up with me for a ride over the Uintas or down to Parashont, or for a boat trip down the Green River and through Glen Canyon, depending on·the season of the year. In the meantime I shall tread the well worn trails in the canyon bottoms of this Borough's Wall Street district and see about as much blue sky as is revealed to the wader in the Little Zion Narrows.[1]

Fraser resumed his desert explorations in 1918 in New Mexico.[2] He climbed Mount Taylor, revisited Laguna Pueblo, and saw the ruins at what would become in the following year Bandelier National Monument.

In 1919 Fraser returned to the Navajo country with his friend George Bird Grinnell, a noted sportsman and conservationist, who was brother-in-law of Fraser's law partner Newell Martin.[3] Traveling mainly by automobile, they stopped at the Wetherills' trading post at Kayenta, Arizona, and rode the canyon trail to the ancient ruins at Keet Seel and Betatakin, part of Navajo National Monument, which Fraser and Rust had missed in 1916. The men also visited Canyon de Chelly, which became a National Monument in 1931. The Hopi pueblos and Petrified Forest National Monument were also on the itinerary.

Several more of Arizona's cliff-dwelling sites were in store for Fraser and his daughter Ann in a 1920 jaunt, including Montezuma's Castle National Monument south of Flagstaff.[4] They also visited the South Rim of the Grand Canyon by train and set off by car across the desert to the Hopi village of Oraibi.

In 1921 Fraser again brought Ann, along with his wife, Jane, to Utah, where they met Dave Rust for a horse-drawn wagon and auto trip through the High Plateaus region. This time they visited Bryce Canyon, still two years away from designation as a National Monument, which Fraser and Rust had bypassed on their 1915 trip. Fraser kept a detailed photo log of this trip, but unfortunately he did not keep a journal. They also stopped by Kanab to visit the Rust home and meet his family. Jane Fraser, in a letter to the Rusts, recalled the stormy weather they experienced on this trip and how they had to heat stones to place next to their feet at night.[5]

Fraser rejoined Rust in 1922 for a horseback journey from Teasdale, Utah, to the historic Crossing of the Fathers on the Colorado River in Glen Canyon.[6] Fraser's daughter Jane ("Jane Jr.") came along, and Rust's eldest son, Jordan, served as horse wrangler. Fraser was interested in retracing part of the Dominguez-Escalante exploration of 1776, especially their desperate search for a crossing of the Colorado on the return leg of their journey. He presented the history of this crossing in an article for *Natural History*.[7] He included photographs from his trip in this article but nothing from his journals. As on his previous Utah trips, Fraser enjoyed his encounters with the local townspeople and ranchers. Attending a Fourth of July celebration in Teasdale early in the trip, Fraser was impressed by the townspeople's patriotic gathering and speeches. Later that day, they attended a town dance: "Coleman Snow took charge of Jane, and made so many introductions that she danced continuously. I sat with a few old men and Miss Snow, and she and I danced the quadrille, i.e., the old-fashioned lancers, with a man in overalls calling out the procedure."

The next day, Fraser and Rust visited their friend Walter Hanks, the forest ranger whose family had entertained them so hospitably on the Aquarius in 1915. Fraser was disturbed to find him "land poor—all signs pointed to extreme poverty . . . a sad change around the old man."

After crossing the Aquarius, they seemed to have followed the Boulder Mail Trail across the deep cut of Death Hollow—a route that for years was the only connection between the towns of Boulder and Escalante. They headed south up onto the Kaiparowits Plateau to climb Canaan Peak, the plateau's highest point, and traversed Fiftymile Mountain, the long escarpment that had beckoned to Fraser on his 1916 trip. Here they reached Navajo Point, where they enjoyed the incomparable view across Glen Canyon to Navajo Mountain. From there they continued to the village of Tropic:

> Stayed with Willis's at Tropic, former hotel owners. Mrs. Willis urged Jane not to attempt the Last Chance country, and invited her to stay as a guest. Mr. Willis said to me "Yer ain't going to take the woman down there, be yer," and shook his head doubtfully when I said yes. Their boys told Jane hair raising stories about snakes, scorpions, centipedes and bad water, and Mrs. Willis assured me that we would get typhoid fever, because the hot days and damp nights always brought it.[8]

Jane and her father made it through the austere landscape below the White Cliffs, however, following Dave Rust's sure lead. Exiting the Paria River drainage, they crossed the broad expanse of lower Wahweap Creek, climbed through the spectacular notch called Gunsight Pass, and descended to the Colorado River, where they attempted to locate the crossing used by the Dominguez-Escalante expedition.

It would be eight more years before Fraser would make another trip with Dave Rust. Business travel brought Fraser to the Southwest several more times, and in 1925 he corresponded with Rust about another trip with Ann and Rust's daughter Emma. It did not materialize. Fraser, by then fifty-three years old, was growing uncertain about his stamina for such journeys:

> I am beginning to doubt whether there will ever be a next trip for me. I know I cannot stand even the moderate pace we made the last time we were out. It is a sad fact that since we rode into Escalante I have had practically no exercise. My appendix, before and after its removal, kept me from doing much for quite awhile. Last Winter I tore the ligaments in my right leg and this Winter tore out the calves of my left leg. Nothing permanent, but decidedly inconvenient and inconsistent with much activity. As you know, my wind has given out. Of course, I can still sit, but unless you have another 'Indian' [the nearly lame horse Fraser's son rode in 1915], it will take more than mere sitting to get across a rough country such as we are talking about.[9]

In 1930 Rust finally got his wish to escort Fraser down Glen Canyon—a trip that did not require strenuous horseback travel. In April,

Fraser had dinner with Frederick Dellenbaugh (of Major Powell's 1871 river expedition) and Clyde Eddy (a contemporary Colorado River explorer and filmmaker) to learn more about the river. In July, Fraser and his youngest daughter, Sarah, journeyed in hundred-degree heat to the desert hamlet of Hanksville, Utah, thence taking a horse-drawn wagon down the washout-prone track to the ghost village of Hite on the Colorado. Fraser accompanied Rust in one of his fourteen-foot rowing canoes, while Sarah rode in a second canoe, piloted by veteran prospector and river guide Bert Loper. Loper had built a cabin in Glen Canyon downstream from Hite, pursuing the river's scattered gold-bearing placers, as Rust had also tried to do more than thirty years before.[10] Sarah Fraser recalled how her father and Dave Rust hiked up the hot, steep trail to Hole-in-the-Rock, where Mormon pioneers had built a precarious wagon track down to the river in 1880. Sarah sat out this climb but joined them on the hike up to Rainbow Bridge, which the two men had visited via the overland route in 1916.

It was, sadly, George Fraser's last visit to the canyon country. Work pressures and, it seems, declining health obviated any further chance to sample the scenic delights of the region. More and more of his geology trips were made in the New Jersey and New York countryside with his children and grandchildren, all of whom were eager to accompany "Peeps," as his grandchildren called him.

Myra Mathers, daughter of Fraser's eldest daughter Myra, recalls taking many long walks with her grandfather in the hills and woodlands of rural New Jersey, studying plants, animals, and geology. "He was never afraid of anything outdoors," she says, and appeared completely comfortable with the outdoor life during their daylong rambles.[11]

In early October of 1935, Fraser traveled to Texas to check on his landholdings. Near Dallas, he fell ill with heart pains and was taken to the hospital. Five weeks later, on November 15, still in Dallas but with family around him, he passed away. Dave Rust's son, Jordan, who had attended Stanford with Fraser's financial assistance, traveled to Morristown to attend the funeral. Fraser's wife, Jane, died the following year.

George Fraser Jr. entered the Army Air Corps and served in Europe during World War I. He had studied at Princeton and after the war entered the business world and worked for Sun Oil in Midland, Texas. Of his sisters, Sarah seemed most to have acquired her father's affinity for travel; among her journeys was a sojourn in Afghanistan and a return to Glen Canyon before it was flooded.

After Fraser's death, Dave Rust continued to guide clients throughout the canyon country, showing them the views from Bright Angel Point, Cape Final, the rim of Little Zion, Table Cliff Plateau, Navajo Mountain, the Aquarius, and Mount Ellen. He always urged his guests to take time to savor these vistas, and he would occasionally read to them a little from Powell or Dutton, as he had learned to do from his friend George Fraser.

Today, most of those panoramas have changed little, though they are (with the exception of Navajo Mountain) easier to reach. Major Powell's writings and Clarence Dutton's *Tertiary History* have been reprinted for a growing audience of canyon enthusiasts. These are still good works to take out of the pack when camped at a high plateau lookoff, as an aid and an inspiration in studying the cliff lines reaching out to infinity.

Notes

Introduction

1. Kidder, "Memorial of George C. Fraser," 372.

2. Jett, "The Journals of George C. Fraser '93," 291. Jett's article, the only published mention of Fraser's journals, provides an excellent scholarly assessment of their meaning and importance. He discusses the journals used in this book as well as those from Fraser's other travels in the Southwest and the Southeast.

3. Pomeroy, *In Search of the Golden West*, 71.

4. Author interview with George C. Fraser III, November 4, 2000.

5. Each journal is bound separately and carries a title page. All are stored at the Princeton University Library's Department of Rare Books and Special Collections. Full citations are given in the "Manuscripts" section of the bibliography (Fraser 1886–1922). The journals were transcribed from microfilm copies graciously loaned by the Peter J. Shields Library at the University of California, Davis. Fraser also wrote several magazine articles on his southwestern journeys. "El Vado de los Padres" (1923) featured photographs taken on his 1922 trip to the Crossing of the Fathers in Glen Canyon. "Glimpses of the South West" (1921) displayed photographs from his various trips. Fraser also wrote an account of his 1914 trip for the *Arrowhead*, a publication of the Union Pacific Railroad, but no copy could be located.

6. Fraser used two cameras on his 1914 trip—a #3 Folding Pocket Kodak and a Vest Pocket Kodak, both of which produced small and indistinct prints. On later trips he added a larger format camera that gave 2½″ by 3½″ prints of better quality, and a panorama camera of approximately 2″ by 6″ format. In 1916 he experimented with a color plate camera, but I could not find any of these images. The poor quality of many of the photographs is partly compensated by Fraser's habit of recording the precise location of every photograph he made. These locations are given on typewritten sheets accompanying the journals and are keyed to the text by a system of letters and numbers. The text references (there are hundreds) are omitted in this book. Duplicate prints of many of Fraser's photographs are found in the David D. Rust Collection.

7. I use the term *canyon lands* to loosely mean the highly dissected portion of the Colorado Plateau physiographic province, athwart the Colorado River, from about Colorado National Monument in western Colorado to the Grand Canyon. The term encompasses far more than Canyonlands National Park, which

includes about 338,000 acres centering on the confluence of the Green and Colorado Rivers. In *Canyonlands Country*, Baars discusses the boundaries of the Colorado Plateau province (8–10).

8. Fraser evidently did not keep his field notebooks. They must have been rather detailed to allow him to dictate more than two hundred pages of manuscript upon returning home. He kept a notebook handy to jot down observations at every halt.

9. This refers to Fraser encountering on the Kaibab Plateau two Harvard seniors whose inhospitality Fraser attributed to the chill New England air (see journal, July 22, 1914).

10. A comprehensive and readable account of early tourist development at the Grand Canyon is presented in Michael Anderson's *Living at the Edge*. M. R. Tillotson, superintendent of Grand Canyon National Park from 1927 to 1938, described the park's visitor facilities in his 1929 book *Grand Canyon Country*. George Wharton James also described South Rim amenities in *In and Around the Grand Canyon* and *The Grand Canyon of Arizona*.

11. James, *In and Around the Grand Canyon*, 78.

12. Ibid., 76.

13. James, *The Grand Canyon of Arizona*, 17. Scenes from the early days of El Tovar can also be found in William Suran's "The Opening of the El Tovar Hotel," which is also found at http://www.kaibab.org/gcps/gcpseltv.htm (accessed February 27, 2004).

14. Anderson, *Living at the Edge*, 71.

15. Bass's son Bill recounted his father's business at the Grand Canyon in Maurer, *Solitude and Sunshine*.

16. Roosevelt's entire speech, as recorded in the *Flagstaff (AZ) Coconino County Sun*, May 9, 1903, along with an interesting article on the president's visit by Bob Ribokas, written for the Grand Canyon Historical Society, can be found at http://www.kaibab.org/gcps/teddy.htm (accessed February 27, 2004).

17. Stephen J. Pyne, in *How the Canyon Became Grand*, addresses how turn-of-the-century writers, artists, and public figures elevated the Grand Canyon to near-mythical status. Earlier, C. Gregory Crampton wrote popular histories of the region (*Standing Up Country*, *Land of Living Rock*) and discussed its development as a tourist attraction.

18. For an account of one such trip, see James, *The Grand Canyon*. He includes excerpts from the diary of Mrs. J. B. Gayler of New Jersey, who made the trip with Bass and James across the Bass Trail and along the North Rim in 1901.

19. The Bright Angel Creek trail was the brainchild of Kanab, Utah, businessman, rancher, and LDS Church leader Edwin D. ("Uncle Dee") Woolley Jr., who helped organize the Grand Canyon Transportation Company in 1903 to carry out his dream of a cross-canyon trail to tap into the tourist traffic at the South Rim. In 1906 he hired his son-in-law, David D. Rust, to oversee completion of the trail and installation of the cable tramway. Rust figures in these journals as the Frasers' outfitter and guide.

20. In 1928 Dave Rust reprinted a portion of Tissandier's journals in the

Mormon youth magazine *Improvement Era*, under the title "A Pioneer Tourist." George Fraser had translated the journals and sent them to Rust, who submitted them to the magazine. The complete journals were reprinted along with a selection of Tissandier's excellent drawings by the Utah Museum of Fine Arts (Francey, *Albert Tissandier*). Tissandier was a journalist engaged in writing a book about his travels and so was not, strictly speaking, a tourist, but the distinction was perhaps not as sharp in those days.

21. Woodbury, *History of Southern Utah*, 190–91.

22. Ibid., 188.

23. Ibid., 196–208.

24. The Cedar City, Utah, *Iron County Record*, for example, announced that "with a good automobile road through Washington County, hundreds of thousands of tourists from Northern Utah and the adjoining states will visit this wonderful section" ("Road Move Commended," quoted in the *Washington County News*, November 27, 1913). The timetable for this traffic was overly optimistic, but visitation to Zion National Park did reach 55,000 by 1930. Still, local writers were hardly in error when they announced that "Southern Utah is destined to be the greatest scenic region in the United States" (R. K. Evans, "Scenery One Of Our Big Assets," *Washington County News*, April 21, 1921).

25. Anderson, *Living at the Edge*, 153.

26. Woodbury, *History of Southern Utah*, 203–4.

27. I briefly sketched Rust's guiding operations in "Canyon Guide" (*Salt Lake Magazine*, July/August 2000, 55–58). William W. Slaughter added to this in "Dave Rust: Pioneering Outdoorsman and Guide" (*Utah Outdoors*, June 2001, 27–29). Excerpts of Rust's notes from his first guided trip down Glen Canyon in 1923 are found in my article "Dave Rust in Glen Canyon: A 1923 River Diary," *Confluence* (Colorado Plateau River Guides), no. 22 (February 2001): 10–14.

28. George C. Fraser to David D. Rust, December 20, 1918. David D. Rust Collection, box 3, folder 5.

29. George C. Fraser to David D. Rust, July 5, 1921. David D. Rust Collection, box 3, folder 6.

30. "Monumental Highway," *Washington County News*, May 24, 1917.

31. For accounts of early-day horseback and motor adventurers in the Navajo and San Juan country, see Topping, *Glen Canyon and the San Juan Country*.

32. Hassell, *Rainbow Bridge*, 78.

33. At this time, homestead entries were still allowed on some national forest lands, and hopeful settlers were taking up agricultural parcels in likely spots. Few survived the return of dry weather in the 1920s and 1930s.

34. Jett, "The Journals of George C. Fraser '93," 298–99.

35. The standard geological works that Fraser carried in his saddlebag (and which retain much of their vitality today) are Clarence Dutton's *Report on the Geology of the High Plateaus of Utah* (1880) and *Tertiary History of the Grand Cañon District* (1882); Grove Karl Gilbert's *Report on the Geology of the Henry Mountains* (1877); and John Wesley Powell's *Canyons of the Colorado* (1895).

36. Pyne, *Grove Karl Gilbert*, 73.

Chapter 1. From Zion to the Grand Canyon, 1914

1. J. Cecil Alter to George C. Fraser, May 5, 1914, David D. Rust Collection, box 3, folder 1.

2. Wallace Stegner, "Introduction," in Dutton, *Tertiary History*, x.

3. The house is now occupied and is listed as a historic site. It is located on the west side of the main road (Utah Highway 17) in Toquerville.

4. Fraser occasionally uses "Virgen River," from its Spanish name, "Rio Virgen." "Virgin River" is substituted for consistency.

5. Stephen Jett, in "The Journals of George C. Fraser '93," cites this as an example of Fraser's observant nature.

6. The bridge is still standing, just upstream from the present-day highway bridge. The hot spring has been developed as a mineral spa.

7. Tonsillitis or perhaps strep throat. "Dioxogen" was a preparation of hydrogen peroxide, an antiseptic.

8. A historic ranch that was located near the present-day Zion National Park history museum.

9. This and subsequent observations suggest considerable erosion was occurring in the headwaters of the Virgin. In his 1915 journal Fraser describes the cause of this erosion as heavy sheep grazing.

10. Parunuweap Canyon encompasses the narrows of the East Fork of the Virgin River. It was explored by John Wesley Powell in 1872.

11. Twelve meridian (noon).

12. Fraser uses the nautical points of the compass somewhat roughly: technically, "east by north" would be one point (1/32 of a full circle) north (counterclockwise) of due east; his bearings are obviously approximate.

13. See note 19 to the introduction.

14. A banquet served on empty plates; that is, to go without. One presumes the women ate in the kitchen.

15. Fraser probably acquired this information from Dave Rust, who had published a favorable account of the women's tenure in his *Kane County News* (January 9, 1914). Fraser included a copy of the article in his journal, opposite p. 102.

16. This roadwork was part of the Forest Service's efforts to improve the road to the North Rim near Bright Angel Point. At that time, the entire Kaibab Plateau was under Forest Service administration. Ironically, roads such as this would eventually bring in so many tourists that the informal generosity Fraser appreciated would become rare.

17. Fire-suppression efforts starting around this time allowed brush and small trees to become established in the forests of the Kaibab Plateau. Ecologists believe that slow-moving ground fires, some of which were probably set by native peoples, allowed the parklike stands of tall ponderosa pine to flourish. See, for example, Will Moir's "Ponderosa Pine Fire Ecology," U.S. Forest Service Rocky Mountain Research Station, Flagstaff, AZ, at http://www.cpluhna.nau.edu/Biota/ponderosafire.htm (accessed February 27, 2004).

18. Ponderosa pine.

19. "Entertainment" here means "hospitable provision for the needs and wants of guests" (*Random House Dictionary of the English Language*, 2nd ed., 1987).

20. Gifford Pinchot was the first chief of the Forest Service (1905–10). Following his firing by President Taft, he was succeeded by Henry S. Graves (1910–20).

21. Probably Walcott, "Precambrian Igneous Rocks of the Unkar Terrane," 492–519.

22. The Wachtung Mountains west of New York City. Navajo Mountain is about eighty-five miles from Cape Final.

23. The famed Kaibab deer herd was believed to have grown to great numbers during the early 1900s, aided by hunting restrictions in the Grand Canyon Game Preserve, grazing-induced vegetation changes, and relentless extermination of mountain lions and other predators. A hard winter in 1924–25 initiated a decline in numbers. Some ecologists dispute the popular story of an immense irruption of the herd due to predator control, followed by a precipitous crash; see, for example, Wuerthner, *Grand Canyon*, 195–200.

24. Fraser inserted into his journal Dave Rust's comment on this campsite: "As was our unique plan, we camped right on the rim, spread out our maps, set the compass and proceeded to consult Dutton and capture the landscape; not simply the skin-deep beauty, but deep down into the interesting structure."

25. Park naturalist Edwin D. McKee, in his *Ancient Landscapes of the Grand Canyon Region*, first published in 1931, ascribed alcove formation in the Redwall more to chemical weathering: "Large amphitheaters, many curving alcoves, caves, and solution funnels are all characteristic features of the great Redwall. It is composed of relatively pure lime so rain and other waters have a chemical action upon it—they leach and dissolve it. Waters all tend to drain toward curving centers, and so increase this curving. Everywhere the rounding off of corners takes place. Thus has the graceful form of the Redwall been brought about."

26. Powell Spring, on the north side of Muav Saddle.

27. Frederick H. Maude was a photographer from Ventura, California, who often visited the Grand Canyon in the company of W. W. Bass and author George Wharton James.

28. Fraser included a "Memorandum As to Cost of Trip" at the end of his 1914 journal, including the following list of expenses:

(a) With Rust from Toquerville to Colorado River.

Rust and his horse, 27 days @ $5.00	$135.00
Extra riding and pack horses at $2.00 each per day in actual service	90.00
Rust's team from Kanab to Camp Woolley, 3 days @ $5.00	15.00
Duffin and his team from Toquerville up Little Zion etc. to Hurricane, 7 days @ 4.50	31.50
Dalton and his team from Hurricane to the Toroweap and Fredonia (8 days) and return to Hurricane (2 days) @ $4.00 (10 days)	40.00

Bedding for George and myself	10.00
Ruesch for meals and board at the sawmill above Little Zion	2.00
Mrs. Naegle, board for Rust, George and myself at Toquerville	4.25
Mrs. McAllister—board and baths for George and myself at Kanab	4.75
Supplies, provisions, etc	$98.50
	$431.00
(b) Other Expenses	
Railroad fares and sleepers (round trip tickets $110.50 each)	$314.50
Bass for horses, guidance and meals	25.00
Automobile at Kansas City	12.00
Automobile from Lund to Anderson Ranch near Toquerville	20.00
Anderson—ranch to Toquer, team	2.00
Ammunition	10.25
Utah Hotel, Salt Lake, room	5.20
El Tovar	9.15
Sundries—meals, telegrams, tips, etc. about	130.90
	529.00
Expenses of trip with Rust as above	431.00
Total expenses of trip, approximately	$1,000.00

29. David D. Rust to George Fraser, August 6, 1914 (Fraser, "Memoranda of a Trip" (1914), 205).

30. George Fraser to David D. Rust, November 28, 1914, David D. Rust Collection, box 3, folder 1.

Chapter 2. The High Plateaus, the Henry Mountains, and the Kolob, 1915

1. See note 35 to the introduction.

2. For a discussion, see Stokes, *Geology of Utah*, 177.

3. Dutton, *Report on the Geology of the High Plateaus*, 284.

4. Sent by Fraser before the trip.

5. Likely the Parry's primrose *(Primula parryi)*, a showy alpine flower.

6. This was Bromide Basin, first developed by Jack Sumner, of Powell's 1869 Colorado River voyage. Rust worked in the basin around 1890, when he was about sixteen.

7. Fraser sent Busenbark a revolver as a Christmas gift that year. Busenbark's letter expressing profuse thanks is included in Fraser's original journal. A sample: "We are having Pretty Hard Work to keep the coyotes away from the sheep & will have a gun I can always Carry. Whenever I shoot it I shall remember you."

Busenbark went on to own his own sheep herd in the 1920s (Murphy, *History of Wayne County*, 162).

8. Now known as the King Ranch. The party had descended from the Henrys into the Sandy Creek valley south of Notom, Utah. Michael R. Kelsey describes the present-day ranches of the area (*Hiking and Exploring Utah's Henry Mountains*, 112–44).

9. Now the Sandy Ranch (Kelsey, *Hiking and Exploring Utah's Henry Mountains*, 125).

10. This is probably Oak Creek. Current maps show Tantalus Creek as a short tributary of Pleasant Creek.

11. The Wingate Sandstone, exposed in the Waterpocket Fold.

12. Earth pillars are found west of Bolzano (Bozen), Italy, in the western Dolomites.

13. Hanks had actually owned the land on which the ranger station was built, and he had constructed a cabin nearby. He traded his land and buildings to the Forest Service in exchange for a lifetime job as ranger. This accounts for his use of the land as a family summer spot. The Forest Service has preserved the ranger station, which was built in 1911, as a historic site. It is located about one-quarter of a mile northwest of the Wildcat Ranger Station visitor information center (itself a historic station)—a pleasant stop along Highway 12 on Boulder Mountain.

14. Hanks's father was Ephraim K. "Eph" Hanks, known for his solo trek to rescue stranded Mormon handcart pioneers in the winter of 1856.

15. Duffin had joined Fraser and Rust on the first part of their 1914 journey.

16. What they took to be Crystal Creek is shown on today's maps as Oak Creek. The former is a tributary of Deep Creek.

17. This is in reference to the eviction of Mormon and other American settlers from northern Mexico in 1912.

Chapter 3. Lees Ferry and the Navajo Country, 1916

1. Cummings, "The Great Natural Bridges of Utah," 157–66.

2. Roosevelt, "Across the Navajo Desert," 309–17.

3. Reilly, *Lee's Ferry*, 188.

4. Powell, *Report on the Exploration of the Colorado River*, 97.

5. Jett, "The Journals of George C. Fraser '93," 297.

6. Autochrome was an early color transparency process introduced a decade or so earlier. Fraser's autochromes, if any survived, were not included with his journals.

7. Fraser's term for the pack stock.

8. Presumably a poached deer. They were in the Kaibab Game Preserve, administered by the U.S. Forest Service.

9. Anderson, *Living at the Edge*, 151.

10. Leaving the horses free to roam at night, although making for much work each morning, was necessary to allow them to forage as needed in the sparse desert grass.

11. That fall Fraser wrote an article describing this encounter, titled "A Desert Incident." In it he tells that Bevard repaid the loan by mail. In 1921, during a family excursion in Utah, Fraser was told that Bevard was known to be a bootlegger who sometimes hid the goods in his empty shirt sleeve.

12. These appear to be the bonytail chub and razorback sucker, both now endangered as a result of impoundments along the Colorado.

13. Charles H. Spencer built a ninety-two-foot steamboat at Lees Ferry in 1911 to haul coal downstream from Glen Canyon to power his prospective hydraulic mining operations near the ferry. The boat could not clear the Colorado's sandbars, however, and mining the Chinle shales at Lees Ferry proved impossible (Crampton, *Standing Up Country*, 141–42).

14. Nathaniel Galloway, a Utah hunter, trapper, farmer, and river guide, was noted for facing downstream when running rapids, a method that now bears his name. He was employed by Robert Brewster Stanton in 1898 as a boatman and hunter and by Stanton investor Julius Stone on his 1909 Green-Colorado River expedition. Rust knew him from his mining days on the river and in the Henry Mountains.

15. W. H. Holmes's drawing, entitled "Midsummerday's Dream—Jurassic—on the Colob" (Dutton, *Tertiary History*, opposite p. 36), shows the pronounced weathering of the cross-bedded layers in the Navajo Sandstone in Zion National Park.

16. Fraser uses the terms *squaw* and *woman* interchangeably; given the current derogatory connotations of the former term, the latter is used here.

17. This may be Chaiyahi Canyon, which leads from Navajo Creek northeasterly to the plateau below Navajo Mountain.

18. This appears to be War God Spring, high on the southeast flank of Navajo Mountain.

19. They evidently ascended south of the present-day route, which comes in from the east via Navajo Mountain village. (The Navajo Nation considers the mountain sacred and in recent years has closed it to the public.)

20. Cha Canyon or possibly Bald Rock Canyon.

21. This upper part of Nasja Creek was named "Surprise Valley" by early explorers.

22. Mapped as point 6140 or 6159 on the 7.5-minute USGS topographic sheet.

23. Fraser uses the terms *arch* and *bridge* interchangeably; current usage holds that a natural bridge (like Rainbow Bridge) spans a watercourse and an arch does not.

24. Fraser provides a description of this conflict, which is omitted here. In 1915, the Ute Tse-ne-gat was accused of killing a Mexican sheepherder and was later arrested by U.S. Army Gen. Hugh Scott, following efforts on the part of local whites to make the arrest, which led to more deaths. Tse-ne-gat was acquitted by a jury in Denver.

25. The Windows section of Arches National Park. It was not established as a national monument until 1929; park designation came in 1971.

Epilogue

1. David D. Rust Collection, box 4, folder 5.

2. Fraser, *Notes of Journeys* (1918).

3. Fraser, *Notes of Journeys* (1919).

4. Fraser, *Notes of a Journey* (1920).

5. Jane Fraser to Ruth Rust, n.d., David D. Rust Collection, box 3, folder 1.

6. Fraser, *Notes of journey* (1922).

7. Fraser, "El Vado de los Padres."

8. Fraser, *Notes of journey* (1922), 46–47.

9. George C. Fraser to David D. Rust, March 9, 1925. David D. Rust Collection, box 4, folder 1.

10. Loper told Sarah Fraser that he left Glen Canyon with five dollars less than he went in with—a common result for miners. He lived in the canyon for eight years in the early 1900s, part of the time with his wife, and built a sailboat to travel up and down the river. Author interview with Sarah Fraser, November 1, 2000.

11. Author interview with Myra Mathers, May 29, 2003.

Bibliography

Manuscripts

Fraser, George C. 1886–89. "Diaries of George C. Fraser, January 1, 1886 to December 18, 1886, during Journey to Egypt, The Holy Land, Ephesus, Greece, Constantinople, Up the Danube, Vienna, Switzerland, Germany and London; March 19, 1888 to April 25, 1888, Through Spain; August 19 to August 30, 1888, Mountain Journey Through Switzerland; Geological Notes 1887 to 1889." George C. Fraser journals. Excerpts published with permission of the Princeton University Library, Princeton, NJ.

——. 1914. "Memoranda of a Trip Taken by G. C. Fraser, Sr. and Jr., to Southwestern Utah and Northwestern Arizona, Sunday, June 28, 1914 to Thursday, August 6, 1914." George C. Fraser journals. Excerpts published with permission of the Princeton University Library, Princeton, NJ.

——. 1914–20. "Note of journeys across the United States in 1914–1920 in company with George C. Fraser Jr. or Ann C. Fraser." Peter J. Shields Library, University of California, Davis.

——. 1915. "Notes of a Journey, June 24 to August 19, 1915 made by George C. Fraser & George C. Fraser, Jr., From New York to San Francisco and Return, Including a 5 Weeks' Trip in Southern Utah." George C. Fraser journals. Excerpts published with permission of the Princeton University Library, Princeton, NJ.

——. 1916. "Notes of a Journey taken by George C. Fraser & George C. Fraser, Jr., June 24 to August 3, 1916, to Acoma, Meteor Crater, San Francisco Mountains and through the Navajo Country." George C. Fraser journals. Excerpts published with permission of the Princeton University Library, Princeton, NJ.

——. 1918. "Notes of Journeys in the South and Southwest 1917 and 1918." George C. Fraser journals. Excerpts published with permission of the Princeton University Library, Princeton, NJ.

——. 1919. "Notes of Journeys into Mississippi, Texas and the Navajo Country, 1919." George C. Fraser journals. Excerpts published with permission of the Princeton University Library, Princeton, NJ.

——. 1920. "Notes of a Journey to Texas, New Mexico and Arizona August 4th to September 15, 1920 with Ann C. Fraser." George C. Fraser journals. Excerpts published with permission of the Princeton University Library, Princeton, NJ.

——. 1922. "Notes of journey, June 23rd to August 11th, 1922, With Jane Fraser, Jr. to southwestern Utah; Portland, Oregon; Victoria, B.C.; Seattle, Washington and east via C.M. & St. Paul Railway." George C. Fraser journals. Excerpts published with permission of the Princeton University Library, Princeton, NJ.

Rust, David D. Collection. Church Archives, The Church of Jesus Christ of Latter-day Saints. Salt Lake City, UT.

Published Works

Alter, J. Cecil. 1913. "To the Grand Canyon of Arizona by Auto." *Salt Lake Tribune*, August 31.

——. 1914. "A Pilgrimage to Little Zion, the Mukuntuweap." *Salt Lake Tribune*, January 4.

Anderson, Michael F. 1998. *Living at the Edge: Explorers, Exploiters and Settlers of the Grand Canyon Region*. Grand Canyon, AZ: Grand Canyon Association.

Baars, Donald L. 1993. *Canyonlands Country: Geology of Canyonlands and Arches National Parks*. Salt Lake City: University of Utah Press.

Crampton, C. Gregory. 1964. *Standing Up Country: The Canyon Lands of Utah and Arizona*. New York: Alfred A. Knopf. Reprint, Salt Lake City: Peregrine Smith Books, 1983.

——. 1972. *Land of Living Rock: the Grand Canyon and the High Plateaus: Arizona, Utah, Nevada*. New York: Alfred A. Knopf. Reprint, Layton, UT: Peregrine Smith Books, 1985.

Cummings, Byron. 1910. "The Great Natural Bridges of Utah." *National Geographic Magazine* 21 (February): 157–66.

Darton, Nelson H. 1915. *Guidebook of the Western United States: Part C, The Santa Fe Route with a Side Trip to the Grand Canyon of the Colorado*. U.S. Department of the Interior, Geological Survey Bulletin 613. Washington, DC: Government Printing Office.

Dutton, Clarence E. 1880. *Report on the Geology of the High Plateaus of Utah, with Atlas*. Department of the Interior, U.S. Geographical and Geological Survey of the Rocky Mountain Region. Washington, DC: Government Printing Office.

——. 1882. *Tertiary History of the Grand Cañon District, with Atlas*. Department of the Interior, Monographs of the U.S. Geological Survey, vol. 2. Washington, DC: Government Printing Office. Reprint, Salt Lake City: Peregrine Smith, 1977. Reprint, Tucson: University of Arizona Press, 2001.

Francey, Mary F. 2001. *Albert Tissandier: Drawings of Nature and Industry in the United States, 1885*. Salt Lake City: University of Utah, Utah Museum of Fine Arts.

Fraser, George C. 1916. "A Desert Incident." *Commerce and Finance* 37 (September 13): 1049–51.

——. 1921. "Glimpses of the South West." *Century Magazine* 101 (March): 609–10.

——. 1923. "El Vado de los Padres." *Natural History* 23 (4): 344–57.

Gilbert, Grove Karl. 1877. *Report on the geology of the Henry Mountains.* Department of the Interior, U.S. Geographical and Geological Survey of the Rocky Mountain Region. Washington, DC: Government Printing Office.

Gregory, Herbert E. 1916. "The Navajo Country: A Geographic and Hydrographic Reconnaissance of Parts of Arizona, New Mexico, and Utah." U.S. Geological Survey Water-Supply Paper 380. Washington, DC: Government Printing Office.

———. 1917. "Geology of the Navajo Country: A Reconnaissance of Parts of Arizona, New Mexico, and Utah." U.S. Geological Survey Professional Paper 93. Washington, DC: Government Printing Office.

Hassell, Hank. 1999. *Rainbow Bridge: An Illustrated History.* Logan: Utah State University Press.

James, George Wharton. 1901. *In and around the Grand Canyon; The Grand Canyon of the Colorado River in Arizona.* Boston: Little, Brown and Co.

———. 1910. *The Grand Canyon of Arizona: How to See It.* Boston: Little, Brown and Co.

Jett, Stephen C. 1974. "The Journals of George C. Fraser '93: Early Twentieth-Century Travels in the South and Southwest." *Princeton University Library Chronicle* 35 (Spring): 290–308.

Kelsey, Michael R. 1987. *Hiking and Exploring Utah's Henry Mountains and Robbers Roost.* Provo, UT: Kelsey Publishing.

Kidder, H. Maynard. 1936. "Memorial of George Corning Fraser." *1936 Year Book.* Washington, DC: American Bar Association.

Maurer, Stephen G. 1983. *Solitude and Sunshine: Images of a Grand Canyon Childhood.* Boulder, CO: Pruett Publishing Co.

McKee, Edwin D. 1931. *Ancient Landscapes of the Grand Canyon Region, the Geology of Grand Canyon, Zion, Bryce, Petrified Forest, and Painted Desert.* Flagstaff, AZ: Edwin D. McKee.

Murphy, Miriam B. 1999. *A History of Wayne County.* Salt Lake City: Utah State Historical Society.

Pomeroy, Earl. 1957. *In Search of the Golden West: The Tourist in Western America.* New York: Alfred A. Knopf.

Powell, John Wesley. 1875. *Report on the Exploration of the Colorado River of the West and Its Tributaries. Explored in 1869, 1870, 1871, and 1872, under the Direction of the Secretary of the Smithsonian Institution.* Washington, DC: Government Printing Office.

———. 1895. *Canyons of the Colorado.* Meadville, PA: Flood and Vincent. Reprint, in excerpt, San Francisco: Chronicle Books, 1996.

———. 1987. *The Exploration of the Colorado River and Its Canyons.* New York: Penguin Nature Classics.

Pyne, Stephen J. 1980. *Grove Karl Gilbert: A Great Engine of Research.* Austin: University of Texas Press.

———. 1998. *How the Canyon Became Grand: A Short History.* New York: Viking.

Reilly, P. T. 1999. *Lee's Ferry: From Mormon Crossing to National Park.* Logan: Utah State University Press.

Richardson, Elmo R. 1965. "Federal Park Policy in Utah: The Escalante National

Monument Controversy of 1935–1940." *Utah Historical Quarterly* 35 (2): 110–33.

Roosevelt, Theodore. 1913. "Across the Navajo Desert." *Outlook* 105 (October 11): 309–17.

Rust, Dave. 1928. "A Pioneer Tourist." *Improvement Era* (July): 752–56.

Stokes, William L. 1988. *Geology of Utah*. Salt Lake City: Utah Museum of Natural History and Utah Department of Natural Resources, Geological and Mineral Survey.

Suran, William C. 1997. "The Opening of the El Tovar Hotel." *Ol' Pioneer* (Grand Canyon Historical Society, Flagstaff, AZ), January.

Tillotson, M. R., and Frank J. Taylor. 1929. *Grand Canyon Country*. Stanford, CA: Stanford University Press.

Topping, Gary. 1997. *Glen Canyon and the San Juan Country*. Moscow: University of Idaho Press.

Walcott, Charles D. 1894. "Pre-Cambrian Igneous Rocks of the Unkar terrane, Grand Canyon of the Colorado." In *U.S. Geological Survey 14th Annual Report for 1892/3, part 2*: 492–519. Washington, DC: Government Printing Office.

Woodbury, Angus M. 1950. *A History of Southern Utah and Its National Parks*. Rev. ed. Salt Lake City: Utah State Historical Society.

Wuerthner, George. 1998. *Grand Canyon: A Visitor's Companion*. Mechanicsburg, PA: Stackpole Books.

Figure Credits

Church Archives, The Church of Jesus Christ of Latter-day Saints

The Frasers at Morristown Station
George Fraser Jr. on Cable Mountain
Colorado River from Toroweap Overlook
Cathedral Valley
Spectacle Lake on the Aquarius Plateau
Zion National Park
Approaching Lees Ferry
George Fraser Sr. and Jr. in the Colorado River
George Fraser and Old Dan
At a hidden waterhole on the Kaibito Plateau
George Fraser changing camera plates
Rainbow Bridge

George C. Fraser III

George C. Fraser

Blanche Rasmussen

Dave Rust
Mount Ellen, Henry Mountains
Walter Hanks, George Fraser, and Dave Rust on Tantalus Point

Dorothy Shore

Approaching the Western Temple of Zion
Little Zion Canyon in Mukuntuweap National Monument
Wading the narrows of the Virgin River, Zion Canyon
E. D. Woolley's outfitting cabin
View southeast from Bright Angel Point
View east from Dutton's Point
Pleasant Valley, Kaibab Plateau

Index